W9-AFO-410

Interpreting Young Adult Literature

The goals of Boynton/Cook's Young Adult Literature series are twofold: to present new perspectives on young adult literature and its importance to the English language arts curriculum and to offer provocative discussions of issues and ideas that transcend the world of the adolescent to encompass universal concerns about the search for identity, security, and a place in life. The contributing authors are leading teachers and scholars who have worked extensively with adolescents and are well read in the genre. Each book is unique in focus and style; together, they are an invaluable resource for anyone who reads, teaches, and/or studies young adult literature.

Titles in the Series

Conflict and Connection: The Psychology of Young Adult Literature, by Sharon A. Stringer

Guide to Young Adult Literature: Critiques and Synopses from The ALAN Review, edited by Virginia R. Monseau and Gary M. Salvner (available on CD Rom)

Interpreting Young Adult Literature: Literary Theory in the Secondary Classroom, by John Noell Moore

Reading Their World: The Young Adult Novel in the Classroom, edited by Virginia R. Monseau and Gary M. Salvner

Reel Conversations: Reading Films with Young Adults, by Alan B. Teasley and Ann Wilder

Responding to Young Adult Literature, by Virginia R. Monseau

Young Adult Literature: The Heart of the Middle School Curriculum, by Lois Thomas Stover

Interpreting Young Adult Literature

Literary Theory in the Secondary Classroom

John Noell Moore

Boynton/Cook Publishers
HEINEMANN
Portsmouth, NH

Boynton/Cook Publishers, Inc.
A subsidiary of Reed Elsevier Inc.
361 Hanover Street
Portsmouth, NH 03801–3912

Offices and agents throughout the world

Acknowledgments for borrowed material can be found on page 202.

Library of Congress Cataloging-in-Publication Data
Moore, John Noell.
    Interpreting young adult literature : literary theory in the
secondary classroom / John Noell Moore.
       p. cm. — (Young adult literature series)
    Includes bibliographical references.
    ISBN 0–86709–414–1 (acid-free paper)
    1. Young adult fiction, American—Study and teaching (Secondary).
    2. Young adult fiction—History and criticism—Theory, etc.
    3. Language arts (Secondary)—United States. 4. Young adults—Books
and reading. 5. Literature—Philosophy. 6. Youth in literature.
    I. Series: Young adult literature series (Portsmouth, N.H.)
PS490.M66 1997
810.9′9283′0712–dc21   97-5045
                                                     CIP

Editor: Peter R. Stillman
Consulting editor: Virginia Monseau
Production: Vicki Kasabian
Cover design: Michael Leary
Manufacturing: Louise Richardson

Printed in the United States of America on acid-free paper
01 00 99 98 97 DA   1 2 3 4 5

For Carol,
Song of Songs

Contents

Acknowledgments

I acknowledge with gratitude the great teachers of my life:

Mildred Patterson Hudson, my grandmother, who first whispered "teacher" in my ear;

Wilma I. Rayburn, my mentor for three decades, who taught me Latin and who opened up the world of language and classical literature;

Dorothy Leech Greer, my favorite pianist, who taught me how to listen, how to play the songs of my imagination, and how to hear the music in everything;

Douglas W. Foard, who showed me that a passion for learning and teaching could sustain a life;

Elsa Nettels, who opened wide the doors of the House of Fiction and taught me the demands and rewards of literary scholarship;

Jan K. Nespor, who helped me redefine my concept of knowledge and self;

Michael G. Squires, who first guided me into the landscape of contemporary literary theory and taught me to trust my own critical voice;

Thomas M. Gardner, who gave me my education in metaphor and taught me how to ride words as far as they will take me;

Virginia C. Fowler, who taught me how to read African American literature and in so doing forever changed my vision of my country's literary heritage;

Patricia P. Kelly, my doctoral advisor and friend, whose cheerful patience and steady hand enabled me to dwell in possibility and to discover that I could make something new.

I thank the ALAN Foundation for Research in Young Adult Literature for an award that helped support my work on the original manuscript.

I thank Peter Stillman of Heinemann Boynton/Cook for showing me the possibilities of that manuscript and guiding my revisions of it.

For her early confidence and continued belief in the ideas that have come to fruition in this text, I am deeply grateful to Virginia Monseau of the English Department at Youngstown State University, Ohio.

I acknowledge with deep gratitude my students over the years, whose curiosity, encouragement, and patience have kept me always happy in the company of Chaucer's Oxford Clerk:

"And gladly wolde he lerne and gladly teche."

Introduction

If you are a teacher or a preservice teacher who feels that you do not know enough about literary theory to use it in your classroom, banish the thought. I invite you to explore contemporary literary theory with me and to discover some intriguing ways of thinking about how language works, how we read books, and how we teach them.

If you are a teacher who knows little about young adult literature, who may never have taught a young adult novel or even read one, prepare for the joy of discovering the wonderful books to which the following chapters will introduce you. Prepare, even, to be amazed.

If you are a teacher who already loves young adult literature, reads it, and teaches it, I hope that this book will give you some new ideas about familiar texts, introduce you to new texts, and offer you some helpful teaching suggestions.

If you teach or take English education courses—methods classes, young adult literature classes, and other classes that examine how we teach language and literature—I hope that you will find this book illuminating and useful in your work.

Context

In offering sustained readings of young adult literature from the perspectives of contemporary literary theories, this book sets out to accomplish something new in a field of inquiry that is itself fairly new. Earlier work in young adult literature has defined the field and described its genre (Nilsen and Donelson 1993), considered the issues of selecting and teaching young adult literature (Monseau and Salvner 1992; Bushman and Bushman 1993; Reed 1994), and demonstrated how specific young adult texts complement the traditional secondary school canon (Kaywell 1993, 1995).

Recent texts that have examined young adult literature from the perspectives of literary theory have usually done so from a single angle of vision, especially reader-response theory (Brown and Stephens 1995; Monseau 1996) and the theory of archetypes (Herz and Gallo 1996). None of these texts, however, attempts to interpret young adult literature from a broad range of contemporary theoretical perspectives as I do in this book. The writers of these texts and I share a common commitment to the belief that the finest young adult literature deserves a place among the familiar classics in the secondary school literary canon.

The relationship of young adult literature to the traditional secondary canon is one of the big issues in the field at the present time. Despite its growing popularity over the last three decades, young adult literature has not yet "come of age"; it remains the "stepchild of the high school curriculum." It is used mostly in upper elementary and middle schools where it is usually selected for reluctant or resistant readers (Christenbury 1995). One study of secondary school curricula concluded that young adult literature was fairly popular in grade nine—38 percent of the teachers reported using it. It had, however, almost disappeared by grade twelve—only 3 percent of the teachers chose it for their students (Applebee 1989).

One of my goals in this book is to convince you that young adult literature can come of age, can lose its stepchild status, only if we treat it with the same respect with which we treat other literatures we teach. This means, simply, selecting the best young adult books to teach, presenting them to all our students without apology, and reading, discussing, and writing about those books in a serious manner.

The Three Circles

This book started to take shape one winter afternoon when I drew three interlocking circles and labeled them "young adult literature," "literary theory," and "social constructivism"—three of my major interests. The story of how I came to draw those circles helps to clarify the purpose of this book.

I had just finished reading and making notes on Katherine Paterson's *Jacob Have I Loved*, Gary Paulsen's *Dogsong*, and Robert Cormier's *The Chocolate War*, and I was thinking about how I might teach these novels in a high school English class. Looking over my reading notes, which included mappings of characters and locales in the novels, key quotations, questions and other doodlings, I noticed that I had, without thinking much about it, been making notations that reflected a number of the literary theories I was studying at the time. For example, Paterson's Sara Louise Bradshaw had raised some important feminist issues about self and community. Early in Paulsen's novel, I had begun mapping out the archetypal quest of his young hero Russel Susskit. And the world of Cormier's Catholic school had set me to thinking about struggles for power and how people construct themselves according to the social pressures they face—which are some of the issues raised by cultural studies.

Studying the notes, I began to marvel at the complexity of these young adult novels, at how much they had captured my imagination, at how much I had to say about them. I was discovering a new literature for myself, one that in my previous secondary school experience had been used mostly in classes of "everyday" English and in classes for reluctant readers and remedial students. I was seeing all kinds of complex interpretive possibilities in these texts. Why was that?

The simple answer is that I was theorizing about these novels, applying critical and interpretive frameworks to books that I had previously thought to be merely quick reads or entertaining stories that were diversionary in comparison to, say, *Great Expectations*. This reflection led me to think about how I had taught fiction for most of my secondary career. In my pretheory days I had confidently taught most novels in the same systematic way, carefully guiding my students in close readings that led to detailed analyses, class discussions, and, eventually, essays on familiar literary elements—plot, character, theme, imagery, metaphor, symbolism. How was theory changing my perspective? For one thing, literary theory was leading me to rethink how we acquire literary knowledge, and my readings in social constructivism had shaken some of my previous notions about how we acquire all knowledge.

In that climate, I drew the three circles. Over the next few days, I realized that the circles encompassed some of the key interests in my life as an English teacher: (1) how we learn, (2) how we read and how we teach others to read, and (3) what literature we choose to teach. In the overlapping of the three circles, I began to envision new ways of knowing literature, new ways of teaching literary interpretation— even new literatures to teach.

In the months that followed the three circles, I continued to read widely in the young adult field and to make notes that affirmed my idea that these novels deserved to be read and studied by all students and that they deserved a place beside the venerated Great Books of the traditional curriculum. In the chapters that follow, I demonstrate my commitment to young adult literature and to literary theory as a way of approaching such literature in new and provocative ways.

The Role of Theory

We can help our students understand what it means to know literature differently if we value multiple readings (or interpretations) over
a single authoritative reading (Applebee 1989, 1990; Probst 1990;
Petrosky 1991; Langer 1992). Literary theory helps us understand that
there are many ways to know texts, to read and interpret them, but
many secondary school teachers are unfamiliar with the changes that
have occurred in literary theory over the last four decades, such as the
emergence of structuralism, deconstruction, black aesthetics, and cultural studies. The prevailing literary theory in secondary school classrooms remains the New Critical approach (Applebee 1989), a way of
reading that gained popularity in midcentury and that continues to
exert tremendous influence on the teaching of literature in secondary
schools and universities. I open the book with this approach, not only
because it is familiar ground but also because many subsequent theories developed in response to that approach.

One of the key issues in teaching students to read involves the
way in which students make meaning or interpret texts. Because the
New Critical approach requires a set of sophisticated skills and a literary vocabulary of little interest to some students, the meaning of a
text often turns out to be what the teacher says it is. We need to
expand our students' understanding of how they read; we need to
teach students how to "develop and defend their own interpretations"
(Applebee 1990, 120). We can accomplish this important goal if we as
teachers have a working knowledge of the literary theories that are
presented in the following chapters.

How the Book Is Organized

Chapter 1 offers an introduction to literary theory and a brief overview of the specific theories presented in this book. The order of subsequent chapters reflects the shifts in emphases that have occurred in
the development of modern theory as its concerns have moved outward from the text itself to the reader and then to the larger cultural
contexts that frame text and reader. While each chapter focuses on
one theoretical perspective, the book demonstrates how these theories have, in their development, borrowed components from competing theories and adapted them to new uses. In practice, we usually do
not work out of one perspective exclusively, and as the book
progresses, I explain how we can be pluralistic in our approaches to
reading and teaching literature. With such a pluralistic approach, we

become comfortable with multiple readings, and we help our students understand the uncertainties and ambiguities of interpretation. The theory chapters are presented according to the reading and interpretive issues they address. Chapters 2 (formalism), 3 (archetypal criticism), 4 (structuralism/semiotics), and 5 (deconstruction) focus on textual structures and on how we read them; these structures represent a move from the autonomous text of formalism to the texts that readers construct through the strategies of archetypes, semiotics, and deconstruction. Chapter 6 introduces theories that are reader centered. Chapters 7 (feminism), 8 (black aesthetics), and 9 (cultural studies) locate the text and the reader in complicated webs of social construction. Chapter 10 demonstrates how multiple readings can enrich our experiences with young adult texts.

What may appear to be noticeably missing are chapters on psychoanalytic theory and on Marxist theory. We can never do all that we wish, and I hope that the following explanation will suffice for any glaring omission. The theory of archetypes in Chapter 3 is based on Jungian ideas; I have worked with Norman Holland's psychological approach in Chapter 6 on reader response, and Marxist thought figures into the cultural studies approach in Chapter 9.

The theory chapters are structured in a pattern that (1) introduces the key concepts and basic terms of the theory, (2) introduces a young adult text and interprets it from that theoretical perspective, and (3) invites readers to join the conversation. The last section of each chapter discusses other young adult texts that might be approached productively by using the theory under study and also suggests critical studies that will be helpful in teaching some of these texts.

The Young Adult Texts

I have chosen books for interpretation that have, for one reason or another, made lasting impressions on me as a reader, books that represent excellence in the field over the last two decades: Virginia Hamilton's *M. C. Higgins, the Great* (1974), Katherine Paterson's *Jacob Have I Loved* (1980), Bruce Brook's *The Moves Make the Man* (1984), Gary Paulsen's *Dogsong* (1985), M. E. Kerr's *Night Kites* (1986), Walter Dean Myers' *Fallen Angels* (1988), Budge Wilson's collection of short stories entitled *The Leaving* (1992), Lois Lowry's *The Giver* (1993), and Ernest Gaines' *A Lesson Before Dying* (1993). Hamilton's and Gaines' novels represent the range of my discussion: *M. C. Higgins, the Great* is an acclaimed children's book, while *A Lesson Before Dying* illustrates the upper range of young adult texts, as do his *Autobiography of Miss Jane Pittman* and *A Gathering of Old Men*.

Young adult literature belongs in the high school curriculum beside the classic canonical texts. A working knowledge of contemporary literary theories, an understanding of the multiple reading strategies they offer, and a commitment to the practice of these strategies can significantly change the way we teach literature. This book aims to bridge the gap between the scholarship of university classrooms where we learn complex ways of reading and the secondary English classroom where we teach others to read. In teaching our students to interpret young adult texts, we teach them to construct texts, to construct themselves, and in some sense, to construct their world.

Works Cited

Applebee, Arthur N. 1989. *The Teaching of Literature in Programs with Reputations for Excellence in English*. Technical Report 1.1. Albany, NY: Center for the Learning and Teaching of Literature.

———. 1990. *Literature Instruction in American Schools*. Technical Report 1.4. Albany, NY: Center for the Learning and Teaching of Literature.

Brooks, Bruce. 1984. *The Moves Make the Man*. New York: HarperCollins.

Brown, Jean E., and Elaine C. Stephens. 1995. *Teaching Young Adult Literature: Sharing the Connection*. Belmont, CA: Wadsworth.

Bushman, John H. and Kay Parks Bushman. 1993. *Using Young Adult Literature in the English Classroom*. New York: Macmillan.

Christenbury, Leila. 1995. Letter to John Moore. Virginia Commonwealth University. November 1.

Gaines, Ernest. 1971. *The Autobiography of Miss Jane Pittman*. New York: Bantam.

———. 1983. *A Gathering of Old Men*. New York: Knopf.

———. 1993. *A Lesson Before Dying*. New York: Vintage.

Hamilton, Virginia. 1974. *M.C. Higgins, the Great*. New York: Macmillan.

Herz, Sarah, with Donald Gallo. 1996. *From Hamlet to Hinton*. New York: Greenwood.

Kaywell, Joan. 1993. *Adolescent Literature as a Complement to the Classics*. Norwood, MA: Christopher-Gordon.

———. 1995. *Adolescent Literature as a Complement to the Classics*. Vol. 2. Norwood, MA: Christopher-Gordon.

Kerr, M. E. 1986. *Night Kites*. New York: Harper.

Langer, Judith. 1992. *Critical Thinking and English Language Arts Instruction*. Technical Report 6.5. Albany, NY: Center for the Learning and Teaching of Literature.

Lowry, Lois. 1993. *The Giver*. New York: Bantam Doubleday Dell.

Monseau, Virginia R., and Gary M. Salvner. 1992. *Reading Their World: The Young Adult Novel in the Classroom.* Portsmouth, NH: Boynton/Cook.

Monseau, Virginia R. 1996. *Responding to Young Adult Literature.* Portsmouth, NH: Boynton/Cook.

Myers, Walter Dean. 1988. *Fallen Angels.* New York: Scholastic.

Nilsen, Alleen Pace, and Kenneth L. Donelson. 1993. *Literature for Today's Young Adults.* 4th ed. New York: HarperCollins.

Paterson, Katherine. 1980. *Jacob Have I Loved.* New York: HarperTrophy.

Paulsen, Gary. 1985. *Dogsong.* New York: Puffin.

Petrosky, Anthony. 1991. *To Teach (Literature)?* Technical Report 5.4. Albany, NY: Center for the Learning and Teaching of Literature.

Probst, Robert E. 1990. *Five Kinds of Literary Knowing.* Technical Report 5.5. Albany, NY: Center for the Learning and Teaching of Literature.

Reed, Arthea J. S. 1994. *Reaching Adolescents: The Young Adult Book and the School.* New York: Macmillan.

Wilson, Budge. 1992. *The Leaving and Other Stories.* New York: Philomel.

One

Inviting Theory
From Formalism to Cultural Studies

The title of this chapter suggests the attitude toward literary theory that this book takes. Theory is inviting in the sense that working with it takes us on an "intellectual adventure" (Jefferson and Robey 1986) as we explore young adult texts in our classrooms. Each theory we use in the interpretation of texts invites us to answer these questions:

1. How does the theory define the literary qualities of the text?
2. What relation does the theory propose between the text and the author?
3. What role does the theory ascribe to the reader?
4. How does the theory view the relationship between text and reality?
5. What status does the theory give to the medium of the text, language? (Jefferson and Roby, 13)

When we think of literary theory in these terms, it is nonthreatening, inviting as a way of working with words.

William Cain (1994) suggests that theory may be threatening to some people as a consequence of the different ways in which it can be defined. Perhaps most intimidating to teachers in secondary schools is the way in which "some scholars define contemporary theory specifically and link it to a concrete form of practice in teaching and scholarship." For example, Marxist or feminist theory "refers to an intricate body of thought—marked by its own history and laced with internal disputes, contradictions, differences in emphasis" (3). Before such gigantic fields of knowledge and inquiry, many teachers easily feel overwhelmed. Cain's second definition defines theory in a broader context as "an array of critiques of New Critical formalism and the development of alternatives" that include "structuralism, feminism, and the black

arts movement in the 1960s" and later theories such as "poststructuralism, deconstruction, new historicism, ethnic studies, gay and lesbian
studies, and cultural studies." Finally, Cain's third definition presents
theory in its most inviting formulation, namely, as "any kind of sustained reflection on practice, any serious question asking how teachers
and critics conduct themselves." According to this third definition, all
of us are already theorists when we think about the work we do in our
classrooms; theory provides us with ways of working with texts and
with ways of reflecting on that work; in this sense, "every scholar-
teacher" "is a theorist to some extent and should feel no unease about
the label" (3).

In this book, I combine the second and third definitions to demonstrate the theories of reading that are explicit or implicit "in all theories of literature" (Jefferson and Robey 1986). The main issues raised
by theories of reading involve "the extent to which a text could be
said to determine its own reading or to be determined by it, on
whether the reader is seen as responding to textual directives, or
whether the text itself is to be seen as a product of the reader's interpretive activity, or something in between" (Jefferson and Robey, 16).
Theory, then, invites us to see texts differently, to look beyond the
closed textual world of a familiar New Critical reading, to investigate
both the reader of the text and the world that produced it.

The etymology of *theory* begins with the Greek word *theorein*,
which means "to look at." When we theorize about a text, we look at
it intellectually; we inquire into it to investigate literary assumptions,
principles, and concepts that we may have previously taken for
granted. To begin theorizing about a text, we treat some element of
the text as a problem to which we seek a solution or several solutions.
For example, we may seek new meaning in a text, rejecting someone
else's familiar interpretation as we use theoretical strategies to work
out our own. Or we might inquire into the history of a text, the conditions under which it was produced, how its first readers received it
and interpreted it, and how and why modern readers interpret it differently. We might also explore the text in the context of other literature of the same period or in the context of cultural forces at work
when the text was written (Graff 1987, 252). Such inquiries constitute the kind of work we do when we theorize about texts.

Working with Theory

How do we begin such inquiry? How do we engage various theories
as we work to answer Jefferson and Robey's five key questions about
the interplay among writer, reader, text, and world? David Richter

uses a series of diagrams to help us visualize this interplay in *The Critical Tradition: Classic Texts and Contemporary Trends*. As a hands-on approach to theory, I invite you to construct each of these diagrams.

We begin with M. H. Abrams' "co-ordinates of art criticism," a theoretical framework familiar to English teachers who have read *The Mirror and the Lamp* (1958). Draw a triangle, labeling the top angle "universe," the left angle "artist," and the right angle "audience." In the center of the triangle, write "work." Now, from "work" draw an arrow to each of the other terms. This is Abrams' map of theoretical concerns. In describing the components of his conception, he first focuses on the centrality of the *work* as artifact, a made thing, moving then to the *artist*, the "artificer," or maker. The third component, *universe*, represents, he says, "existing things," an "objective state of affairs" from which the work takes its subject. Finally, he defines the *audience* as "the listeners, spectators, or readers" who pay attention to the work (Abrams 1958, 6). Abrams' approach, typical of New Critical formalists, places the work of art at the center of inquiry.

In another map, Richter changes some of Abrams' terminology to reflect changes in theoretical thinking that have occurred since Abrams' original diagram (Richter 1989, 3). Again, construct a triangle, labeling the top angle "world," the left angle "author," and the right angle "audience"; write "poem" in the center. Consider for a moment what Richter's changes mean. First, in contrast to the word *work* which suggests a finished product, something already complete, the word *poem* suggests a structure in which the language is more open, inviting some ambiguity and, therefore, perhaps inviting a wider range of interpretive possibilities. *Artist* often connotes the creator in the world of fine art, while *author* specifically denotes a maker of texts, a word worker. *Universe* suggests that a work might have some enormous cosmic significance, while *world*, at least in its most immediate sense, limits the scope of theoretical inquiry to the sphere we readers inhabit.

Young Adult Reading

In *Becoming a Reader: The Experience of Fiction from Childhood to Adulthood* (1990), J. A. Appleyard reads Abrams' diagram in explaining the process through which young readers, or, as he calls them, "apprentice literary critics" (148), develop theoretical perspectives within the context of their psychological development. In tracing readers' growth, Appleyard observes that our earliest responses to books are mostly spontaneous, mostly reactions to the pleasure of story. He reads Abrams' diagram clockwise, starting with *world*. In adolescence, he says, we begin to investigate the world in the text, and we construct that world from our perspective as *readers*, seeing it as a representation of experience or of a world we might wish to inhabit. We are not, of course, aware that we are theorizing a text. As we become more sophisticated readers, we move beyond the world and ourselves to focus on the *author* who created the text and on the point of view from which the textual world is presented to us. In our evolution, we finally engage the language of the *text* specifically (Appleyard 1990, 147).

More sophisticated reading, Appleyard continues, focuses on what is beyond the text—the sign systems, language structures, and ideologies that surround the text. In his analysis of interpretation, Appleyard concludes that "the project of studying literature" may have gone far beyond practical and eclectic approaches to "a kind of reading whose object is the reconstruction of a self and a vision of the world adequate to the totality of one's lived experience" (152). The theories that are presented in succeeding chapters provide teachers and students with frameworks for constructing these kinds of readings.

In this book, I use the word *reading* to mean a performance in language and about language. Theories of reading teach us how to enact these performances; they provide us the tools with which we can create or construct our interpretations of texts. Interpretation is an act of analysis and synthesis. By its definition, a *text* is a made thing, woven of words, as its etymology illustrates: Middle English; from Middle French *texte*; from Middle Latin *textus*; from Latin "texture," "context," from *texere*, "to weave" (see *Webster's Collegiate Dictionary*, 10th ed., s.v. "text"). One metaphor for interpretation sees it as a process, a way "to trace the weave of thoughts, feelings, words, figures, sounds, and representations in a text, a weaving that constitutes readers' diverse responses" (Marshall 1992, 166). I use this metaphor for interpretation to introduce the theories explored in this book, and I weave it throughout my text.

Theories About Structures

New Critical Formalism

This theory, to use William Cain's designation, views the work of literature as self-contained, a finished work of art understandable without reference to its author or to the emotional response of the reader (William Cain, 1994, 4). We trace the weave of images, plot, character, and theme, and our close reading reveals patterns that produce order, harmony, and unity in the structures, the forms, of the work.

If we are properly trained, this theory contends, we can arrive at one "correct" reading of a text. Subsequent theories have developed as responses to the narrowness of this approach.

Archetypal Theory

This theory also focuses on patterns, but it sees the text as woven into the larger patterns of literary history. Archetypes are plots, characters, images, and themes that are continuations and reworkings of familiar elements in myths and folktales. In our reading we trace these recurring elements and consider them to be manifestations of a shared human experience. Archetypal criticism often explores the human psyche, especially through dreams.

Structuralism

Language is a system of signs (semiotics) through which we structure and organize our ideas and understand our experiences. Language is a cultural code, and when we read, we make meaning by decoding these signs. Signs, however, have no meaning by themselves. They depend on relationships with other signs within a system; and when we read, we trace the weave of these relationships within the text. Structuralists see language as the unifying element in the text and in the world.

Deconstruction

According to deconstructionists, theorists who responded critically to structuralism, a language system cannot produce unity. A single text is not a unified whole. It is, instead, a compilation of many texts, or intertexts, and we find meanings in the ways in which these intertexts relate to each other. No single "correct" reading exists because multiple meanings emerge as we examine the complicated ways in which the language of the text contradicts itself. Deconstruction claims that texts are in the process of falling apart. When we trace the weave, then, we discover how the text unravels as we read it.

Reader-Response Theories

According to these theories, reading is an event, a process that takes place between reader and text. Reader-response approaches consider the ways in which we respond personally to texts and how our personal history gets embedded in the text. Some reader-response approaches investigate gaps or indeterminancies in the text; through these we explore what has been left out of the text. All reader-response theories see the reader as an active participant in the creation of the text, so our interpretation arises out of the ways in which we weave ourselves into the text as we read it.

Culturally Based Theories: Feminism, Black Aesthetics, Cultural Studies

Feminism operates on the principle that gender is the fundamental category for literary inquiry. Similarly, the new black aesthetics sees race as the fundamental category. Both theories affirm the importance of locating the literary text in broader cultural contexts. The realm of cultural studies is broadly interdisciplinary and intertextual. The text is located in a complex web of discourses—including psychology, anthropology, sociology, politics, economics, and ethics—that may seem nonliterary. The realm of cultural studies calls into question what actually constitutes a text and includes film, advertisements, television programs, and other elements of the popular culture as texts that can be "read."

Summary: Changing Perspectives

If we think of the changes in theoretical perspectives from New Critical formalism to cultural studies, we notice the moves (1) from aesthetics to ideologies; (2) from the work of art to the text, context, and intertext; (3) from the work centered to the text decentered; (4) from the author as artist to the question "Who is the author?"; (5) from the reader as audience to the reader as writer or co-writer; (6) from one correct reading to no correct reading; (7) from a canon of great works to an exploded canon; (8) from microscopic vision to telescopic vision. From formalism to cultural studies, literary theory opens up the concepts of writer, reader, text, and world.

Getting Started

How do we enter the world of literary theory? Since the field is so enormous that we cannot master it or even try to cover it, and since there are "innumerable entries," the best advice, according to theorist Jonathan Culler, is to "always begin where you are." He offers a clever metaphor for beginners. We are, he says, like shoppers who face shelves full of brand name detergents, each claiming its superior powers, each encouraging us to give it a try. Which one should we buy? No single detergent can do all that the hyperbole of its advertising claims. Similarly, no single theory can fulfill all of our interpretive needs. Given the range of possibilities, we simply choose the theory that seems to suit the material with which we are working. In critical practice, Culler tells us, some theories suit some texts better than others. For example, feminism offers a useful framework for exploring relationships between the sexes in a novel, for investigating the condition of the women characters, or for connecting those characters to women in history or in the contemporary world. Deconstruction offers provocative excursions into the ways in which the language of a novel works, often exposing that language as unstable and the world that it portrays as falling apart (Culler 1992, 225).

A note of caution: I do not wish to suggest that readers attempt to develop an eclectic theory of reading from the interpretive frameworks of the following chapters. I emphasize the importance of pluralism rather than eclecticism, and I hope that these chapters encourage teachers to explore the power of multiple readings in the intellectual and critical development of young readers.

Works Cited

Abrams, M. H. 1958. Introduction to *The Mirror and the Lamp: Romantic Theory and the Critical Tradition*, 3–29. New York: Norton.

Appleyard, J. A., and S. J. 1990. "College and Beyond: The Reader as Interpreter." In *Becoming a Reader: The Experience of Fiction from Childhood to Adulthood*. 121–54. Cambridge: Cambridge University Press.

Cain, William E. 1994. "Contemporary Theory, the Academy, and Pedagogy." In *Teaching Contemporary Theory to Undergraduates*, eds. Dianne F. Sadoff and William E. Cain, 3–14. New York: Modern Language Association.

Culler, Jonathan. 1992. "Literary Theory." In *Introduction to Scholarship in Modern Language and Literature*, ed. Joseph Gibaldi, 201–35. New York: Modern Language Association.

Graff, Gerald. 1987. "Tradition and Theory." In *Professing Literature*, 247–62. Chicago: University of Chicago Press.

Jefferson, Ann, and David Robey. 1986. Introduction to *Modern Literary Theory: A Comparative Introduction*, 2d ed., 7–23. Totawa, NJ: Barnes and Noble.

Marshall, Donald G. 1992. "Literary Interpretation." In *Introduction to Scholarship in Modern Language and Literature*, ed. Joseph Gibaldi, 159–82. New York: Modern Language Association.

Richter, David H. 1989. Introduction to *The Critical Tradition: Classic Texts and Contemporary Trends*, ed. David H. Richter, 1–11. New York: St. Martin's.

Two

Formalism
Structure and Idea in *M.C. Higgins, the Great*

An Introduction to Formalism

Formalism offers a way of reading that needs little introduction. This approach is so familiar that one critic calls it "normal criticism" because its strategies dominate the criticism practiced in most universities (Culler 1988, 13). This approach dominates English teaching in secondary schools as well. Formalism has its roots in Russian literary criticism of the 1930s. The American version, developed during the 1940s and after, was called New Criticism. The terms are often interchanged, and William Cain even combines them (Chapter 1) into New Critical formalism, which clearly indicates New Criticism's roots. For convenience in this chapter, I use *formalism* to keep the idea of structure foremost in our minds as we read Virginia Hamilton's *M.C. Higgins, the Great*.

The basic vocabulary for working with formalism in fiction consists of the familiar literary elements: plot, character, theme, setting, point of view, conflict, and style. The central strategy, a detailed close reading, allows us to trace the interconnections of these literary elements and to discover how they interpenetrate each other to create a harmonious and unified structure, a work of art. Form, explored in this way, becomes more than a mere external container of the story; it becomes the "total principle of organization" (Brooks and Warren 1959, 684). In reading and interpreting *M.C. Higgins, the Great*, we will concentrate on the interrelationships of plot, character, and theme. A brief summary of the novel will help contextualize these basic formalistic elements.

Black and poor, thirteen-year-old Mayo Cornelius Higgins lives with his family halfway up the side of Sarah's Mountain, just a few miles from the Ohio River. Strip-mining operations threaten the family's safety and future as a dangerous spoil heap perched atop the mountain ominously slides in its own seepage toward the family home built against the side of the mountain. M.C.'s view of the world changes during the three late summer days that the action covers. His view of the world expands as a result of (1) his encounters with two strangers, (2) his discovery of the strong bonds that connect his mother Banina and his father Jones to the mountain, and (3) his discovery of the complex worldview of his strange neighbors, the Killburns.

The novel's first day (Chapters 1–6) begins as M.C.'s secret friend Ben Killburn reports that he has seen a stranger, a man with a tape recorder. M.C. stalks another stranger, a mysterious young woman, but she disappears. Later, James K. Lewis appears with his recorder and sets into motion M.C.'s fantasy: Lewis' recording of her voice will make Banina a star. At lunch M.C. tells his father about Lewis; but his father, Jones, is disinterested and prefers to talk about family history. Near day's end, M.C. stalks and scuffles with the strange young woman who subsequently disappears. In the evening, when Lewis returns to record Banina's voice, Jones and Lewis argue about how the spoil heap endangers the family's home. That night M.C.'s nightmares symbolize his growing conflict with his father over the family's safety and future.

Early on the second day (Chapter 7–13) M.C. meets Lurhetta Outlaw, the mysterious stranger of the first day. Lurhetta, a free spirit, boldly challenges M.C.'s authority; and in a childish display of ego, M.C. jeopardizes both their lives in a potentially fatal swim through an underwater tunnel. At lunch Lurhetta meets Jones, discovers the Higgins' superstitious fear of the Killburns, and challenges M.C. to accompany her to Killburn's Mound. There, superstition gets the best of M.C., and he flees, leaving Lurhetta behind. In the evening Lewis returns with the tape of Banina's voice, explaining that he cannot make her famous. He leaves, resolving one of the novel's conflicts by destroying M.C.'s fantasy. That night M.C. dreams of romance, of Lurhetta, of escape from the mountain, and of future happiness.

On the final day of the novel (Chapter 14), when M.C. learns that Lurhetta is gone, the dream of a romantic escape dies. M.C. decides to start building a wall to protect his home, resolving the conflict with his father and casting his lot with family and history. Later in the day, his siblings and Ben help him start the wall, and the novel ends.

Plot

Formalists distinguish between *plot* and *action*, defining *plot* as the structure of the action presented and *action* as a series of connected events that move through the logical stages of beginning, middle, and end. These stages create a dynamic unity in which change occurs. The importance of change, which occurs as the dramatic structure unfolds, is crucial: "No change, no story." An *exposition* opens up the story, often locating its characters in a setting characterized by stability. Complications develop through *conflict*, which creates instability and moves the story toward its *climax*, the point of highest tension. From this point, the story's tensions resolve in the unraveling of the plot, the *denouement*, as a new stability emerges in the fictional world. The proportion of these narrative movements is not mechanical; it depends on the materials of the story (Brooks and Warren 1959, 78–82). For example, the movement from exposition to climax in *M.C. Higgins, the Great* takes up most of the novel because M.C.'s final action, for its effectiveness, must come as a surprise to the reader as it brings the novel to a swift close. Consequently, there is little or no denouement. The final action provides no conclusion; instead, it actually points to the next phase in the Higgins family history, which, we may guess, is M.C.'s continued commitment to its preservation.

Character

Plot is "character in action" (Brooks and Warren 1959, 80). This disarmingly simple statement about the interpenetration of character and plot provides an excellent point of entry into the study of character in *M.C. Higgins, the Great*. In the broadest sense, characters in fiction are presented by what they do, say, and think. The technicalities of point of view through which the author creates character are familiar to us in their range of possibilities, among them the external omniscient third-person narrator, the first-person narrator, the multiple voices of other characters, and the interior monologue. We are also familiar with the three basic kinds of fictional conflict: conflicts with external forces, such as nature and society; conflicts with other characters; and conflicts within the self (Brooks and Warren 1959, 172).

M.C. Higgins, the Great operates as an intricate web of character juxtapositions, the total effect being an accumulation of world views that influence the changes beginning to take place in M.C.'s thinking near the end of the action. Hamilton juxtaposes other major characters with M.C. by weaving them in and out of his experience in the three days of the action. To visualize this weaving, imagine a piece of fabric loosely woven with distinctively colored threads, one of which is prominent throughout the texture. Imagine that M.C. is that most prominent thread, running the full length of the fabric. Imagine that Jones, Banina, Lewis, Lurhetta, and the Killburns are woven all around that thread, sometimes visible, sometimes hidden in the texture. In this way you can see how Hamilton creates the texture of her fictional cloth.

Theme

Theme may be simply defined as "what a piece of fiction stacks up to." Regarding the formalist principle that plot, character, and theme interpenetrate, theme develops gradually as "the characters act and are acted upon, as one event leads to another" (Brooks and Warren 1959, 273–74). Theme may not be literally expressed in a work. Rather, events or situations may "act as metaphors for a state of mind," or a narrative theme might evolve as a "metaphorical image of a psychological process" (Robey 1986, 85). Hamilton creates an increasingly complex web of mental images and balancing structures to reveal the psychological processes of M.C.'s coming of age.

When the novel begins, M.C. is a child watching other children; he often sits atop a gleaming steel flagpole equipped with a seat and bicycle pedals, all anchored in his front yard. The pole is a gift from M.C.'s father, a celebration of M.C.'s athletic accomplishments. M.C.'s primary responsibility is to take care of his younger siblings, Lennie Pool, Macie Pearl, and Harper while his parents work in Harenton. When Lewis arrives from Cleveland to record and preserve the authentic songs of the Ohio Mountain people, he sets into motion M.C.'s fantasy that his mother's beautiful singing will make her famous and that the family must move off the mountain if this fame is to materialize. His fantasy conflicts with his father's conviction that they must stay on the mountain to preserve the legacy of Jones' great-grandmother Sarah's escape from slavery to freedom.

As the theme develops, events in the novel become metaphors for the state of M.C.'s mind. On the opening morning of the novel, M.C. is the self-proclaimed hero of his own life. At first the flagpole represents his youthful pride, his wide-eyed innocence, and his creative spirit. As the days pass and M.C. is frustrated by events that he cannot control, he mounts the flagpole and pedals wildly, accomplishing nothing, going nowhere. After Lewis and Lurhetta leave, he descends the pole for the last time, and the wall he begins to build serves as a symbol of his developing sense of personal responsibility, as a solid affirmation of the novel's theme that we are our history, that we cannot escape it, and that we are ennobled in our efforts to preserve it. M.C.'s surprising final act—his commitment to an idea much greater than himself—redefines him as a character and amplifies his greatness.

The Method: Close Reading

The early Formalists practiced their theory by reading short works, usually poems, line by line, pointing out how the language of images and ideas created a unified structure. This kind of reading would be impossibly cumbersome in a novel as complex as *M.C. Higgins, the Great*, where there are at least thirty-three internal stories (Mikkelsen 1994, 29). To demonstrate how close reading focuses on the language of the text and how Hamilton uses an image to unify the narrative structure, I here explicate parallel scenes that frame the plot of the novel. Taken together, the scenes symbolize the changes that take place in M.C.'s character as the coming-of-age theme develops.

When we first meet M.C., he is greeting the sunrise, raising his arms high to the sky and opening them wide. In the imagery of this grand gesture, he literally opens up the world of the novel in which he is the center. He senses himself beyond the control of gravity ("I'm standing in midair") and declares his power to "bounce the sun beside me if I want" (2). In a complementary scene that opens Chapter 2, we see M.C. perched atop the flagpole. There, almost godlike, he imagines himself as creator of the natural world. He traces the curves of the hills, fluffs the trees, and smoothes the sky until everything is still and orderly, "the way he liked to pretend he arranged it every day" (27). Similarly, he imagines himself constructing the human world; the nearby town of Harenton seems close enough to touch, so he pushes and shoves pieces of it together until he has it "just right." In grand gestures he sweeps dust from the smoke stacks of the steel mill and places boats in the river until he is content, commenting "you're looking good" (28). This set of images, the open arms that frame the world and the joyful pole ride, help us understand M.C.'s innocent worldview: He is great, and he can do, he believes, anything. The action changes his thinking so that on the third day he awakens with a very different perspective on the world.

In the final pages of the novel, Hamilton balances these early open-armed gestures with a pair of contrasting images that symbolize the changes in M.C.'s thinking. In his last pole ride, frustrated by the departures of Lewis and Lurhetta, M.C. imagines himself a destroyer. Clutching a hunting knife that Lurhetta has left behind, he rides the pole in a wide arc, thrusting the knife into the clouds and stabbing the river below until he cuts it into two pieces. He yells out as he slices the chimneys of the mill town of Harenton, now "shrouded" in mist. The image of the shroud suggests the death of a world that M.C. had created so joyfully a few mornings ago. M.C. descends the pole, and arms closed, he stabs the soil in a desperate gesture.

Paradoxically, though, this stabbing becomes an impetus for an act of creation as M.C. begins to build a wall of earth to protect his home should the spoil heap come crashing down the side of Sarah's Mountain. He uses the knife to tear loose chunks of earth, and his action indicates what he is learning: However unlovely, this mountain is his world, and he has responsibilities to it and to the family history it preserves. Structurally, then, the novel traces another pattern, comes full circle, from an act of creation born of fantasy and innocence at the beginning of the first day to an act of creation born of responsibility and experience at the end of the last day.

Tracing the Weave of *M.C. Higgins, the Great*

One way to study the unity of the novel is to explore how plot as "character in action" creates theme, how M.C. comes of age as a result of challenges to his innocent vision of life. Jones represents the historical worldview of the power of ancestral identity and the responsibility to preserve it. Banina reinforces Jones' vision and makes M.C. aware of the bonds of a deep love that cannot be threatened by her son's delusions of grandeur. Lurhetta also reinforces Jones' worldview as she introduces M.C. to the economic view of the power of land and of ownership. She also challenges him to face the unknown represented by Mr. Killburn's philosophical worldview in which spirituality connects family, history, and the natural world. The magnitude of M.C.'s change becomes clear when, having heard all these voices, he discovers and listens, finally, to his own.

Jones: The Responsibilities of History

Events in Chapters 3–5 help M.C. to understand how Jones Higgins is inextricably bound to Sarah's Mountain and how his history eliminates the possibility of the family's moving to the city so that Banina can become a star.

After telling his father about Lewis on the first day, M.C. goes into his room—a dark, cool, windowless cave dug out of the side of Sarah's Mountain. Ironically, the mountain is not just in M.C. through his historical connection to Sarah; but in the cave, M.C. is also literally *in* the mountain. He falls into a reverie that represents the conflict he feels between his fantasy and Jones' history. M.C. enjoys hunting, which is a recurring motif in the novel; and in his reverie, a literal hunt is transformed into a psychological event that locates M.C. between childhood and manhood. Deep in his mind he hears the roar of a wild creature. He sees himself as a hunter, a man-child who is "not quite old enough for the silence and the darkness," and, although tracking the animal of the dream, "not yet brave enough" to handle the dark landscape around him. M.C. sees a silhouette in the imaginary forest, and his identity splits. Is he the hunter? Or is he the silhouette, "waiting for another part of himself to reach it?" As he tries to move toward the image, he is numbed by a coldness that rises from his ankles, climbs to his knees, then to his neck. He cannot run. He is "rooted to the mountainside,"and mud from the spoil heap oozes into his mouth and nose (66). The imagery of paralysis suggests M.C.'s suspension between past and future, and the root image suggests his organic connection to the land and to his father's history.

A scene in Chapter 4 structurally balances the imagery of M.C.'s reverie in Chapter 30. When Jones comes home from work, M.C. expresses his fear that a landslide will destroy them all, that the spoil heap will grow "like its alive," finally tear loose, perhaps without warning, and roar down the side of the mountain, "trying to climb my pole" (76–77). The sliding spoil heap threatens both the family's safety and M.C.'s freedom to sit atop the pole and create the world anew. From his historical perspective, Jones presents a contrasting image of the mountain as "a feeling": "A solid piece of something big belongs to you. To your father, and his, too." It's as if, he continues, you belong to it, too, and have for a long time (77). Jones then tells the proud story of Sarah's arrival, pregnant with his granddaddy and singing a song. This song from the past is another thread that unifies the novel, continued in the present by Banina's singing.

In one of the novel's crucial moments, Jones circumscribes M.C. in history by chanting a fragment of an African song, "*O bola, Coo-pa-yani, Si na-ma-gamma, O deh-kah-no.*" He explains the family tradition regarding the song: "Sing it always to the sons. One son to another, down the line" (78). He explains how his history lives, how in the heat of the day he can hear "Sarah, as of old" climbing the mountain, her baby crying. Earlier conflicts momentarily resolve as father and son fuse in history. M.C. reveals that sometimes, up on the flagpole, he, too, senses Sarah's approach. The image frightens him, he says, but his father comforts him with the idea that Sarah just wants to show M.C. a vision of herself: "No ghost. She climbs eternal. Just to remind us that she hold claim to me and to you and each one of us on her mountain" (79). Following this image of how history stays alive, Jones repeats the African song and casts the mantle of preservation on M.C.: "You are the one responsible." In an image that recurs as a unifying thread in the novel, M.C. feels "the rope within" that binds him to the mountain, a rope that is always present "like a pressure on his mind" (80).

After this conversation, Jones leaves, singing a courting song as he goes. M.C. has three metaphorical visions that represent his internal conflicts and create more structural balances in the novel. In the first, his imagination unconsciously rewrites history. He sees Sarah running so fast that she trips and falls, dropping the bundle she is carrying. Something bloody splatters on the ground, and the image perhaps symbolizes M.C.'s unconscious desire to be free of the burden of his father's history. The second vision reiterates the imagery of M.C.'s afternoon reverie (Chapter 3); but now he sees Jones, not himself, trapped in the spoil, mud oozing into his ears. "Woven through his thoughts" is the courting song that Jones was just singing. M.C. tries to free himself from the song, but he cannot: "Nothing, not even his pole, could keep away the sad feeling, the lonesome blues of being grown, the way either his mother or his father could with their singing" (83–84). Here M.C.'s description of maturity as a blues hints at his fear of what growing up means, and it also links him to the musical symbolism of the novel. Reading from the formalist perspective, Jones and Banina's song becomes a metaphor, a song of experience, a shared view of the world that is beyond their son's comprehension.

Banina: The World of Romance

This shared worldview becomes clear to M.C. in the evening of the first day when (Chapter 5) he encounters the powerful metaphoric light of his mother's knowledge. In her first important dialogue of the novel, Banina complicates M.C.'s idea of Jones by illuminating more family history. Before this moment, we have seen Banina only as M.C. perceives her—idealized, beautiful, a future star. Now she tells her son to stop bothering Jones about leaving the mountain. M.C. does not understand the whole story, which Banina explains. When Banina came to the mountains to live, she insisted that the family have a yard, so Jones cleared away the family tombstones to make one. Jones soon filled the space with junk, mostly car parts. M.C. already knows that the yard is a burial ground, but until now he has not comprehended the significance of the flagpole, which his mother reveals. In fact, the flagpole is more than a tribute to M.C.'s athletic abilities; it is a "marker for all the dead" who have lived on Sarah's Mountain (105). Ironically, then, while he has dreamed of escaping the mountain, M.C. has been metaphorically riding the pole through family history. Darkness and light serve as metaphors as this new knowledge fills M.C.'s brain, "as if someone had lit up a screen hidden so long in the darkness" (106).

The bond between mother and father becomes even clearer later that evening when Lewis returns (Chapter 6) to record Banina's voice. M.C. fails to register a number of important moments. First, Lewis makes it clear to Jones that he has no plans for Banina's voice beyond the taping; thus, Lewis assures Jones that he is "just a collector" (114). Second, M.C. fails to notice the interweaving of his parents' voices. Banina is not the only singer; Jones actually begins the call-response from which Banina's wine song emerges. Banina follows the wine song with a Juba song, ghostly in its melody. As Banina sings, we notice Jones' face "contented and closed" and "impenetrable" (118). Their lives are as intertwined as their songs, but in his innocence M.C. cannot comprehend this connection.

The next morning when M.C. and Banina go for a predawn swim, they pass through a familiar forest now "changed and ghostly" (127). Formalists carefully trace patterns of allusion that unify a work, and this misty surrealistic world symbolizes M.C.'s romantic fascination with his mother by locating mother and son in a fairy-tale setting where a doe springs up among the trees "like a wind-up toy, swift and magical" and where the mountains emerge "like swollen, smoky giants" (127–128). Paradoxically, in this fantastical world Banina warns M.C. to stay away from the Killburns and their magical powers. This moment foreshadows and structurally balances M.C.'s visit to the Killburn Mound later in the day.

When Banina offers more practical advice ("Don't dream too hard"), she juxtaposes M.C.'s innocent dreams with her realistic philosophy: "You live wide awake, or you quit living." When M.C. asks his mother to whom "you" refers, she replies with a vision of unity: "All. All together. All part. But all." M.C. understands that Banina has gone "beyond him to know something he hadn't yet come to know" (133). This is a vision of family unity that experience has not yet taught him to grasp, but it is a vision that his father understands and a vision that M.C. will ironically find acted out when he goes to Killburn Mound.

Lurhetta: Economic Necessities

More parallel scenes create structural balances in the novel when Lurhetta Outlaw appears later in the early morning of the second day. First, Banina has awakened M.C. for the predawn swim. When Banina leaves to go to work, Lurhetta enters the novel, and M.C. feels her "waking most certainly in his mind" as she literally awakens in a tent that she has pitched near the lake where M.C. and his mother have been swimming (139). Second, the narrator's description of Lurhetta near the end of Chapter 7 surrounds her with a magical aura similar to the descriptions of Banina and the forest at the beginning of the chapter. Lurhetta appears as if "standing in a halo of shadow" (141). Third, Lurhetta appears at the very center of the novel's fourteen chapters, replacing Banina as the most important woman in M.C.'s life. Her entrance into the action foreshadows the changes that she will bring about in M.C.'s thinking.

A close reading of the language describing this crucial moment illustrates how imagery interweaves to unify plot, character, and theme in the novel. Emerging from the tent as sunlight shimmers off

the lake, Lurhetta "looked like a figure living in darkness. Some premonition, dream he hadn't thought to have. Bright flashes cut into his
eyes as he looked at her, distorting his vision. She seemed to be standing in a halo of shadow" (141). Lurhetta emerges from *darkness* as
M.C. begins to emerge from his innocence about the world. So much
of his world has been made up of *premonition, dream,* and *thought.*
Metaphorically, he cannot see, and the novel's bright *flashes* of experience *distort his vision.* Now, at the very center of the novel, he too
stands metaphorically in the mysteries of the *shadow* created by
Lurhetta's *halo* of illuminating light. He is poised for change, although
he does not know it as he introduces himself as "M.C. Higgins, the
Great" (141).

Lurhetta challenges M.C.'s confident self-image and his innocent
perceptions of life, and she introduces him to a worldview based on
economic reality (Chapter 8). When Lurhetta asks M.C. who owns
the lake and surrounding land, he replies nonchalantly that he knows
of no one who ever "bothered with owning it." Older than M.C. by a
few years, Lurhetta presents a more mature attitude about the land.
Somebody owns it, she says, because "Somebody owns everything."
Lurhetta's grasp of economic reality exceeds M.C.'s childish concepts
as she goes on to say that "land's the basis of all power" and "people
hold on to their land" (153). This contrast in perspectives sparks the
conflict that ensues.

M.C. begins to feel inferior to Lurhetta not only because she is
older than he but also because she appears to be fiercely independent.
She has a job, makes her own money, and owns not only the car in
which she has driven to the lake but also the tent in which she has
spent the night. Furthermore, despite her mother's disapproval,
Lurhetta travels around alone, camping out and seeing the world. In
the face of Lurhetta's apparent superiority, M.C. describes his own
greatness; but Lurhetta notes that she has seen M.C. sitting atop the
pole "with nothing to do and no place to do it!" (156). This is more
than M.C.'s ego can endure, so he brags about his ability to swim
through a water tunnel. When Lurhetta challenges M.C. to take her
through the tunnel, he fails to ask if she can swim. She cannot, and
the episode nearly ends in tragedy (Chapter 9). When they are safely
out of the water, M.C. typically glosses over the potential danger to
which he has exposed Lurhetta with a romantic vision of their future
happiness in which they will only play: "Day after day, they swam the
lake. Hour upon hour, they sunned themselves on the shore" (164).
Again, M.C. is imagining himself in an unrealistic world of play and
pleasure—no work, no economics, and no real responsibilities.

As M.C. and Lurhetta continue to interact, changes take place in
M.C.'s thinking. He invites Lurhetta to lunch; and at the foot of

Sarah's Mountain, Lurhetta again raises the question of land ownership. This time M.C. responds with pride: "Been in the family forever.
And someday, it's going to be mine." He explains the history of the
place, linking himself to it and to his father: "It's always handed down
to the oldest son. . . . My oldest son will take it from me" (178). M.C.
is perhaps unaware of the symbolic nature of these words with which
he defines himself for the first time as a crucial actor in the drama of
his family's history.

Lurhetta's ideas overwhelm M.C. so much that he gets a head-
ache, a metaphor for the conflict between his romantic worldview
and Lurhetta's challenges to it. He feels "as if his head contained two
minds," one of them intent on leaving the mountain, the other knowing that his family will never leave. Psychologically, M.C.'s identity
crisis is symbolized here as he is torn between these two minds, "not
knowing what to believe" (179).

The Killburns: Organic Philosophy

Lurhetta forces M.C. to confront his fear of the Killburns on the afternoon of the second day. Although Ben is secretly M.C.'s best friend,
the Higginses fear the Killburns' alleged strangeness, their intermar-
riages, their light skin, and their red hair. Like Lurhetta, the Killburns
are outlaws. With their supernatural powers they are not subject, so
their neighbors think, to the laws of nature. When, after lunch, three
Killburn men come to bring ice to the Higginses (Chapter 10), Lurhetta's interest in the Killburns is provoked by Jones' inordinate fear of
them and by his rudeness to them, as well as by M.C.'s superstition
that he has been contaminated by the touch of Mr. Killburn's six-
fingered hand. Although his father has taught him that the Killburns
are dangerous in their witchiness, M.C. is of two minds about the
Killburns now: "Part of him believed and part disbelieved" (195).
When Lurhetta challenges M.C. to take her to the Killburns' compound, he feels change sweeping over him: "He knew he would never
be the same" (199).

M.C. and Lurhetta's afternoon visit to the Killburn's Mound
(Chapters 11 and 12) sets the Killburn world symbolically against
M.C.'s world. From the formalist perspective, this new setting contributes to the novel's structural unity. The location of Killburn's Mound
geographically balances Sarah's Mountain: a plateau connects the two
settings. As M.C. and Lurhetta approach the mound, it seems to be
located out of time. Walking on the shiny, smooth footpath, M.C feels
that Lurhetta and he are neither "here nor there" (210).

The magic of the Killburn world echoes the magical forest of the
predawn swim with Banina and creates another internal balance in

the novel. The Killburns live in a compound where the barns and sheds seem to be "chocolate and silver," taking on "the appearance of a fairyland." This is not only an "unearthly" world, but it looks "slightly sinister" as well (214). The whole enclosure is a cultivated garden, suggesting an Edenic paradise, offering another opportunity for formalists to explore allusions in the text.

Watching the busy activities going on around him, M.C. falls into a reverie, in which time seems suspended, as if he were in both dreamworld and real world, past and present. His mind translates the sound of talking into two images. In one image the sounds are like an internal clock that is ticking off the loneliness of his daydream. In the second image, the sounds seem like the "staccato of a time bomb set to go off" (217). This pair of images symbolizes his internal turmoil, the clock perhaps ticking off the end of childhood dreams, the time bomb on the verge of bursting like the festering boil perched precariously at the top of Sarah's Mountain.

In contrast to the conflicts in M.C.'s internal and external worlds, the central image of the Killburn world is an image of unity, a giant web, a net that links all the houses and that enables the Killburn children to swing from row to row as they harvest the vegetables that cover the earth. In contrast to the Higgins children who spend all their time at play, the Killburn children are productive members of their world. Ben's ninety-six-year-old grandmother sits at the center of the compound, another point of structural balance in the narrative. Like M.C.'s Sarah, Ben's grandmother exists in the ever present truth of mythology. When asked where his grandmother came from, Ben replies, "She was always here" (221).

The climax of this brilliant journey comes when Mr. Killburn expounds a worldview totally unfamiliar to M.C., a view that reveals the man's complex thinking and that contrasts with the Higgins' perception that the Killburns are witchy people. Even the smallest children, Mr. Killburn explains, "understand that vegetables is part of the human form," part of the body of earth. People pull these vegetables up "by the root," eating them if they are healthy, disposing of them if they are diseased. His root image balances and provides a counterpoint to M.C.'s earlier reveries in which he dreamed himself imprisoned, rooted inextricably to the mountain. When Mr. Killburn extends his imagery to the larger world, his vision of ownership contrasts with Lurhetta's: soil, streams, and mountains are all part of a body that no one owns. Humans are only "caretakers," he tells M.C. Finally, in a brilliant image, Mr. Killburn joins the human body to the earth, describing humans as "a body just wiggling and jiggling in and out of the light" (229). While Mr. Killburn's metaphor of the dance of life refers to the joys of the human experience, it also accurately describes M.C.'s predicament in the novel, his vacillating thinking, his frenetic movements through darkness and light, his sense of uncertainty about himself and his future.

Mr. Killburn continues to offer his philosophical perspective when he takes M.C. and Lurhetta to see the compound's storehouse. When Lurhetta admires the rope design above them as a spider web, Killburn tells her that it is "*A eye* of Gawd" (230). The ceiling is literally a form of basket weaving known as a God's-eye pattern, but Mr. Killburn extends the act of making the basket to a metaphysics in which humans are watched over benevolently by a higher being. This image negates the Higgins' fear of the Killburns' malevolence—their witchiness. In an elegant balancing of images, the rope that threatened M.C. in his earlier dream is transformed into the unifying cord of the Killburns' world.

Fear gradually gets the best of M.C.; and leaving Lurhetta behind, he flees. But his way of thinking is changing. Now he realizes that his previous knowledge of the Killburns and what he has seen on Killburn's Mound have become "mixed in disorder in his mind" (238). Simple dichotomizing will no longer work as he tries to bring order to his disordered thinking. What lies ahead is work that he can only do by himself, and in a symbolic concluding image to the chapter, we see M.C. "alone" (239).

His Own Voice: A Vision

When Lewis returns (Chapter 13) for his final visit to the Higgins' house, it is only to bring a copy of the tape he has made. When he departs, M.C.'s dream dies as "everything" seems to "sink and perish inside" of him (247). Once the dream of freedom on the wings of his mother's song is dead, M.C. hopes that Lurhetta will return and that he will escape to her world: "Go where she lives. Maybe get a job like she has" (249). M.C.'s problem has been that he looks to others for his vision of freedom, that he has not been able to act on his own thinking and cannot commit himself to an action for which he must assume responsibility and accept the consequences. Late in the second day of the novel, M.C. realizes that Lurhetta will not come back, and an approaching storm heightens his fear for her and for his family. The storm is an external parallel to his internal turmoil. As M.C. falls into a fitful sleep, his mind tries to come together, to work out resolutions to his conflicts. In two romantic visions, M.C. sees himself running to the lake after the storm and finding Lurhetta waiting there for him.

When he awakens, however, and goes out into the early morning, fog obscures his vision. The mood of this poststorm morning stands in sharp contrast to the brilliant opening of the novel's first day and the surrealist magic of the second. M.C. walks to Lurhetta's camp near the lake and finds that she has disappeared, leaving behind her hunting knife. Walking back home with the knife, he has visions about it and thinks how he will hunt with it or how "he could easily thrust it into his own heart" (264). The first vision recalls the joy of his frequent early morning trapping excursions, and the second affirms the bitter awareness of the death of dreams and the potential for the hunter to become ultimately the hunted, to die at his own hand. This is the darkest moment in the novel.

Arriving home, M.C. rides the pole for the last time, imagining himself slicing open the world of Harenton with the gleaming hunting knife. He finds, however, that he cannot stab to death the surrounding hills because they are an integral part of him: "He could feel their rhythm like the pulse beat of his own blood rushing. If they faded never to return, would his pulse stop its beat as well?" (267). Achieving this moment of personal truth, M.C. descends the pole and begins to stab the earth. His action seems destructive, but then the "perfect idea" (268) comes to him and resolves, at least for now, his internal conflict. He begins to build a wall of earth to protect his home should the spoil heap slide. Looking around, he gets the idea of reinforcing the dirt with the auto parts that have held the pole aloft. As he pulls out a fender he thinks how he will make it stand with rocks and dirt. The symbolism is clear: As he dismantles the heap of junk that holds the pole aloft, he builds another kind of ride, a metaphoric car that will transport him into the future.

Jones comes home at noon; realizing what M.C. is doing, he contributes a broken-handled shovel to make the work easier. In the final conversation between M.C. and his father, Jones offers advice on building the wall, to which M.C. responds: "It's *my* idea" (272). This is perhaps the most important sentence in the novel because M.C. makes a declaration of independence. The sentence does not insist selfishly, as a child might, on having his own way. It is a different voice from the one we have heard during most of the novel. And as M.C. continues, his words signal his coming of age. Rather than think about play and the pleasures of the immediate moment, he now thinks about his future. He announces that next summer he will be working for Mr. Killburn. If Mr. Killburn cannot pay him in money, he says, "I'll take his vegetables for pay" (272). The *vegetables* take on a powerful significance as we realize their centrality in Mr. Killburn's philosophy of organic wholeness. M.C. intends to be a part of that cosmic worldview, and his plans negate his former superstitions of the witchy people. He will weave himself into the fabric of a formerly forbidden world as he insists now on thinking differently from both his father and mother. A related manifestation of the change taking place in M.C. is his declaration of friendship for Ben: "I play with anybody I want" (273). When M.C. invites Ben to join him out of the shadows, M.C. stands poised, ready to fight Jones should he try to stop Ben.

Jones' final gesture in the novel is a tender one, symbolic and sacrificial. As if in affirmation of the greatness of M.C.'s idea, Jones gives his son Sarah's tombstone, which he has hidden years earlier under the porch. The stone is a gift that will strengthen the wall and that signals M.C.'s connection to past and future. As storm clouds mass, Jones goes off to work, and M.C. bids a symbolic farewell to his childhood: "Sarah, good-by," then "Lurhetta, good-by," and finally, "*Good-by, M.C., the Great*" (277–78). The Sarah he names is perhaps the Sarah of his fears, the ancestor that has kept him rooted to the mountain. The wall seems to indicate that he, like his father, will keep the Sarah of history alive, that she is essential to the future that the wall will help protect.

Another change is apparent as the novel closes: M.C. is no longer alone. He has become, instead, the catalyst for a young community as Lennie Pool, Macie Pearl, Harper, and Ben work alongside him. Finally, then, the solitary dreamer becomes integrated into the world of the mountain. The imagery of the final sentence of the novel positively affirms the power of these young people to construct a world for themselves as they work on the wall: "And it was rising" (278). The wide arc circumscribed by the flagpole on the first morning of the novel has disappeared, and in its place, the imaginary arc of Sarah's Mountain encircles the widening world of M.C. Higgins, the Great.

On Balance

The Novel

In this richly complex narrative, unity of plot, character, and theme is achieved through multiple balancing structures—locations, events, characters, images, and symbols. At the highest level, M.C. is suspended in time, in the patterns of history—past, present, and future—a tension that he resolves, at least momentarily, as he begins building the wall. Suspended in geography, M.C. dreams of leaving the mountain, of going to the city of his mother's stardom or of accompanying Lurhetta into her world. He resolves this tension, at least for the moment, by staying. He is also suspended in the topography of the novel's landscape: Sarah's Mountain on one side, Killburn's Mound on the other. These external physical suspensions are balanced internally with M.C.'s psychological state as he struggles with the choices that experience offers him, as his head aches in the confrontation of old knowledge and new knowledge. What M.C. discovers is that independence exacts a great price, that life forces him to make difficult choices. When we leave M.C. as he is building the wall, we realize that his "greatness" lies in his having forsaken the easy ride in order to help others survive in a dark and threatening world.

Formalism

Since its advent in the early decades of this century, what has been the effect of formalism on the study of literature? One effect is that, according to Donald Childs (1993), the "habit of close reading" has become an accepted part of critical practice: "Few, if any contemporary approaches to literature can forego the careful reading of irony, paradox, ambiguity, and contradictions that New Critics offered as the sine qua non of literary study." As other theories have emerged, they have shared some formalist perspectives. For example, formalism and structuralism share an ahistoricality, locating meanings in the structures within a text, "denying, ignoring or de-emphasizing a poem's involvement in the ideological projects of its time and place." Formalism, poststructuralism, and deconstruction are all "alert to the play of literary language," and all are "happy to acknowledge the death of the author." A fundamental difference exists, however, in the formalists' and deconstructionists' attitude toward the centrality of language. Formalists believe that we can rely on the meaning of words to support our one, correct reading, that meaning is centered in the words of the text. Deconstructionists, on the other hand, base their theory on the crucial idea that words are not centered, that meaning does not hold, that there is no correct reading (122–23). Formalism has also influenced reader-response theories (Willingham 1989, 38). In the following chapters, consider tracing the weave of formalistic thinking in the reading strategies of the new theories that you encounter.

Joining the Conversation

In using the formalistic perspective to teach young adult fiction, it is important to remember that the goal is not merely to study the literary elements of a text separately but to show how those elements interpenetrate to create a unified structure. One approach might be to emphasize how setting, for example, contributes to the unity of a text in its interconnections with plot, character, and theme. Nilsen and

Donelson (1993) suggest some good choices for this kind of work (80–88). In Bette Greene's *Summer of My German Soldier* (1973), the setting in Jenkinsville, Arkansas, serves as the stage for the dramatic story of twelve-year-old Patty Bergen, a Jewish girl, and her encounter with Anton Reiker, a German soldier who is a prisoner of war. The central theme of the effects of racism is woven throughout the rural Christian world of Jenkinsville, where Patty comes to understand something about herself and the nature of love. Another good choice is Robert Newton Peck's *A Day No Pigs Would Die* (1972), in which the setting in a rural Vermont Shaker community offers the chance to explore the family values of the main characters. The themes of maturation, the acceptance of death, and the strength required to run a farm are woven into graphic descriptions as the plot unfolds. Nilsen and Donelson (1993) offer an insightful reading of how the setting works in Sue Ellen Bridgers' *Permanent Connections* (1986), where, they point out, setting "serves as a metaphor and a symbol for what is happening in people's minds." In a clear formalistic conclusion to their analysis, Nilsen and Donelson observe that young adult readers will "get more" from fiction "if they are sensitive to the way in which authors incorporate setting in plot, characterization, theme, tone, and mode" (87–88).

One of the key ideas of my book is that young adult fiction can be read from multiple perspectives. Formalism can easily serve teachers and students in the reading of the texts that we explore in successive chapters. Using setting as the element again, a reading of Gary Paulsen's *Dogsong* (1985) could focus on the nature of the Arctic tundra and on how Russel Susskit's struggle to survive in this frozen winter world shapes the person that he becomes. In Bruce Brooks' *The Moves Make the Man* (1988) effective starting points for discussing the novel's complicated characters and themes would be the integrated high school in Wilmington, North Carolina, Duke Hospital in Durham, North Carolina, and Jerome's home, especially the attic room in which he writes the story of his relationship to Bix Rivers. Similar interweavings could grow out of a study of dystopic landscapes in Lois Lowry's *The Givers* (1993), Vietnam and Harlem in Walter Dean Myers' *Fallen Angels* (1988), the Nova Scotian settings in Wilson Budge's *The Leaving* (1992), the black-and-white worlds of Ernest Gaines' *A Lesson Before Dying* (1993), the worlds constructed by class differences in M. E. Kerr's *Night Kites* (1986), and the Chesapeake Bay and Appalachian mountain settings of Katherine Paterson's *Jacob Have I Loved* (1980). Setting provides just one thread for tracing the weave of these texts. Characters, plot structures, and themes are equally fertile ground from which to begin a formalistic reading.

A Final Note

The exploration of new theories of reading does not mean that we abandon the familiar formalism. Better to build on it, to dialogue with it, to understand that theories that have emerged in response to it have done so because the proponents of those theories found formalism alone to be restrictive and unrealistic with respect to the ways in which we make meaning with words in a complicated world. Nothing stops us as teachers from opening a discussion with a reader-response approach or a feminist reading and then moving to some of the technical aspects of texts that formalism helps us to explore.

Works Cited

Bridgers, Sue Ellen. 1986. *Permanent Connections*. New York: HarperCollins.

Brooks, Bruce. 1988. *The Moves Make the Man*. New York: Harper and Row.

Brooks, Cleanth, and Robert Penn Warren. 1959. *Understanding Fiction*. 2d ed. New York: Appleton.

Childs, Donald J. 1993. "New Criticism." In *Encyclopedia of Contemporary Literary Theory*, ed. Irena R. Makaryk, 121–24. Toronto: University of Toronto Press.

Culler, Jonathan. 1988. *Framing the Sign: Criticism and Its Institutions*. Norman: University of Oklahoma Press.

Gaines, Ernest. 1993. *A Lesson Before Dying*. New York: Vintage.

Greene, Bette. 1973. *Summer of My German Soldier*. New York: Dial.

Hamilton, Virginia. 1974. *M.C. Higgins, the Great*. New York: Macmillan.

Kerr. M. E. 1986. *Night Kites*. New York: HarperKeypoint.

Lowry, Lois. 1993. *The Giver*. New York: Bantam Doubleday Dell.

Mikkelsen, Nina. 1994. *Virginia Hamilton*. New York: Twayne.

Myers, Walter Dean. 1988. *Fallen Angels*. New York: Scholastic.

Nilsen, Alleen Pace, and Kenneth L. Donelson. 1993. *Literature for Today's Young Adults*. 4th ed. Glenview, IL: Scott, Foresman.

Paterson, Katherine. 1980. *Jacob Have I Loved*. New York: HarperTrophy.

Peck, Robert Newton. 1972. *A Day No Pigs Would Die*. New York: Dell.

Robey, David. 1986. "Anglo-American New Criticism." In *Modern Literary Theory: A Comparative Introduction*, 2d. ed., eds. Ann Jefferson and David Robey, 73–91. Totawa, NJ: Barnes and Noble.

Willingham, John. 1989. "The New Criticism: Then and Now." In *Contemporary Literary Theory*, eds. G. Douglas Atkins and Laura Morrow, 24–41. Amherst: University of Massachusetts Press.

Wilson, Budge. 1992. *The Leaving and Other Stories*. New York: Philomel.

Three

Archetypes
The Monomyth in *Dogsong*

When I read Gary Paulsen's *Dogsong* (1985) for the first time one sunny June morning, I heard echoes of Homer and of ancient mythologies, legends, and stories of struggle and survival, tales of heroes and triumphant journeys that had fascinated me as a young adult reader. Why did I hear these echoes as Russel Susskit's dogsled sped over the Arctic ice? The answer: I have been mythologically conditioned to trace the weave of ancient story and song in all literatures.

This way of reading reflects the principles of archetypal theory, a perspective on literature that results from our cultural inheritance of a "mythological universe":

> Man lives, not directly or nakedly in nature like animals, but within a mythological universe, a body of assumptions and beliefs developed from his existential concerns. Most of it is held unconsciously, which means that our imaginations may recognize elements of it, when presented in art or literature, without consciously understanding what it is that we recognize. (Frye 1982, xviii)

Reading young adult novels based on the quest motif and the hero's journey, as *Dogsong* is, makes us "more aware of our mythological conditioning" (Frye 1982, xviii).

Writers as well as readers are mythologically conditioned; archetypes are so pervasive in cultures that storytellers use them unconsciously. Some years ago, I heard Paulsen speak on survival stories in young adult literature, and I asked him if he was aware of the archetypal patterns in *Dogsong*. His reply, "If it's there, it's in the people" (Moore 1994), attests to the power of myth in human life.

Understanding the Archetypal Perspective

Understanding the relationship between the words *myth* and *archetype* is crucial to working with this literary theory of archetypes. Early in our educations, we learn that myths are stories with which primitive peoples explain why things happen in nature. Usually we get the sense that myths are not "true" because they often contain exaggerated and fantastic characters and events.

Archetypal theory, however, redefines myth for us: Myths are stories that are *always* true, that have specialized social functions in a culture, "stories that tell a society what is important for it to know, whether about its gods, its history, its laws, or its class structure" (Frye 1982, 33). As a culture advances, certain myths become interconnected, and, taken together, they create a mythology that then becomes a component in the creation of a cultural history. In this definition of the term, myths are not simply direct responses to the natural environment. They encircle a culture, drawing "a circumference around a human community," looking inward toward the community in such a way that the mythology becomes part of the "imaginative insulation," a "social skin that marks the boundary between ourselves and the natural environment" (Frye 1982, 33–51). Expanding this concept to include all cultures, basic story patterns that recur from culture to culture become community property for the human race.

The meaning of *archetype* emerges from this concept of community. At the simplest level, certain story patterns connect the mythologies of all cultures. We refer to these story patterns as *myths*, and we refer to the universal significance that these stories share as *archetypes*. These interconnections serve as the basis of archetypal theory. In hearing echoes of classical literature in *Dogsong*, I responded to this interconnectedness in my recognition of the archetypal pattern of the quest myth. In this familiar story, the hero is initiated into manhood through a series of tests and trials from which he emerges victorious. This is the central myth of all literature (Frye 1963, 18–19), and archetypal critics refer to it as the *monomyth*.

Joseph Campbell and the Monomyth

Joseph Campbell's *The Hero with a Thousand Faces* (1968) explores the monomyth, with particular emphasis on its psychological significance. Campbell examines archetypes as recurring story patterns as well as manifestations of psychological phenomena, elaborating the monomyth through Carl Jung's analytical theories about the nature of dreams and what they reveal about the human psyche. Jung posited a collective, or universal, unconscious that lay below the threshold of the individual unconscious. In this context he studied certain elements that he found in human productions, from the ancient to the moderns. These elements—the components of archetypal theory—included story patterns, characters, themes, symbols, and images. Jung explored these patterns in a tremendous range of cultural productions, including literature, paintings, dances, carvings, dreams, and sacred rituals. He declared these productions to be timeless manifestations of the human psyche, created in all cultures and stored in the repository of humankind's collective unconscious (Leitch 1988, 118).

The physical journey of the hero in the monomyth has a psychical correspondence: The hero locates his real difficulties in the "causal zones of the psyche," faces them, eradicates them, and breaks through them (Campbell 1968, 17–18). The work of dreams is crucial to the hero's fulfillment as he resolves these difficulties. The structure of *Dogsong* weaves together the physical world and the psychical world, built as it is on an alternating pattern of movement in the Arctic cold and Russel's dreams.

The monomyth takes place in three stages: (1) separation, (2) initiation, and (3) return. A brief description of the events and their significance goes something like the following: The hero breaks away or departs from the local social order and its context where he has an identity. Next, he takes a long retreat, not only backward in time but also inward, deep into the psyche. A series of darkly terrifying and chaotic encounters leads him to a centering experience that brings harmony to his life and gives him courage. The return journey is a rebirth to life in which the hero sometimes bestows favors or blessings on his people (Campbell 1972, 208–209). *Dogsong* reflects Campbell's pattern, especially in the book's recurrent imagery of centering and its focus on birth and rebirth in Russel's return to the community.

The Pattern of the Monomyth

In *The Hero with a Thousand Faces*, Campbell works through a complex cyclical schema for the monomyth. In "The Adventure of the Hero," he elaborates the full heroic cycle. Part I, Departure, moves through five stages: (1) The Call to Adventure, (2) Refusal of the Call, (3) Supernatural Aid, (4) The Crossing of the First Threshold, and (5) The Belly of the Whale. In Part II, the pattern includes six stages: (1) The Road of Trials, (2) The Meeting with the Goddess, (3) Woman as Temptress, (4) Atonement with the Father, (5) Apotheosis (elevation to divine status), and (6) The Ultimate Boon. Part III, the final phase of the cycle, also contains six stages: (1) Refusal of the Return, (2) The Magic Flight, (3) Rescue from Without, (4) The Crossing of the Return

Threshold, (5) Master of the Two Worlds, and (6) Freedom to Live (Campbell 1968, 36–37). Stories the world over fit within this pattern, but the pattern is adapted in a variety of ways. Some storytellers isolate or enlarge one or two of the elements, or they string parts of the cycle together into a single series, as Homer does in the *Odyssey*. Storytellers may shape their tales by fusing certain characters or episodes or by repetition and change within a single element (Campbell 1968, 246). Paulsen's novel extends the departure phase of the monomyth in "The Trance," spends most of its narrative time in the initiation phase in "The Dreamrun," and only implies the impact of the return in the short final section, "Dogsong."

Dogsong: An Introduction

Departure: "The Trance" (Chapters 1–5)

Russel Susskit lives with his father in a small Eskimo village. Troubled and uncertain in his early adolescence, he visits the old shaman Oogruk who provides him a historical context for their communal life. Their people have abandoned the traditions of hunting and consequently have lost the songs of their identity. Russel answers the call to adventure by deciding to experience the old ways; the metaphor for this journey is that Russel wants to become a song, but he lacks knowledge of both what to do and how to do it. Oogruk functions as the supernatural aid in this version of the monomyth, instructing Russel in the ways of survival until his death, when Russel sets out alone to find his dogsong.

Initiation: "The Dreamrun" (Chapters 6–14)

Chapters 6 through 13 parallel the tests and obstacles of the monomyth, alternating in a pattern of "The Run" and "The Dream" that fuses in Chapter 14, "The Dreamrun." The complex imagery of these chapters unifies Russel's mythic journey; after each run, a dream moves him back and forth in the cultural memory, the Jungian collective unconscious that mixes Russel's present journey with the archetypal journeys of his ancestors. Finally, Russel discovers the connection of his quest to the traditions of Eskimo hunters before him. The tests include finding meat for himself and the dogs (Chapter 6), surviving a devastating storm (Chapter 8), rescuing Nancy, a young pregnant woman (Chapter 12), confronting a polar bear, and, finally, racing to safety in a northern village (Chapter 14).

Return: "Dogsong"

This final, short section of the novel, written in italics, represents the completion of Russel's quest as he sings the song of his becoming a man.

In each of the novel's three parts, Paulsen sets contrasting worlds against each other. "The Trance" juxtaposes the modern village of government houses, snowmobiles, and television sets with Oogruk's memories and primitive lifestyle. "The Dreamrun" chronicles Russel's journeys in the icy landscape of the Arctic and in the troubled land-scape of the human psyche—the two landscapes linked by the appear-ance of Nancy who folds the hero's vision of the past into a vision of the future. "Dogsong" celebrates the union of myth and everyday experience.

Dogsong: **An Archetypal Reading**

Part I: "The Trance"

The title of this opening section reflects several situations in Part I. First, it refers literally to the suspended state between waking and sleeping into which Russel falls as Oogruk instructs him. Second, it symbolizes Russel's suspension between present and past, between modern ways of living and the old ways of Eskimo culture. Each untitled chapter in this section opens with an epigraph from the past that foreshadows the events that take place in the narrative present and future.

The Two Worlds. The juxtaposition of the old and the new is sig-naled in the first words of the novel, an epigraph in which an old Eskimo man relates the memory of his birth:

> *I came wet into the world.*
> *On both sides there were cliffs,*
> *white cliffs that were my mother's thighs.*
> *And I didn't cry though it was cold*
> *by the white cliffs and I was afraid.*
> *I came wet into the world.* (3)

This epigraph introduces several ideas that are central to the novel. Although the first line refers to a literal birth, it also serves as a met-aphor for Russel's birth as the hero of the novel, which begins epic-like *in medias res*, that is, in the middle of things. These lines also sig-nal Paulsen's use of poetry and poetic prose in the novel. The "white cliffs" of the poem are strongly sexual, and they point both to Russel's subsequent rebirth in the Arctic tundra as well as to the stillbirth of Nancy's baby. The novel does not develop issues of sexuality in depth because Paulsen is aware of the "tacit censorship that exists in books for young people" (Paulsen 1994, 44).

As the story begins, Russel is living with his father in a small, sixteen-by-twenty-foot government house, his mother having run off years earlier with a white trapper. His father is a Christian, converted by missionaries. When Russel tells him that he is troubled, his father suggests that Jesus might help him. The Christian myth is one version of the monomyth, but Russel quickly rejects Christian mythology ("He was sure Jesus wouldn't help"). His father sends him to Oogruk, the wise old man of the village who "tells good stories" (10). Paulsen's novel affirms the transformative power of storytelling.

This first chapter introduces another powerful metaphor in the novel. Russel's father instructs his son to take Oogruk a gift of two deer heads because Oogruk likes to eat the eyes. The image points to Oogruk's powers of sight; although the eyeballs are literal, they will become metaphor as Oogruk helps Russel see into the old ways.

The Call to Adventure. The prose epigraph of Chapter 2 both returns us to the old world and sets up the next events in Russel's story. An old Eskimo tells a story of his youth, a time when there was no meat, and, in desperation, he and his comrades ate their dogs in order to survive. Again, a woman figures prominently in the story, connecting it to the epigraph of Chapter 1. The ironic story focuses on the mother as nurturer. In their desperation, the old Eskimo and his people asked their mother if they could kill her and eat her body until a deer came to provide food. He insists that they would have carried out this plan, but a deer came, and they killed it, sparing their mother's life. The epigraph emphasizes that the world of the old man's story is a man's world; women bring men into the world, and they serve men in whatever way circumstances demand. The story may shock modern ears, but its point is clear: *Dogsong* is a novel of survival, and eating is one of its central images.

Russel hears the call to adventure as he moves into Oogruk's world. On the outside, Oogruk's dwelling looks like all the other village houses; but inside, Russel learns that he must see differently, both literally and metaphorically. Oogruk lives without electricity, light provided only by a seal-oil lamp. More important for the hero's transformative journey, Oogruk's ways require "a different thinking" (13). Oogruk appears almost mystical, clad only in a breechcloth, his hair so white that it seems to have come from and to be part of the smoke from the seal-oil lamp. Against a backdrop of harpoons, lances, bows, arrow bags, and clothes made of the skins of squirrels and caribou, Oogruk gives Russel a history lesson in a voice that moves "like strong music" (14). Many passages in the novel are fluid, poetic and musical, reminiscent of the oral traditions of ancient poetry when poets sang stories of heroes.

Oogruk recalls a world where songs had so much power that a whale song would bring whales to a hunter's harpoon. Oogruk eats the deer eyes Russel has brought; and when Russel refuses the delicacy, Oogruk announces that on the youth's future journey he will wish that he had eaten them. Oogruk's words point to the new ways of seeing that Russel will need as he returns to the old ways of living. At this crucial moment, Russel realizes that Oogruk is literally blind, almost simultaneously concluding that now he wants to see as the old man sees, both backward and forward.

As Oogruk explains how Christian missionaries destroyed the Eskimos' love of hunting and singing with their tales of heaven and hell, Russel hears the call to adventure, to "go back and become a song" (29). He and Oogruk share a meal of deer meat and water-blood soup, a ritual communion, after which Oogruk speaks and Russel falls into a trance, suspended between waking and sleeping, between the world outside and the world inside, between past and future. Heightening the mystery of the old ways, Paulsen omits the words Oogruk speaks as well as the details of the trance.

The Education of the Hero-Hunter. The epigraph to Chapter 3 again slides us backward in time. An Eskimo woman tells a story of her youth, introducing herself as once beautiful, a woman who had three husbands before she was twenty. All three were killed, she says, the third by a great bear. She finally got a husband, she concludes, that lasted. Her story literally foreshadows Russel's later meeting with Nancy and his battle with the great polar bear. On a more symbolic level, however, it illustrates cycles of loss and renewal in human life, the kind of movement that Russel will experience as he rejects the new ways in order to experience the old ways. As a consequence of his journey, Russel, too, will replace something that has been lost with something that lasts.

Chapter 3 opens in forward motion with Russel in action, learning how to work with Oogruk's dog team and sled. The dogs and sled, the last in the village, are powerful symbols in the novel. By giving them to Russel, Oogruk provides him with the vehicle for the quest and connects him to Eskimo history. The dogs are similar to the animals in traditional quest stories; they are the hero's helpers who possess special knowledge and magical powers without which the hero could not succeed (Auden 1962, 44). A series of short runs to hunt ptarmigan (grouse) and deer test Russel's ability to apply the knowledge that he is gaining from Oogruk.

Dressing himself physically for life in unfamiliar territory, Russel also dresses himself psychologically, remembering Oogruk's thoughts, "as if they had been his own" (*Dogsong*, 33). Standing stark naked, he puts on Oogruk's hunting clothes—bearskin pants, sealskin mukluks, a squirrelskin innerparka, an outerparka of thick deerhide with a wolverine ruff, and deerhide mittens. In the tradition of epic poems, this moment recalls the hero's arming himself for the tests and trials that will define him as a man.

Similarly, Russel's equipment recalls the brilliant and magical creations with which the ancient gods sent their favorites into battle. Oogruk's dogsled, with its birch side rails and elegantly carved stanchions, seems to have an element of such mythic unreality about it; it is a work of art that is more "like a carving of a sled" than a real sled (35). In another archetypal connection, Russel's commandeering of the dogs opens with the kind of ritualistic formula common in epic poetry: "Then a thing happened" (36). As Russel's journey continues, these recurring formulas recall the phrases with which ancient poets seamed their stories together as they sang.

Although Russel handles the team awkwardly on the first run, the dogs and sled become agents of his birth into the history of his people. He feels that he is "alive and the sled is alive and the snow is alive and the ice is alive and we are all part of the same life" (39). Simple repetition creates poetry that runs across the page and into the mind as the sled glides over the ice.

When Oogruk sends Russel on a second run to hunt meat, further transformations occur in the young hero. When at first Russel fails to kill ptarmigan with his bow, he remembers one of the powerful messages of the trance: "Look to the center of the center of where the point will go. Look *inside* the center" (42). This advice functions as a metaphor for the whole experience of the monomyth: The journey centers the hero spiritually as well as centering him in the experience of his culture. After he kills ptarmigan, Russel begins to feel the changes taking place in him, sensing that the sled is becoming an "extension of his body" as he is becoming an "extension of the dogs" (45). In an affirmation of this oneness, Russel hears for the first time a dogsong in his mind: "*Out before me they go / I am the dogs*" (50). Perhaps a song from the Eskimo consciousness, a song of the old days, it foreshadows the day when Russel will sing his own dogsong.

More Preparation for the Departure. The imagery of the epigraph of Chapter 4 returns us to the world of Eskimo myth and contrasts with Russel's successful hunt and his respect for nature in Chapter 3.

An Eskimo tells the story of early Russian fur hunters who abused the Eskimos, taking the women for themselves, using the men as beasts, and leaving them starving. The epigraph's emphasis on hunting and eating remains the focus as Russel's narrative continues and as Russel endures several tests of his ability to apply what he is learning.

Two tests, the central events of this chapter, illustrate the role of the dogs in Russel's success. The first test comes in a snowstorm in which Russel, trying to guide the dogs, gets lost, finally trusting the dogs to find the way back. In the second test, a break in the ice threatens to carry Russel and the dog team to a watery death; but Russel engineers a floating ice bridge by swinging a chunk of ice around and forcing the dogs to cross it. Both tests symbolize the process of Russel's transformation as the hero. The tests recall the episodic nature of poems such as the *Odyssey* in which Homer tells the story of Odysseus by linking together episodes that reveal the hero's ingenuity in overcoming obstacles, represented by the one-eyed giant Polyphemus and the sorceress Circe. Russel's struggle with the breaking and shifting ice especially recalls Odysseus' confrontation with the watery dangers of Scylla and Charybdis.

Leaving Home. The final chapter in "The Trance" opens with another epigraph that juxtaposes the ancient and the modern worlds. Speaking from memory, an old woman recalls the great power that shamans had "before the church came" (67), a link to Oogruk's memory of the missionaries (Chapter 2), whose theology replaced the mythology of his people. In the old woman's story, one shaman had two heads that couldn't resolve their differences; when one head told the body to kill the other head, the whole body died. How do we interpret this story in the context of Russel's quest? Perhaps the two heads symbolize the conflicts between two ways of knowing; perhaps they point to the death of Oogruk, suggesting that the hero cannot listen at once to two heads, that he must learn to keep his own counsel and be of one mind in his resolve to fulfill his destiny.

In the next hunt, Russel is accompanied by Oogruk, but once they are out on the ice, Oogruk instructs Russel to leave him. Oogruk's final advice prepares Russel for his future. If the boy is to become a man, Oogruk explains, he cannot go back home. Instead, he must make a journey of self-discovery: "Run long and find yourself." He cannot accomplish this alone: "Run with the dogs and become what the dogs will help you become" (72). In an eerie moment Russel leaves Oogruk, knowing that his friend will freeze to death. Later, overcome with guilt, he circles back to find the old man sitting upright, frozen, staring, it seems, far beyond the edge of the ice "where his spirit had flown, out and out" (74). Russel understands the significance of Oogruk's death. Equipped with weapons, dogs, and a fine sled, Russel knows that the rest of his knowledge must come from the basic elements of the world: "Everything would come from the land" (75). The young hero stands poised on the brink of great adventure as he sets out alone to continue his quest.

Part II: "The Dreamrun" and Initiation

"The Dreamrun" illustrates the initiation phase of the monomyth. The journey is outward toward the north, away from the village; it is backward in time into the collective unconscious of the Eskimo race; and it is inward, psychological and spiritual. In this complex multilayered texture, Paulsen intertwines the mystic and mythic world of dreams with the cold and challenging world of the Arctic tundra, the landscape in which Russel's dreams come to life.

Russel's initiation is framed by "thresholds of transformation"— events, moments that demand changes in both the physical and psychological patterns of life (Campbell 1968, 10). With the death of Oogruk, Russel crosses the first threshold into an unknown, dark, and dangerous world. His physical appearance has been transformed because he wears Oogruk's hunting clothes, carries his treasured weapons, and, most important, takes charge of his sled and dog team. Psychologically, Russel has been transformed by Oogruk's words, his vision of the journey. At the end of this adventure, when Russel crosses the return threshold and rejoins his community, he will have been transformed by the quest for selfhood and song.

Landscape: The Journey Outward. Crossing the first threshold, Russel faces a series of tests, often referred to as the "difficult tasks" motif of myth (Campbell 1968, 97). In the first run, Russel finds the terrain so unfamiliar that he thinks it looks otherworldly, "like something from another planet" (80). His purpose on this run is to hunt for meat. He kills a caribou with his arrows; and, as if foreshadowing his fulfillment in the quest, he sings a "poem song," praising his arrows because they have been "true" (87). Content after he makes camp and eats, Russel lets his mind "circle and go down" into the first dream (89). This circular psychical motion that occurs in the dream sequences of the novel parallels the circular pattern of the quest, the hero's journey from home to home.

Dreamscape: The Journey Inward. As his mind circles down, Russel enacts the archetypal descent into the psyche, into the "crooked lanes" of his "spiritual labyrinth" where he finds himself in a "landscape of symbolical figures." In this labyrinth he will experience moments of insight, of illumination, which are necessary for his transformation (Campbell 1968, 101–09).

Russel's dream opens in swirling fog, a metaphor for the transition from consciousness to dream. This curtain of fog rises to reveal the symbolic figures of the dreamscape: a man, his young wife, and two small children. The dream moves forward in three scenes that Paulsen presents almost cinemagraphically. In the first scene, the family appears inside its warm home; in the second, the man leaves on a hunt (crossing a threshold); and in the third, the man appears out on the sweeps, killing a mammoth. This initial dream sequence enacts the departure and test motif of the monomyth, and Russel's subsequent dreams will complete this dream story.

In the first scene, Russel identifies with the man, feeling "more than close somehow" (93). In the second scene, the figures in the dream assume mythic proportions as the man leaves the warmth of the tent to harness dogs that seem "more than dogs," standing like gigantic shadows. The sled, "all of bone and ivory" is a work of art, reminiscent of Oogruk's carved sled (94).

The curtain of fog swirls away the second scene, clearing to show the third, a hunt in which the man works the dog team in silence. The man encounters a huge shape, phantasmagoric, as in a nightmare; a woolly mammoth with great tusks emerges, angrily whipping back and forth, its red eyes tearing through the fog "like a demon's from the Below World" (96). This Below World can be interpreted as a manifestation of the underworld of classical mythology, and the dream of the mammoth represents a symbolic visit to that underworld, a visit that provides Russel with knowledge he will need later in his own journey. The image of the mammoth symbolically looks forward and backward, prefiguring Russel's climactic test in the confrontation with the polar bear and situating him in prehistory. When Russel recognizes the prehistoric man in the dream as an older, hairier version of himself, he realizes what this person symbolizes: He, too, will have to fight and kill a mammoth. As this recognition fills him with tremendous fear, the dream hunter kills the beast and bursts into a song of exultation. Russel makes a connection; he can feel "all those songs inside his soul" (98), a backward connection to Oogruk and a foreshadowing of journey's end when he sings his own dogsong.

Landscape: Storm on the Sweeps. In the second run onto the sweeps, Russel stays connected to the scenes in this dream. He can still smell the inside of the "dreamigloo-tent," the stench of the mammoth "voiding itself in death" (101), and the hot smell of the beast's blood as it runs down the shaft of the hunter's lance. Making camp under an overhanging stone ledge, Russel finds an old stone lamp that recalls Oogruk's seal-oil lamp—another connection to history and Eskimo tradition.

An approaching storm transports us into the second dreamscape. Russel begins to realize his power to create a world and to create himself: "Where there had been nothing he now had shelter and food and heat and comfort. Where there had been nothing he had become something" (108).

Dreamscape: Feasting and Storytelling. The second dream, emerging in the envelope of fog, connects to the end of the first dream as Russel thinks "He was the man and he was the dream. He was the fog" (98). In this new monochromatic dreamscape, the hunter drives his gray dogs out of gray fog; it seems as if the dogs are not "animals but fog that had come alive" (109). Traveling more deeply into the collective unconscious of his race, Russel possesses extraordinary vision now. The dream hero, having killed the mammoth, finds a village; Russel is simultaneously himself and the hunter, a connection he senses so clearly that he can see the dream hunter's "mind working" (110). Russel and the dream hunter travel in "a new land" where "the people were known to him as all people are known to all other people" (110). This passage illustrates the power of archetypes: The hero's story is one story for all the world.

The dream showcases the art of storytelling; in ancient epics the hero must often establish his identity and credibility in strange lands by telling his story. Odysseus tells such a story, for example, at the palace of Alcinous and Arete in *Odyssey, Book 7* when he recalls his experience on Calypso's Island. Storytelling in this section of *Dogsong* serves a similar purpose. Ritualistic feasting often provides the stage for such storytelling in ancient epics, as it does in the familiar *Beowulf* where heroes ensure their fame with tales of supernatural strength. The villagers of Russel's dream feed the hunter and his dogs, hoping that the stranger will tell stories of the killing of the large beast and of journeying through unknown lands. Perhaps, they think, the stranger will "sing his song" (111), the same kind of song that motivates Russel's quest.

Dreamscape: Foldings. The second scene of this dream fulfills the epic storytelling practice and introduces the metaphor of "a new folding" as a way of connecting the mythic world, the dream world, and the waking world. After the dream feast, the hero, clad only in a breechcloth, appears larger than life. Russel sees that he is unified with the earth: Rather than standing on the ground, he seems, almost magically, to be "growing up *from* the ground," and he continues to grow larger as he takes his strength from the earth (112). This is the perfect metaphor for the transformation that is occurring as Russel journeys toward manhood, growing through the knowledge he acquires in his connection to the land. Knowing that he *is* the man in the dream, Russel lets that knowledge "carry him into the man" (113). Here, then, Russel folds into the symbolic figure in the dream, and the image of growing up from the earth recalls the final words of "The Trance": "Everything would come from the land" (75).

Dreamscape: Transformation. Now an extraordinary transformation occurs in Russel's dream, complicating the levels of the hero's experience. The hunter is transformed into the mammoth in a ritualistic choreography that is "more than a dance, more than a story": He *"became* the mammoth, down to the smell, the foul smell that came from the beast" (113). Such a symbolic metamorphosis from man to beast was typical of initiation rites in early hunter/warrior cultures. As part of their military initiation, young warriors were ritually transformed into a predator, a "raging carnivore," in a "magico-religious experience" that radically changed their way of being in the world (Eliade 1972, 6). This identification of the hunter/warrior with a predator was "so universal that we may reasonably characterize it as archetypal" (Fields 1991, 62). In Indo-European cultures, which originated in the steppes, the transformation was most often into a bear or wolf, the cult of the bear having its earliest history with northern Paleolithic hunters who were the ancestors of the Indo-Europeans. How did such a transmutation take place? Young warriors, like the hunter in Russel's dream, "danced themselves into identity" with the bear; in their initiation, however, they wore masks and pelts of fur as they imitated the howls and growls of the bear. The symbolism of the bear also relates to its mysterious hibernation, to the symbolic winter death from which it is reborn in spring (Fields 1991, 62–63). In this context, the killing of the mammoth in the dream prefigures Russel's literal killing of the polar bear and signals the most important single moment of his transformation: his birth into manhood.

As the dream continues, Paulsen increases the rhythmic intensity of his poetry in a series of concentric circles, catching the reader up into the swirling dance occurring in Russel's mind. In the dance, the mammoth grows in strength and rage, attacking the hunter and his dogs. When the mammoth falls on the hunter's spear, it dies.

This dance initiates another circle as the hero-hunter, exhausted, falls to the floor and others rise to sing and dance songs that continue through succeeding days and nights. These circles of stories and days again symbolize the power of myth through which generations have defined themselves and their culture in storytelling.

The dream sequence ends in a fusion of two metaphors for the landscapes of the novel as "the dream folded back into the fog" (115). Folding suggests how a simple physical motion may change the shape of something, just as the fog reshapes the physical and psychical worlds of Russel's experience.

Landscape: Riding the Storm. When the storm hits (Chapter 10), Russel follows Oogruk's advice to ride it out and sleeps for two days. Then he sets out for new country, unsure of where he is, again trusting Oogruk's advice that the destination does not count, that he must "pay attention to the journey" (119). Letting the dogs run at will, he discovers snowmobile tracks that appear "as if by magic" (121). Modern life seems to be intruding on his journey into the past, and he senses that the presence of a snowmobile is "out of place, opposite, wrong" (122). The dogs run on for two days and nights, and, again, Russel's mind begins to circle and slip down into a dream. This time, however, he does not dream but hallucinates a series of three vignettes that point backward and forward. In the first vignette, he thinks he sees someone riding in his sled, a foreshadowing of his rescue of Nancy. In the second vignette, he sees small lights on the dogs' feet, symbolic of their power to guide, to see for him in the storm. In the third and most complex vignette, a mirror serves two functions by symbolizing his location in both past and present and by transporting him into the next dream. The opening of his parka hood seems to be a mirror in which "everything he saw in front of him was somehow in back of him." As he drives on into the dark night, "the mirror vanished and he had the dream" (124). Since the dream occurs as the dogs run into the darkness, landscape and dreamscape now become one.

Landscape/Dreamscape. This dream (Chapter 11) circles back to the hero-hunter of the first dream, but much is changed. The gentle gray fog is transformed into a violent and destructive gray storm, and the whole dream has "an air of madness to it" (125). The darkest moment of the psychical journey occurs as the dream hunter, having stayed too long to enjoy the hospitality of the strange village, returns to his family. This dream is composed of two scenes. In the first, the hunter almost dies in the storm. In the second, the dream mother and her children await death in their tent as the mother considers mercifully strangling her two children. The "hungry wind," a negative form of the eating imagery of the novel, threatens to devour the people in the dreamscape (128).

Landscape: The Meeting with the Goddess. "The Run" (Chapter 12) picks up the narrative in the icy landscape as Russel comes upon the snowmobile that made the tracks he saw earlier. Although another storm threatens, Russel follows human tracks in the snow until he finds the frozen shell of a pregnant "girl-woman" (135) who corresponds to the mother in the dream. She is about to give birth, and Russel's rescue of her symbolizes his approaching birth into manhood and rebirth into the Eskimo community. Formalists would point out that this frozen image of Nancy near the end of the journey balances the frozen figure of Oogruk at the beginning of the quest. Both figures represent the protective guardians of the threshold in the monomyth. Only by advancing beyond the bounds represented by such figures can the hero pass into "a new zone of experience" (Campbell 1968, 82). While Oogruk's frozen death formerly moved Russel out into the dangerous and solitary struggles of the hero's adventure, Nancy's rebirth from her frozen shell will move Russel inward, toward the safety of community.

After finding the girl, Russel makes camp, and his construction of it is highly symbolic and archetypal. Positioning the dog team so that it creates "a living screen" against the wind, he makes a lean-to by turning the sled on its side and covering it with animal skins. Considering the girl's pregnant state and the hero's transformation, this lean-to suggests a form of what Campbell calls the "Belly of the Whale," a "world-wide womb image" out of which the hero is reborn. In Campbell's explanation, this womb image occurs at the first threshold of the journey, but in *Dogsong* it occurs before the second threshold. In some myths, the hero, in order to be born again, undergoes a symbolic death by going inward (Campbell 1968, 90–91), as Russel does here. The lean-to in the storm, then, can be interpreted as a pattern of concentric circles. Working from the outside inward, from the (1) swirling storm outside, we see that Russel constructs (2) a womb for his own rebirth into the landscape after the storm, a womb that protects (3) the round body of Nancy whose (4) womb encircles the unborn child.

Dreamscape: Two Worlds in One. In the insulated world he creates, Russel falls into the final dream that fuses his earlier dreams with his rescue of Nancy. By dream's end, he knows "in his center" that "the dream had become his life and his life and the run had become the dream" (144). In the dreamscape (Chapter 13), the storm clears, and the hunter heads home. As the dreamdogs come near the family's tent, Russel senses an "end to things," senses that he is "out of the dream but still in it" in a way that he does not understand (141). This sensation is part of the process in which the two worlds of the journey, the physical and the psychical, become one world.

A tragic scene emerges in the dreamscape as Russel sees the hunter's tent and contemplates "the end that came to all things" (142–43).

Only two bones remain in the tent as visible evidence of the former existence of mother and children. In the scene, though, Russel sees a signal of hope—the shallow stone lamp, an image that has been woven throughout the novel. This lamp is an imaginary form of other real lamps—Oogruk's lamp and the lamp Russel found earlier when he camped in the snow. The image of the dreamlamp shifts back into reality as Russel awakens to discover the flickering light of his own lamp and to realize that the girl beside him is "the same woman as the woman in the dream" (144).

The Meeting with the Goddess. The meeting with the "girl-woman" is a variation on one of the events of the monomyth: the meeting with the goddess, "the ultimate adventure," often represented as a "mystical marriage." This meeting may occur at the farthest points of experience, zenith or nadir, at the "outermost edge of the earth," in the center of the cosmos, or within the "darkness of the deepest chamber" of the human heart (Campbell 1968, 109). This event is not worked out in *Dogsong* as it is in Campbell's pattern, but Nancy clearly represents the goddess principle as Campbell describes it in the monomyth. Woman, he explains, "represents the totality of what can be known." The hero is the person who comes to this knowledge by progressing through the slow initiation of human life. The goddess may be transfigured a number of times; she can never be greater than the hero, but together goddess and hero "will be released from every limitation" (Campbell 1968, 116). As a result of his encounter with the woman in the dreams, Russel realizes that he has changed:

> At the other end of the dreamrun nothing was the same as when he started. At the other end, Russel was no longer young, but he wasn't old, either. He wasn't afraid, but he wasn't brave. He wasn't smart, but he wasn't a fool. He wasn't as strong as he would be, but he wasn't ever going to be as weak as he was. (145)

These seem to be perfectly realistic claims for an adolescent on the threshold of manhood. At the end of the dream and at the end of the storm, Russel emerges from the womb of the lean-to and acts as both husband and father.

Landscape: The Final Test. Chapter 14, "The Dreamrun," brings the cycle of stories in Part II full circle. Its title, identical to the section title, suggests how this chapter fuses the alternating scenes of the "dreamrun" sequence and ends them. The strands of the landscape and dreamscape narratives are fused by (1) the imagery of "a great folding" and (2) the repetition of the statement "These things happened" (146). The language supports our archetypal reading as the narrator says, "These things happened. Either in the dream or the run, either in one fold or another fold, these things happened" (146). This sentence itself is a microcosmic narrative of *Dogsong*: What happened is folded inside both dream and reality.

This final folding reveals the rest of the story. As Nancy tells Russel about her premarital pregnancy, her subsequent disgrace and homelessness, she folds out of Russel's dream and into his life. Leaving the lean-to, they set out, running north. When their food runs out, Russel goes to find meat; he leaves Nancy at the camp, but he is haunted by the memory of the dream family's death. Days later, unsuccessful in his search and sensing failure, he finally encounters the great polar bear.

The battle with the bear is the climactic event of the novel. Russel succeeds in wounding the bear as his lance slides "into the center of the center of the bear" (*Dogsong*, 160). Even near death the bear strikes his adversary, and for a moment Russel senses his own imminent death as his life flashes before him. This is the near-death experience, but Russel is reborn when he comes "back into his life from where the bear had knocked him away" (160–61).

When Russel returns, he finds Nancy, and a new cycle begins: "Where there had been an end there was once more a beginning" (163). In a folding of life into death, Nancy gives birth "from the center of her center" to a stillborn child. In this act, she, too, is transformed by the journey, wherein "girl-woman became a woman in the night" (165). She loses the life inside her, but she does not lose herself. Russel takes the dead child out into the snow, and at this moment the most problematic sentence of the novel occurs: "And he wished that he had stayed in his village" (166). What does this imply about the nature of the hero? Despite his manly acts, this thought reveals the delicacy of the balance between adolescence and manhood, a moment in which a young man, in deep travail, might wish never to have begun that journey.

Crossing the Return Threshold. Part II of the novel ends with a race to safety. The poetic incantation "So began the race" punctuates the final journey to an unfamiliar village on the northern coast, a village symbolically on the edge of the land. Heroism is imperative now, and Russel thinks, "I must win this race" (169). The action of the novel ends in a suspension not unlike the one with which it began. Paulsen indicates that we are in a halfway world with the "man-boy" and the "woman-girl" on the edge of adulthood, and he signifies their return with a final word, "Back" (171).

Part III: "Dogsong"

Although the novel's action ends in the northern village, time obviously passes between Parts II and III. "Dogsong" locates us back in Russel's home village to complete the cycle of the myth, the 360 degrees signifying totality (Campbell 1968, 223). The song provides evidence that Russel has grown up, has become a man, is connected to the land on which so much has depended: *"I stand on the earth and I sing"* (176). It alludes to his wife, his children, his dogs, his village and his history: *"I stand by the sea and I sing. / I sing of my hunts / and of Oogruk* (177). From a journey backward in time, outward to the edge of the world, and inward to his soul and to the collective unconscious of his race, Russel sings of the future, the perpetual hunt with his dogs as they go before him "in the long line out." The final image of unity wraps up the journey experience in one image: *"They go, I go, we go. They are me"* (177). This is a moment of the greatest pride—when Russel sings himself into the grand hunting tradition of his race.

The Significance of Archetypes

This reading of *Dogsong* demonstrates the general principles of archetypal theory. First, most archetypal critics agree that creating myths answers a basic human need and that creating myths is inherent in our thinking process. Second, myth creates a matrix from which literature emerges historically and psychologically. Consequently, plots, characters, themes, and images in literature are essentially complications and displacements of elements in myths and folktales. Third, in addition to stimulating the creative artist, myth provides the critic with concepts and patterns to use in the interpretation of literary works. Fourth, the mythic quality of literature is part of what moves us deeply as we respond to what we read (Vickery 1966, 119–120).

The way in which the monomyth pervades contemporary culture is attested to by Campbell's popularity, heightened as a result of journalist Bill Moyers' public television series "The Power of Myth," which is based on Campbell's thinking and writing. Moyers affirms the power of archetypal criticism in the world outside the schoolroom. Recalling his boyhood fondness for movies, he explains:

> Not until I met Joseph Campbell did I understand that the Westerns I saw at the Saturday matinees had borrowed freely from those ancient tales. And that the stories learned in Sunday School corresponded with those in other cultures that recognized the soul's high adventure, the quest of mortals to grasp the reality of God. He helped me to see the connections, to understand how the pieces fit. (Moyers 1988, xviii)

Not only do myths pervade elements of the popular culture in the way that Moyers describes, but script consultant Linda Seger (1994) contends that many successful films are based on these universal stories. She explains the monomyth to aspiring screenwriters, encouraging them to read Joseph Campbell and Greek mythology as well as to explore archetypes in Jungian psychology. In language specific to the film world, she describes the steps in the monomyth as "story beats," noting that their significance is to tell "who the hero is, what the hero needs, and how the story and character interact in order to create a transformation." Affirming the power of these myths, Seger observes that filmmakers, including George Lucas, Steven Spielberg, Sylvester Stallone, and Clint Eastwood, have dramatized the monomyth in creative ways. She encourages young scriptwriters to add mythic elements to their stories, because "myths are marketable" (Seger 1994, 252–58).

In the broadest philosophical context, Campbell suggests that the monomyth is at the very heart of our knowledge and our experience of becoming. In making human life a metaphor, a journey of obstacles, myth helps us achieve a higher level of consciousness, and myth criticism helps us see through literature in more powerful ways (Campbell 1968, 121). *Dogsong* is both about Russel Susskit's experiences and simultaneously about our life journey from childhood through adolescence toward adulthood. At the very center of the novel are issues about the conflict between the worlds into which we are born physically and psychologically and the worlds to which we aspire.

Joining the Conversation

The archetypal pattern of the quest that occurs in *Dogsong* is the foundation of many coming-of-age stories in the field of young adult literature. Leila Christenbury (1993) offers a way to join the theoretical conversation in exploring this pattern in "Leaving Home to Come Home: The Hero's Quest in *Great Expectations* and Three Young Adult Novels." Her ideas create a bridge from our reading of Paulsen's novel to other young adult fiction. After a critical assessment of Dickens' novel, a staple in the secondary school curriculum, Christenbury comments on the challenges it offers in the contemporary classroom: its language, its length, its portrayal of female characters, its improbable twists and turns of plot. Observing that today's young adult readers might be less fascinated with Dickens' novel than their Victorian counterparts were, Christenbury suggests how three young adult novels can complement and illuminate the mythic theme in Dickens' *Great Expectations*.

After examining the archetypal journey of Dickens' hero, Christenbury explores how Cynthia Rylant's *A Fine White Dust*, Paulsen's

Dogsong, and Robert Lipsyte's *The Brave* complement Dickens' story. She provides specific questions to guide teachers' inquiry into each of the young adult novels.

In "Teaching, Learning, and Archetypes: Images of Instruction in Cynthia Voigt's *Dicey's Song*," Tom Albritton (1994) applies an archetypal approach to the schoolteachers in the novel. He works out of Carol Pearson's *The Hero Within: Six Archetypes We Live By* (1989), an adaptation of Campbell's heroic archetypes. According to Pearson, personal power is achieved by moving through six archetypal stages: the Innocent, the Orphan, the Wanderer, the Warrior, the Martyr, and the Magician (Albritton 1994, 56). Answering the question "Do the archetypal patterns of heroic growth really fit the characteristics of pedagogical growth? Albritton concludes that they do and that as we teach *Dicey's Song* we "may be sending and receiving powerful messages about teaching itself." Teaching, he believes, can "be heroic, and teachers' journeys can lead to magic" (Albritton 1994, 59).

Another coming-of-age novel that fits Joseph Campbell's archetypal pattern is Denis Johnson's *Fiskadoro* (1985). Set in a nuclear wasteland in the middle of the twenty-first century, this work of science fiction explores how people cope with the destruction of a world and its mythologies.

An intriguing novel that can be put into conversation with Paulsen's *Dogsong* is Markoosie's *Harpoon of the Hunter* (1970), a quest story in which sixteen-year-old Kamik, an Inuit, is subject to tremendous trials as he attempts to follow in his father's footsteps as a great hunter. Although Kamik completes his quest, nature deals him a tragic blow that leads him to take his own life with the harpoon that has made him a hero.

Tolkien's *The Hobbit* (1986), set in the fantastical land of Middle-Earth in The Third Age, offers another variant on the quest pattern. An Anglo-Saxon scholar, Tolkien tells the story of the adventures of Bilbo Baggins, a less-than-auspicious hobbit, who goes on a journey to find treasure, but who, like many of the central characters in young adult quest stories, finds out some valuable things about himself. He returns as a changed hobbit. With its mixture of Celtic, English, Scandinavian, and Germanic elements, this often humorous tale makes an intriguing counterpoint to the study of *Beowulf* and the realistic quest stories discussed here.

Robin McKinley's high fantasy *The Hero and the Crown* (1984), set in the mythical kingdom of Damar, presents the archetypal quest for identity from the perspective of a female character. Eighteen-year-old Aerin, the only daughter of King Arlbeth, is the rightful heir to the throne, but she must prove herself worthy by overcoming gender stereotypes. Her transformation, in the sense of Campbell's monomyth, occurs when she gains her identity and self-esteem by defeating the evil Agsded and regaining the Hero's Crown that the mage has stolen. At the end of the novel, she becomes Queen of the Damarians.

Cynthia Voigt's *Orfe* (1992), a retelling of the Greek myth of Orpheus and Eurydice, invites comparison with the original story to understand how Voigt has transformed the myth. In "A Teaching Guide to Orfe," Elizabeth Poe (n.d.) describes the novel as "a fascinating journey into the worlds of rock music, drug addiction, and human yearnings" (2). She suggests other young adult novels with archetypal connections that might be paired with *Orfe* for classroom study (3). Biblical archetypes appear in Cynthia Voigt's *David and Jonathan* (1992) and in Katherine Paterson's *Jacob Have I Loved* (1980) (see my discussion of these archetypes in Chapter 10). Neal Shusterman's *The Eyes of Kid Midas* (1992) and Paul Zindel's *Harry and Hortense at Hormone High* (1984) both contain archetypes from Greek mythology. Fairy-tale patterns appear in Adele Gracas' *Pictures in the Night* (1993), *The Tower Room* (1992), and *Watching the Roses* (1992). To Poe's suggestions, I add Robin McKinley's retelling of the fairy tale "Beauty and the Beast" in her novel *Beauty* (1978) and the amazing fairy-tale twists and transformations that Francesca Lia Block creates in *Weetzie Bat* (1989).

Poe mentions other texts that would be useful in a cultural studies (see Chapter 10) reading of *Orfe*. An ancient version of the story occurs in Ovid's *Metamorphoses* (I recommend the Rolfe Humphries translation). Familiar retellings of the myth appear in the mythology collections of Thomas Bullfinch and Edith Hamilton. *Black Orpheus*, a 1959 film by Marcel Camus, relocates the myth in the setting of modern Brazil (Poe, 2).

Nilsen and Donelson (1993) discuss "archetypal initiation rites" in a variant on the quest motif that they call the "adventure/accomplishment romance." Their description of this story pattern follows the separation-initiation-return sequence of Campbell's monomyth. They discuss Cynthia Voigt's *Izzy, Willy-Nilly* (1986) as an example of this pattern that focuses on the mental trials that a tenth-grade cheerleader named Izzy must face when she loses her leg in an accident. Other young adult novels that they cite as representative of this kind of story include Virginia Hamilton's *M.C. Higgins, the Great* (1974) (see Chapter 3); Robert Lipsyte's *The Brave* (1991), a rewriting of *The Contender* (1967); and Bruce Brooks' *The Moves Make the Man* (1984) (see Chapter 5). Their inclusion of Hamilton's and Brooks' novels underscores one of the key ideas of my book: Many texts may be read from multiple theoretical perspectives. Such pluralistic approaches to interpreting young adult fiction can enrich the reading by teachers and their students as they work to make meaning of the texts they share.

Works Cited

Albritton, Tom. 1994. "Teaching, Learning, and Archetypes: Images of Instruction in Cynthia Voigt's *Dicey's Song.*" *ALAN Review* 21 (Spring): 56–59.

Auden, W. H. 1962. "The Quest Hero." *Texas Quarterly* 4:81–93. Reprinted in Neil D. Isaacs and Rose A. Zimbardor, eds., *Tolkien and the Critics: Essays on J.R.R. Tolkien's* The Lord of the Rings. South Bend, IN: University of Notre Dame Press, 1968: 40–61.

Beowulf. 1963. Trans. Burton Raffel. New York: New American Library.

Block, Francesca Lia. 1989. *Weetzie Bat.* New York: HarperCollins.

Brooks, Bruce. 1984. *The Moves Make the Man.* Harper and Row.

Bullfinch, Thomas. 1970. *Mythology.* New York: Crowell.

Campbell, Joseph. 1968. *The Hero with a Thousand Faces.* 2d corrected ed. Princeton: Princeton University Press.

———. 1972. "Schizophrenia—the Inward Journey." In *Myths to Live By*, 207–239. New York: Bantam.

Camus, Marcel. 1959. *Black Orpheus.* Loper Films.

Christenbury, Leila. 1993. "Leaving Home to Come Home: The Hero's Quest in *Great Expectations* and Three Young Adult Novels." In *Adolescent Literature as a Complement to the Classics*, ed. Joan F. Kaywell, 117–26. Norwood, MA: Christopher-Gordon.

Dickens, Charles. 1967. *Great Expectations.* New York: Macmillan.

Eliade, Mircea. 1972. *Zalmoxis: The Vanishing God.* Chicago: University of Chicago Press. (Quoted in Rick Fields, *The Code of the Warrior in History, Myth, and Everyday Life.* New York: HarperPerennial, 1991, 61–62.)

Fields, Rick. 1991. "The Warrior's Dilemma: The Indo-Europeans." In *The Code of the Warrior in History, Myth, and Everyday Life*, 55–79. New York: HarperPerennial.

Frye, Northrop. 1963. "The Archetypes of Literature." In *Fables of Identity: Studies in Poetic Mythology*, 7–20. New York: Harcourt, Brace, and World.

———. 1982. *The Great Code: The Bible and Literature.* San Diego: Harcourt Brace Jovanovich.

Gracas, Adele. 1992. *The Tower Room.* New York: Harcourt Brace Jovanovich.

———. 1992. *Watching the Roses.* New York: Harcourt Brace Jovanovich.

———. 1993. *Pictures in the Night.* New York: Harcourt Brace Jovanovich.

Hamilton, Edith. 1942. *Mythology.* Boston: Little, Brown.

Hamilton, Virginia. 1974. *M.C. Higgins, the Great.* New York: Macmillan.

Hardin, Richard F. 1989. "Archetypal Criticism." In *Contemporary Literary Theory*, eds. Douglas G. Atkins and Laura Morrow, 42–59. Amherst: University of Massachusetts Press.

Homer. 1990. *Odyssey.* Trans. Robert Fitzgerald. New York: Vintage.

Johnson, Denis. 1985. *Fiskadoro*. London: Chatto and Windus.

Leitch, Vincent B. 1988. "Myth Criticism." In *American Literary Criticism from the Thirties to the Eighties*, 115–47. New York: Columbia University Press.

Lipsyte, Robert. 1991. *The Brave*. New York: HarperCollins.

———. 1967. *The Contender*. New York: Harper and Row.

Markoosie. 1970. *Harpoon of the Hunter*. Montreal: McGill-Queen's University Press.

McKinley, Robin. 1978. *Beauty*. New York: Harper and Row.

———. 1984. *The Hero and the Crown*. New York: Greenwillow.

Moore. John N. 1994. Conversation with Gary Paulsen. Orlando, FL.

Moyers, Bill. 1988. Introduction to *The Power of Myth*, by Joseph Campbell. New York: Doubleday.

Nilsen, Alleen Pace, and Kenneth Donelson. 1993. "The Old Romanticism of Wishing and Winning." In *Literature for Today's Young Adults*, 4th ed., 141–69. New York: HarperCollins.

Ovid. 1983. *Metamorphoses*. Trans. Rolfe Humphries. Bloomington: Indiana University Press.

Paterson, Katherine. 1980. *Jacob Have I Loved*. New York: HarperCollins.

Paulsen, Gary. 1985. *Dogsong*. New York: Puffin.

———. 1994. "Write What You *Are*." Interview by Cheryl Bartky. *Writer's Digest* (July): 42–45, 65.

Pearson, Carol. 1989. *The Hero Within: Six Archetypes We Live By*. New York: HarperCollins.

Poe, Elizabeth. N. d. *A Teaching Guide to* Orfe *by Cynthia Voigt*. New York: Scholastic.

Rylant, Cynthia. 1986. *A Fine White Dust*. New York: Bradbury.

Seger, Linda. 1994. "Creating the Myth." In *Signs of Life in the U.S.A.: Readings on Popular Culture for Writers*, eds. Sonia Maasik and Jack Solomon, 250–59. Boston: St. Martin's.

Shusterman, Neal. 1992. *The Eyes of Kid Midas*. New York: Little, Brown.

Tolkien, J.R.R. 1986. *The Hobbit, or There and Back Again*. New York: Ballantine.

Vickery, John B., ed. 1966. *Myth and Literature: Contemporary Theory and Practice*. Lincoln: University of Nebraska Press.

Voigt, Cynthia. 1992. *David and Jonathan*. New York: Scholastic.

———. 1992. *Orfe*. New York: MacMillan Children's Group.

———. 1982. *Dicey's Song*. New York: Fawcett Juniper.

———. 1986. *Izzy, Willy-Nilly*. New York: Aladdin.

Zindel, Paul. 1984. *Harry and Hortense at Hormone High*. New York: HarperCollins.

Four

Structuralism
Decoding Signs in *The Moves Make the Man*

> *Every work, every novel, tells through its fabric of events the story of its own creation, its own history. . . . the meaning of the work lies in its telling itself, its speaking of its own existence.*
>
> Tzvetan Todorov

In the first sentence of Bruce Brooks' *The Moves Make the Man* (1984) (hereafter known as *Moves*), thirteen-year-old Jerome Foxworthy declares himself a storyteller: "Now, Bix Rivers has disappeared, and who do you think is going to tell his story but me?" (*Moves*, 3). The first chapter centers on the act of writing. Jerome tells us that he has the tools (sharpened, dark-green enamel, number-three pencils and four black-and-marble composition books), plenty of time (all summer) and a good place (his own room). He has knowledge ("I can tell you some things"), and he has us as an audience. If we listen, he assures us, "you'll be getting the story, all you want." More important than materials, time, space, knowledge, and audience, Jerome is motivated to tell this story: He is really mad at the lies going around town about Bix Rivers, and he encourages us not to pay any attention to "this creepy jive," because "It's me gets to tell the truth" (*Moves*, 3–5). From the beginning of the novel, we know that this story is more than a tale of friendship between Bix and Jerome; it is a story about how language constructs us in the world—either as "creepy jive" or "the truth"—and about how a storyteller constructs a world in narrative. A structuralist reading of *The Moves Make the Man* explores the linguistic elements of the text that Jerome writes.

An Introduction to Structuralism

A Perspective on the Word Structure

In structuralist theory, the meaning of *structure* differs from its use in formalism and in archetypal theory. Formalism defines a work of art as a unified whole achieved through the repetition of structural and imagistic patterns. Archetypal theory moves beyond the concept of *form* as an internal governing principle to locate a work as a recurring structure within the larger framework of literary traditions. These theories share with structuralism an intense interest in system, but structuralism differs from the other two because its system is based on linguistic structures inside the work. Like formalists, structuralists work inside the text itself; but instead of looking for patterns of architectural unity, structuralists analyze the ways in which the language itself produces meaning.

Linguistics and Literature

What does this kind of structuralist work mean for the practical reader and interpreter? Simply put, it means that we must rethink the way in which we analyze the language of a text. Structuralist analysis has its own grammar, the result of the pioneering work of the father of modern linguistics, Ferdinand de Saussure. Saussure's grammar describes the basic processes by which language functions to enable us to construct meaning and to communicate with one another (Rowe 1990, 27).

Words and Signs

A few basic principles and definitions will clarify the structuralist approach. First, in structural analysis a word is no longer a word because Saussure redefined the word as a basic unit of thought and communication. He explained that in traditional usage a *word* meant something fixed, solid, self-contained, independent. In his grammar, however, Saussure replaced *word* with *sign*, defining a *sign* as something fluid, changing, dependent. This unit is composed of two functions. The first is the acoustic function, what we hear when the word is spoken; Saussure called this the *signifier*. The second is the conceptual image, the picture into which the sound is translated as it enters the mind of the hearer (or reader); this Saussure called the *signified*. Most important, Saussure explained that a sign could not possibly have one universally accepted meaning because there are too many languages in the world. Instead, what a sign means is based on its usage inside the culture that speaks the language. This theory of signs is called semiotics, a way of making meaning that occurs when we read the signs of a culture. Semiotics operates on two basic principles:

1. The meaning of a sign can be found not in itself but in its *relationships* (both differences and similarities) with other signs within a *system*. To interpret an individual sign, then, you must determine the general system in which it belongs.

2. What we call social "reality" is a human construct, the product of a cultural *mythology* that intervenes between our minds and the world we experience. Such cultural myths reflect the values and ideological interests of their builders, not the laws of nature or logic. (Massik and Solomon 1994, 14).

In semiotics, then, meaning depends on social relationships within a culture, and the meaning of a sign can change over a period of time and from place to place.

Binary Oppositions and Truth

Saussure said that meaning was produced in a social context of relationships between signs: Every term had an opposite term that was necessary to establish meaning within a sign system. Saussure referred to this concept as *difference*. Later theorists elaborated this *difference*, renaming it "binary opposition," a concept critical to our reading of *Moves*. In the opening pages of the novel, Jerome designates a binary opposition that will govern his story: the "creepy jive" of lies and "the truth." *Truth* is a problematic term in structuralist theory because reality is not *a priori*, that is, it does not exist as a universal idea outside the specifics of human experience. In semiotic terms, cultures construct their own versions of truth within their own concept of reality, and language is the most important tool in these constructions. The words *truth, lies*, and *fake* are the essential threads out of which Jerome constructs his text, and our reading traces his weaving of these terms into his version of reality.

The Structuralist Activity: Creating a World

A structural/semiotic reading (the words have become interchangeable) is systematic, a series of mental operations in which readers have the specific goal of understanding a text, or more exactly, of understanding the linguistic rules by which the language of the text functions. Interpretation results as we decode the signs of the text from the perspectives of our own cultural mythologies; consequently, our reading results in a unique text that only we can produce. There is no universal, accepted reading of the text, so we produce a "veritable fabrication" of the world of the text (Barthes 1967, 1196–97). *Fabrication* in this sense does not mean deception; it means creation and invention. Through structural analysis, then, we *create* the text in contrast to the formalistic act of *discovering* unifying patterns and the archetypal act of *classifying* the text within a larger structural system.

In a complex way, reading *Moves* involves us in a double structuralist activity: Jerome Foxworthy constructs his story out of his memory and out of the words he finds in Bix Rivers' notebook. In reading the novel, we construct the world of Wilmington, North Carolina, out of Jerome's language—that is all we have to work with. In this respect, then, we must remember that Jerome Foxworthy's determination to tell us the truth is only, in the end, his version of the "truth" of Bix Rivers. Our analysis of *Moves* is the process through which we render the "truth" of the novel intelligible to ourselves as readers and interpreters of its sign system.

Structuralism and Teaching

Structuralism offers exciting possibilities for our teaching when we consider that it actually calls into question what we do when we teach literature. We are no longer teaching only the text itself, but we are teaching a "literary system" through which we decode or figure out the meaning of the signs of the text. We stand back, in a sense, and examine the ways in which we analyze; we look at *how* we arrive at an interpretation of a text (Eagleton 1983, 123–24).

Ways of Working: Dissection and Articulation

In a structuralist reading, we perform two operations: dissection and articulation. First, we dissect the text to find "mobile fragments" or units, each of which has no meaning in itself but acquires meaning from its relationship to other units in the text. These fragments taken together create a group, an "intelligent organism" that we can know because it is different from all other groups in the text. Once we have discovered these units through our dissection, we articulate the grammar rules that associate them, and in this way we construct our version of the text (Barthes 1992, 1197–98).

Applying this dissection/articulation process to *Moves*, we come up with a structure that is based on units of Bix's presence and absence in the text:

First Part

Absence	1. Jerome sets up the story.
	2. Jerome gets Bix's notebook.
Presence	3–6. (Spring) Jerome first sees Bix play baseball and sees Bix's mother.
Absence	7. Bix and his mother disappear.

Second Part

Absence	8–14. (Summer) We are introduced to Jerome's world. (Fall) School starts (classes and basketball tryouts).
Presence	15–19. "Braxton Rivers, the Third" is introduced. Jerome's mother has an accident. Jerome and Bix team up. The mock apple pie story is told.
Absence	Bix breaks down in class, then disappears.

Third Part

| Absence | 20–21. Jerome's mother gets well. Jerome wins an unusual nighttime game. |
| Presence | 22. Bix reappears as a voice in the darkness and then disappears. |

Last Part

Presence	23. Jerome teaches Bix hoops. Bix refuses to fake and then disappears.
Absence	24. Two months pass.
Presence	24. Bix returns with a plan to beat his stepfather in basketball.
	25. The game is played: Bix finally fakes and wins.
	26. Bix is at Jerome's for dinner, and the mock-apple pie is served.
	27. Bix goes to Duke and pulls the ultimate fake: Bix denies his mother's identity and then disappears. Jerome is injured.
Absence	28. (Summer) Jerome recovers and writes the story. Bix sends a postcard without a message. Fall and school approach.

The final image of the messageless postcard ends the novel in another form of the absent/present opposition: silence/speaking. This binarism constitutes an appropriate structural balance to the first sentence of the novel in which the present Jerome begins to tell the story of his absent friend.

Reading and Interpreting *The Moves Make the Man*

A Brief Overview

Jerome's story covers one calendar year. After he first sees Bix Rivers playing baseball, Jerome becomes his classmate in the largest white high school in Wilmington, North Carolina, where Jerome is the first black student to attend. The binary opposition of black/white is constant in the story.

The narrative traces the developing relationship between the two boys whose families exist almost as binary oppositions. Jerome's fatherless home nurtures him and gives him security and identity in the guidance of his powerful mother, while Bix lives with the uncertainty of his brooding stepfather and the trauma of his mother's hospitalization for mental illness at Duke Hospital. Another set of oppositions, then, governs the structure of the story: present mother/absent mother; present stepfather/absent father.

The "moves" of the novel's title refer to the game of basketball that draws Bix and Jerome together in the novel's central action. Bix's stepfather has not allowed Bix to see his mother since her hospitalization. Therefore, to earn the right to visit her, Bix challenges his stepfather to a game of basketball. If Bix wins, his stepfather agrees to take him to Duke to visit his mother. Jerome teaches Bix the moves. Bix wins the challenge and goes to Duke, taking Jerome along. At Duke, Bix makes his most complex and difficult move and then disappears from Durham at the end of the novel.

Language Codes

Jerome codes and decodes his world in a number of sign systems: (1) the figurative language he uses to construct others and himself, (2) the language he uses to describe education at Chestnut Street Junior High, and (3) the color-coded language of basketball.

Coding Others/Coding Self. When Jerome tells the story of his first seeing Bix at the baseball game, he describes him as a "flashy white dude" with an angelic, Vienna choir boy face (14). Recalling his first sight of Bix's mother, Jerome observes that she had such a strong effect on him that looking at her was like looking at a painting hanging in the state museum. She appears, in his simile, to be classically beautiful, a work of art; she is such a vision of white light that her skin seems golden and her hair appears to be flashing brilliantly. In his language, Jerome has constructed Bix's mother in language that codes traditional Caucasian beauty. He detects something missing, however, and constructs a simile for it. Seeing her, he explains, is like being in gym class and seeing someone without an arm. His language functions metonymically, suggesting a broken/unbroken binarism. This opening section of the narrative provides a good introduction to how Jerome uses language to tell his story: He is fond of figurative language, and he has a wonderful eye for detail.

Coding the Self: The Moves. Recalling the summer that followed his first sight of Bix, Jerome explains how *moves* define and construct him. His moves in basketball, he says, are like "little definitions" of himself, and he codes himself in basketball language: "Reverse spin, triple pump, reverse dribble, stutter step with twist to the left, stutter into jumper, blind pass. These are me. The moves make the man, the moves make me" (44). During this summer, he has constructed an imaginary opponent—a bad dude, an alter ego, a second self that he comes to realize is Bix Rivers. Jerome got inexplicably mad at Bix after the baseball game; and in constructing Bix as an opponent, Jerome builds Bix up in his imagination so that he can tear him down on the court. Jerome realizes that he has never needed such an imaginary opponent to define himself. This opposition will move the novel forward when the two adolescents meet again.

School: The Language of Race. Chapters 8–14 explain Jerome's life before Bix Rivers enters it again; they reveal how sign systems construct the world for Jerome and how he decodes signs in those systems. The most pervasive system is the language of integration, governed by the oppositions white/black and inside/outside. Jerome discusses "crackers," white people who keep "jigaboo boys and girls" out of their schools (49). Here Jerome mixes two sign systems: In one system, blacks disparage poor Southern whites as "crackers"; in the other system, whites demean blacks as "jigaboos." Jerome has been chosen to integrate Chestnut Street Junior High School, and when he arrives, the principal, Mr. Terence, codes him into the white system as a "new racial item" and a "new intellect item." Jerome is not bothered by the principal's language, nor does he mind when some of his black friends later call him "Crackerjack," code for a black person who likes white people better than black people (53).

English and Narrative Truth. Two classes at Chestnut enable Jerome to notice the ways in which language constructs identity—English and French. Jerome objects to the "crap" that Miss Burno the English teacher picks for them to read aloud in class; he sees the exercise as a manifestation of the unreal/real nature of education. The stories are actually lies, he says, "magic-kingdom kiddie jive," in which the hero, their age, is designed to suck them into the narrative world as they identify with him. Jerome can see through these lies, telling us that it's dishonest for adults to treat kids this way. In the human world, things don't work the way they do in these stories, he says. The stories trick you by getting you interested in a "system of things" in which you have a good conflict, for example, a magician against a mad king and his dragon. Instead of complicating this situation and working it out imaginatively, the writer simply bails the good guy out of trouble; and Jerome tells us that this kind of writing is dishonest (58). This method, he implies, is no way to tell a story. Jerome's storytelling does not resort to such quick fixes and happy endings.

French and the Construction of Social Reality. The inside/outside opposition in Jerome's world takes on a different meaning in French class where his perceptions reflect the structuralist concept of the construction of social reality, of how we create ourselves and our world in language. Walking into the class, Jerome feels "completely new." Before this class, he has never realized "how much my way of talking was what made me who I thought and other people thought I was." What he likes most is the idea that he can "start from scratch" and build himself "a personality step by step through the words" he uses, knowing all the time what he is doing (60). This process also describes the way in which he tells us the story: He selects details from his experiences with Bix and from Bix's notebook that he has "borrowed" from the Rivers' house, decides on the order of these experiences, and constructs a story. The story is a social construction, a product of the world that Jerome has shared with Bix.

Coding/Decoding Basketball: Playing White. When Jerome goes to the basketball tryouts at Chestnut Street Junior High, the coach informs him that participants have been "specially invited," another coding for the inside/outside world that Jerome has described earlier in his thinking about integration. Nonetheless, he moves onto the court and makes a brilliant play that the coach calls a "typical jig trick shot" (71). Undeterred, Jerome challenges the white athletes to a game of one-on-two. "Nigger ball?" they respond, by which Jerome understands that they mean "make it-take it" (72). During the game, the coach calls the plays, always against Jerome; signals the turnovers with "White ball"; and finally declares the white players the winners, telling Jerome "Take a hike, boy" (76). The racial epithet "boy" suggests two binary oppositions: slave/free and black/white. *Boy* is a sign that is culturally coded to emasculate black men, to deny them the power to construct themselves as Jerome has done in his challenge to the white players and as he is doing in telling his story.

Coding/Decoding Basketball: Playing Black. Jerome's observations suggest the kind of behavioral analysis that anthropologists make when they study cultural systems, the ways in which people live. Anthropologist Dan Rose's analysis of the cultural code represented by the black game of "make it-take it" illuminates the game that Jerome plays with the white students at Chestnut. In "Knowing Ourselves," the first chapter in his ethnographic study *Black American Street Life: South Philadelphia, 1969–71* (1987), Rose writes about an experience he had just after he moved to Philadelphia

Coming upon a group of black youths who were playing basketball in an abandoned school yard, Rose was attracted to the moves they made. As he joined the game, he immediately became aware that "some of the moves they were trying were so exaggerated and risky that none of us had any hope they would work." These moves alerted him to "differences between the way I had grown up playing in the white middle class of small midwestern towns and the way the game was played in urban, black Philadelphia" (Rose 1987, 1–2). As the game proceeded, Rose realized that the black youths were "playing at playing" and that he could not push himself "into the style of what they were saying and doing." In other words, he could decode neither their language nor their behavior. He explained that the white boys he had grown up playing with broke basketball up into its components— jump shots, free throws, two-handed and one-handed shots, dribbling, driving: "Each fake, each type of shot—whether jump shot, set shot, or layup—was a single Cartesian piece. We only assembled the pieces when we started the game" (Rose 1987, 2).

Later, Rose came to understand that the play of the black youths resulted from the way they had constructed the game. Their game was conceptually different from the white construction of play in basketball: "There were no discrete moves, no special, bracketed shots. It was as if the game was a continuous flow from the beginning to the end." He saw that the "entire repertoire of adventurous tactics —dribbling, driving, shooting, passing, faking, running a play— formed an unbroken performance" in which "the emphasis was on performing when one received the ball, not as an isolated *star*, but within an organic flow of self and other, ball and basket" (Rose 1987, 2). As Rose, an anthropologist reading the sign system, decoded the game he had witnessed, he saw it as a black/white binarism:

> I was in a zone of American life that revealed cultural differences separating us. Our dialects were different, our styles of playing the game were different, the rules were different, and the kind of humor on the court was different. (3)

This same difference structures Jerome's life at Chestnut Street Junior High, where whites play inside and blacks remain outside.

Teaming for Truth and Lies

Faking It. Bix Rivers is present in Chapters 15–19, which conclude Part Two of the novel. Bix and Jerome meet in a home economics class to which they are assigned because school officials think the class will help them learn how to take care of themselves in their mothers' absence. Members of the class team up to make a mock apple pie from Ritz crackers. This whole section reinforces the truth/deceit opposition in the novel as Bix and Jerome win the contest for best "apple" pie, a win that leads to Bix's breakdown in front of the class. He cannot accept the idea of winning through a lie; and as the class proceeds, he grows hysterical, yelling, "NOBODY IS TELLING THE TRUTH!" (117). Scratching his hand until it bleeds, he ends up in the nurse's office and subsequently disappears from school for two months.

Learning Hoops. When Bix returns (Chapter 22), Jerome teaches him hoops, comparing the process to the act of writing a book: "The thing is, you can't do it all at once, no more than you can sit down and write a book like this all at once either. You have to go day by day in pieces. So with hoops, what piece do you pick first?" (167). This reflexivity about the act of creation underscores the construction of a text in which a writer picks narrative pieces to create a story. This construction is already once removed from the experience, so it amounts to the truth as the writer perceives it. Readers who are interpreting from the structuralist perspective pick out pieces of the constructed story and then reconstruct, refabricate, the writer's text.

When Bix has learned all the fundamentals of basketball, Jerome announces that Bix is ready to learn the moves. Bix's refusal creates the greatest tension between the two adolescents. Bix will not fake a play because a fake is a lie. In his response Jerome refers to some of the truth/lie binarisms that have structured the story so far. Fakes, cracker pies, and jokes are all lies, he tells Bix, and everything that Bix thinks is a lie "is just a move to everybody else" (179). Structurally, what Jerome is trying to tell Bix is that truth is not an absolute, that he is demanding too much of the concept of truth if he wants to survive, to play, in the world. Bix replies that he will not participate in Jerome's "fancy jigaboo stutter crud," and Jerome is so frustrated that he tells Bix to go ahead and stick with his absolute insistence on truth, to play the game straight. Bix disappears for two months as the absence/presence opposition continues to structure the story.

Faking in the Game for Truth

Three games structure the remainder of the novel. In the first, a literal game, Bix finally makes a move, a fake, to beat his stepfather and win the right to visit his mother at Duke Hospital. In the second, a social game on the eve of his departure for Duke, Bix fakes out Jerome's family. In the third, a metaphoric game, which takes place at Duke Hospital, Bix makes the biggest fake of his life. After that, he makes his final disappearance.

The Challenge Game. Bix returns from the two-month absence with a plan: He challenges his stepfather to a basketball game, asking Jerome to referee. He explains that he will not fake to win, that he must win the game straight, because it is "the game for the truth" (199). The relationship between the boys reaches its turning point as Jerome lashes out at Bix, challenging him to stop his mystery jiving in all his talk about truth. When Bix asks Jerome to go with him to Duke, Jerome asks why: "To keep you on the truth, to make sure you don't tell no lies to your momma?" (201). He realizes that he has gone too far in this question and that he will not be able to help Bix anymore. This is the point in the novel where Bix begins to (re)construct himself as a combination of truth and lies.

Before the game, however, we discover why Bix is so obsessed with the truth. Bix's stepfather tells a bitter story of a lie that Bix told his mother, one lie that pushed her over the edge of sanity. As her mental illness worsened, Bix's mother came one night to Bix's room, naked and holding a knife in her hand. When she awakened Bix to ask if he loved her, he said no, but she did not understand his answer. In the frightening context of her appearance, Bix meant "No" only as "not now." She read his response as "not ever." Distraught, she ran into the hall, stabbed herself in the wrist and elbow, and then thrust her arm through the window, jerking it back and forth on the broken glass. This violent story of Bix's lie sets the stage for the game for truth that Bix cannot win until he makes "the first fake of his life" (223). That fake, however, is the move that isolates him, pushes him over the edge, too, and insulates him so that, as Jerome realizes one year later, he and Bix's stepfather were at that moment "out of the picture" (224). Bix constructs himself in this inside/outside world for the rest of the story.

The Dinner Game. Binarisms structure the second "game" as the novel moves to its conclusion. The world of the dinner game—which Bix constructs alone—reflects the opposition of black/white in the language Bix uses and Jerome decodes. When Bix arrives and is introduced to Jerome's brother Henri, he says, "Dig it." Bix is speaking in an unfamiliar code, one that he does not understand; Jerome points out that "dig it" is a "stupid thing to say" when you are introduced to someone. This fake is only the beginning, however, as Bix greets Jerome's other brother: "What be happening, Maurice, my man?" a question that Jerome labels as "jive talking 'junk'" (233). Jerome describes how Bix appears to be trying to win everybody's favor as he creates a "whole flow" of moves that culminate in the biggest move of the evening (238).

Bix has brought along the dessert that appears to be an apple pie, but it turns out to be the mock apple pie of the home economics class. Although the brothers do not discover the fake, Jerome and his momma do. Bix cannot sustain this move, this deception, and he falls apart, his constructed self ("a balloon toy") deflating into a "slinky pale scared kid" in a matter of seconds (241).

From a structuralist perspective, this is a critical moment defined in the word/wordless binarism that is woven throughout the novel. In his anger at Bix's disrespect for his family, Jerome tells him that he is "too screwed up for words." Jerome senses that Bix has moved outside his sign system: "There really were no words for Bix when he went off my map" (243), this map being language and language being one way to map the world. The encounter leaves Jerome with a new perception about the way we think, about what happens when the sign system fails, "when your thinking itself does not come in words anymore like packages of meaning" (244). All of a sudden, he explains, you begin to feel that you cannot control the language passing through your mind, as if it has passed in and out of you and you have never read the text, or, as Jerome puts it, you have never "seen the printing" (244).

The Duke Hospital Game. When Jerome sees Bix's mother in the hospital, he responds to her in language that represents the absence/presence opposition. She is emaciated, her beauty faded. For Jerome, her eyes symbolize her absence, and he constructs a simile to express the look. The eyes are deep, he notices, but there is nothing behind them, "only an empty room far away" filled by whatever image passes before them (264–65). This image of the empty room also reflects this moment in the novel. For Bix's mother, there is no son in the room. She does not recognize Bix; and when he attempts to give her flowers, she asks whose little boy he is. Her question precipitates the big move that Bix makes in this final game of the novel.

Bix fills the room with a fake mother in what Jerome describes as "the greatest single move in history" (267). Bix goes over to Hazel, the woman in the next bed, embraces her and sobs loudly, "MOTHER, MOTHER, MOTHER" (268). At this point, Bix's mother begins to realize who Bix is, but, sensing this recognition, Bix makes another move: Just as he is about to become present as his mother's son, he walks out of the room, absenting himself from her life. As he leaves, Bix snaps "a quick head fake" to get by an old man who is in his way.

Writing about this scene a year after it happened, Jerome interprets his relationship to Bix as a state of presence and absence:
"Watching Bix until he vanished—that is just what I always did,
wasn't it?" He recontextualizes the room metaphor: "I stood outside
Bix's door where it was a little crazy inside and I watched." The whole
friendship, he is able to understand, has been an inside/outside one,
and he finally acknowledges that he could not "get into Bix" (272).
The act of writing becomes the act of discovery, the construction of a
story becomes one way to interpret a relationship, to try to get inside.

In the scene at Duke Hospital, Bix's mother literally knocks Jerome
out. She recognizes Bix only after he has gone; and as she tragically
screams out his name, she twists wildly about, her elbow striking Jerome between the eyes, both literally and metaphorically cutting off his
vision. This knockout sets up the remainder of the story.

Semiotics as Construction

The final images of the novel remind us of the binary oppositions that
have structured Jerome's story: presence/absence, speaking/silence,
truth/lies.

Jerome's knockout results in a concussion, so he is absent from
school for the rest of the year. He has remained silent about what
happened in the hospital, and this novel is about how he breaks the
silence. For his part, Bix communicates his own absence with a postcard from Washington, D.C.—also a sign of his silence: He has not
written a word in the message spot. Now, a year later, Jerome decodes
this blankness as presence/absence: "He could find his way in that city
and lose his way for everyone else" (279). He interprets the possibilities of the empty postcard in the context of the truth/lies opposition.
The truth might be that it represents a tender side of Bix that wants
to reach out to Jerome, to make a connection. Or it could be "the next
in a long line of great fakes." Jerome expresses the ambiguity of
human experience in the language of basketball: "The fact is—if you
are faking, someone is taking." This faking/taking binarism conditions
the world that Jerome has experienced: It is "true" for him, "juking
through the woods with my ball," and it also true for Bix, "cutting
through the streets of D.C. with his life" (280). Jerome's word *juking*,
a relatively new addition to our language (1967), means to fake out
of a position. Its counterpart, *cutting*, with which he describes Bix,
sports an etymological history dating back to the thirteenth century
and suggests multiple meanings for Bix's actions, from sharply pene-
trating the city, to moving swiftly, dissolving, intersecting, and absenting oneself—as from a class. Or, we might add, from a story, or from
a world.

From a structuralist perspective, we can interpret the last sentence of the novel from the way we read Jerome's story: "There are no moves you truly make alone" (280). As readers we are part of the writer/reader binarism necessary for the story to exist, to be heard. We make moves as readers, working through the writer's text, understanding the words in the context of our cultural mythology, decoding them as we interpret the story. One critic observes that "the form of structuralist research . . . turns into a proposition about content: Literary words are about language and take the process of speech as their essential subject matter" (Jameson 1972, 198–199). Reading *The Moves Make the Man* within this theoretical context reveals that it is a novel about writing a novel, that its language is about the ways in which we use language, that its story is about the storyteller.

Beyond Structuralism

Although deconstructionists critiqued their theoretical assumptions, structuralism and semiotics continue today to have many adherents. The general premises of structuralist theories have been "taken for granted as a starting point" (Marshall 1993, 51) for later critical perspectives, including deconstruction, reader-response, and feminism. Deconstruction finds that texts contain not one but several competing signifying systems. Some reader-response theories focus on the subjectivity of the receiver of the text, thus making it possible to construct an infinite number of meanings in transaction and interaction with the text. Feminist criticism uses the concept of coding to explain the process by which the female body has been negatively inscribed into a patriarchally dominated culture where binary oppositions consistently oppress women both in texts and in life (Lefkovitz 1989, 71). Subsequent chapters work out some of these implications of structuralist thought in the literary theories that followed it.

Joining the Conversation

Jerome Foxworthy is conscious of himself as a writer, and because he often comments on the process of trying to tell his story, *The Moves Make the Man* is a natural choice for working with the structuralist perspective. The field of young adult fiction offers many opportunities to explore the language of characters who are reflective about their writing and who often aspire to become writers. Carl Anderson (1990, quoted in Reed 1994, 386–87) describes Bobby Marks, the central character in Robert Lipsyte's *One Fat Summer* (1977), *Summer Rules*

(1981), and *The Summerboy* (1982), as a "walking writer's handbook."
From a semiotic perspective, Bobby constructs his version of reality;
he is always conscious of recording the world around him. For example, in *Summer Rules*, he observes that "a writer has to get his good
lines down or he'll forget them" (9). He is aware of himself as an
observer of the world, noting that his location is important in how he
sees the action. "Writers," he explains, "should sit in the back, or off
to one side, so they can observe the entire scene" (12). Describing his
idea of what it takes to become a writer, sixteen-year-old Bobby
declares that he wants to work "on a landscape gardening crew with
rough guys who drag raced and hunted and had girl friends who went
all the way. I was going to get into great physical shape and have the
kind of exciting adventures I needed to become a writer like Ernest
Hemingway" (1). This is, of course, the image of the rugged, romantic writer, a very different image from Jerome's sequestration in his
attic while he writes his version of the "truth." Anderson's aim, to
make the connection between student readings of young adult literature and their own writing, is not connected to literary theory and
ways of interpreting the novels; but the novels that he discusses provide a good starting point for teachers who want to explore semiotic
approaches with their students.

In a response to Anderson's ideas, Jean Pollard Dimitt (1993) continues the conversation about young adult literature and student writers, and some of her selections are good for a semiotics approach,
especially Robert O'Brien's *Z for Zachariah* (1974), S. E. Hinton's *The
Outsiders* (1967), and Joan Blos' *A Gathering of Days* (1979).

For our structuralist purposes, Ann Burden keeps a journal in *Z
for Zachariah* as a way of reading and writing her post–nuclear holocaust world; alone, her language becomes her companion: "I thought
writing it might be like having someone talking to me" (4). Similarly,
writing is a way of understanding and constructing the reality of her
devastated world: "I am writing this partly to get it clear in my head,
and to help me make up my mind" (45). Writing helps her keep a
grasp on reality, she says: "I will try to write it down in order. That
may help me to think clearly and decide what I must do" (163, quoted
in Dimmitt 1993, 27).

The Outsiders shares a similarity with *The Moves Make the Man* because the novel that we read is the product of fourteen-year-old Ponyboy Curtis' need to tell a story. While *Moves* opens with Jerome's
affirmation of his intent to write about Bix Rivers, *The Outsiders* ends
with Ponyboy's revelation that the book we have just read is the story
he has told. The novel completes a circle as the last sentence repeats the
first one: "When I stepped out into the bright sunlight from the darkness of the movie house, I had only two things on my mind" (188).

Studying Ponyboy's language in constructing the world of rival gangs and survival in hostile environments provides a good semiotics project. For example, Ponyboy explains how the gangs are named as signs of class distinctions: "We get jumped by the Socs. I'm not sure how you spell it, but its the abbreviation for the Socials, the jet set, the West-side rich kinds. It's like the term 'greaser,' which is used to class all us boys on the East Side" (10). Explaining how words signify in his cultural mythology, he says that "tough and tuff are two different words. Tough is the same as rough; tuff mean cool, sharp—like a tuff-looking Mustang or a tuff record. In our neighborhood both are compliments" (20–21). Studying the language of the dialogue that Ponyboy constructs in *The Outsiders* affords more opportunities for semiotic work.

In Joan Blos' *A Gathering of Days: A New England Girl's Journal, 1830–32* Catherine Hall writes "to know her own mind" (Dimmitt 1993, 27), and in that sense to construct her version of her world—a farm community in the rural New Hampshire of the early 1830s. A foreword and an epilogue, written when Catherine is an adult, frame the journal text and offer insight into what the recorded experiences have taught her. From a semiotics perspective, the journal offers valuable insight into a period of American history, and its language closely resembles the style of historical documents of the period it covers. The vivid details of its construction of history should fascinate students and teachers as they investigate Catherine's language.

Other novels that are cast as diaries or journals make good places to work with students who are using semiotics. In *Using Young Adult Literature in the English Classroom* (1993), John and Kay Bushman explore the reading/writing connection as Anderson and Dimmitt do, but they offer more extensive lists of books in which writing is a central process. In a list entitled "The Writing Process At Work," the Bushmans include *The Outsiders* as well as Hinton's *Taming the Star Runner* (1988), Avi's *The Man Who Was Poe* (1989), and Gary Paulsen's *The Island* (1988). In their list entitled "Journals/Diaries," the Bushmans cite O'Brien's *Zachariah*, Blos' *Gathering*, Ouida Sebestyn's *The Girl in the Box* (1987), Joyce Carol Thomas's *Marked by Fire* (1982), Chris Crutcher's *Stotan!* (1986) and Peter Dickinson's *Eva* (1988). Consider my presentation of these lists as an invitation to explore these texts with students.

Semiotic analysis figures into some of the following chapters. In Walter Dean Myers' *Fallen Angels* (1988) (Chapter 6), the language of Richie Perry's letters represents different constructions of war; the languages used to describe different concepts of the hero (in the war, in the movies) make good sites for semiotic study. In Chapter 8, the analysis of Ernest Gaines' *A Lesson Before Dying* (1993) is based on its signifying practices within the contexts of African American language and literatures, but further opportunities for semiotic work exist in that novel. One rewarding subject for inquiry is the counterpoint between the dialect with which Jefferson tells his story in the diary and the language with which college-educated Grant Wiggins tells the story of how his life becomes intertwined with Jefferson's. In Chapter 10, part of the analysis of Sara Louise's character in Katherine Paterson's *Jacob Have I Loved* (1980) relies on semiotic signification.

Finally, I suggest a novel that is a wonderful semiotic romp, namely, Kathyrn Lasky's *Memoirs of a Bookbat* (1994), in which fourteen-year-old Harper constructs herself and her world from books. Her version of reality is at odds with that of her parents, whom she refers to as "migrants of God," as they travel about the country in a fancy motor home, provided to them by the religious organization they represent. The self and world that Harper constructs originate in the library. Often she describes herself in relation to the world of books. For example, remembering *The Three Little Pigs*, Harper recalls that she wasn't "into pig," but she "was into houses—houses that weren't shaped like shoeboxes, houses without wheels" (*Memoirs*, 15). She is even more drawn into the world of the books she reads when she begins writing to Rosemary Nearing, the illustrator of her copy of *Goldilocks*, and to Delores Macuccho, a science fiction writer. The extremes of the imaginary worlds created in these texts represent Harper's connection to childhood and to the fascinating unknown. She discovers a secret compartment of a closet wall in the mobile home and names it her Narnia cubby, an allusion to C.S. Lewis' cycle of fantasy novels for children. The books that she recalls and the way in which she responds to them allow us to see how she constructs her world, and they allow us to construct her as well. Other examples abound. Harper describes one episode as a "very Judy Blumish thing to do," echoing Blume's *Are You There, God? It's Me, Margaret* in her "Are you there, Judy? It's me, Harper" (*Memoirs*, 88). In other episodes, she takes "comfort in the stars the way Huck Finn did on his trip down the mighty Mississippi" and declares herself to be "Huck Finn at his worst" in her ridicule of another character in the novel (*Memoirs*, 183, 194). In the end, she escapes her parents, imagines herself on a raft with her friends "Gray and Huck and Mr. Twain—and Jim," a scene in which she says "I can taste the freedom" (*Memoirs*, 207). In the final image of the novel, Harper imagines herself and many of the authors whom she has read as "floating down the mighty Mississippi in the long evening shadows" as "a bat flies into the night" (*Memoirs*, 215). She declares herself a bookbat rather than a bookworm because books allow her to soar into new worlds and to construct herself beyond the prosaic reality that her parents present to her.

Works Cited

Anderson, C. A. 1990. "Young Adult Writers in Adolescent Literature: Models for Student Writers." *The ALAN Review* 17 (Spring): 12–14. Quoted in Arethea J. S. Reed, *Reaching Adolescents: The Young Adult Book in the School*, 386–87. New York: Macmillan, 1994.

Avi. 1989. *The Man Who Was Poe*. New York: Avon.

Blos, Joan. 1979. *A Gathering of Days: A New England Girl's Journal, 1830–32*. New York: Aladdin.

Blume, Judy. 1970. *Are You There, God? It's Me, Margaret*. New York: Bradbury.

Barthes, Roland. 1967. "The Structuralist Activity." Trans. Richard Howard. *Parisian Review* 34 (Winter). Quoted in Hazard Adams, ed., *Critical Theory Since Plato*, 2d ed., Fort Worth: Harcourt Brace, 1992, 1195–96.

Brooks, Bruce. 1994. *The Moves Make the Man*. New York: HarperCollins.

Bushman, John H., and Kay Parks Bushman. 1993. "The Reading/Writing Connection." In *Using Young Adult Literature in the English Classroom*, 63–99. New York: Macmillan.

Crutcher, Chris. 1986. *Stotan!* New York: Dell.

Dickinson, Peter. 1988. *Eva*. New York: Dell.

Dimmitt, Jean Pollard. 1993. "More on Model Writers in Adolescent Literature." *ALAN Review* 21 (Fall): 26–29.

Eagleton, Terry. 1983. "Structuralism and Semiotics." In *Literary Theory: An Introduction*, 59–112. Minneapolis: University of Minneapolis Press.

Gaines, Ernest. 1993. *A Lesson Before Dying*. New York: Vintage.

Hinton, S.E. 1967. *The Outsiders*. New York: Viking.

———. 1988. *Taming the Star Runner*. New York: Dell.

Jameson, Frederic. 1972. *The Prison-House of Language: A Critical Account of Structuralism and Russian Formalism*. Princeton: Princeton University Press. Quoted in Terence Hawkes, *Structuralism and Semiotics*, Berkeley: University of California Press, 1977, 99.

Jefferson, Ann. 1986. "Structuralism and post-structuralism." In *Modern Literary Theory*. 2d. ed., eds. Ann Jefferson and David Robey, 92–121. Totowa, NJ: Barnes and Noble.

Lasky, Kathryn. 1994. *Memoirs of a Bookbat*. San Diego: Harcourt Brace.

Lefkovitz, Lori Hope. 1989. "Creating the World: Structuralism and Semiotics." In *Contemporary Literary Theory*, eds. Douglas Atkins and Laura Morrow, 60–80. Amherst: University of Massachusetts Press.

Lipsyte, Robert. 1977. *One Fat Summer*. New York: Harper and Row.

———. 1981. *Summer Rules*. Harper and Row.

———. 1982. *The Summerboy*. Harper and Row.

Maasik, Sandra, and Jack Solomon, eds. 1994. Introduction to *Signs of Life in the U.S.A.: Readings on Popular Culture for Writers*, 1–14. Boston: St. Martin's.

Marshall, Donald. 1993. "Structuralism and Semiotics." In *Contemporary Literary Theory: A Selective Bibliography*, 50–51. New York: Modern Language Association.

Myers, Walter Dean. 1988. *Fallen Angels*. New York: Scholastic.

O'Brien, Robert. 1974. *Z for Zachariah*. New York: Macmillan.

Paterson, Katherine. 1980. *Jacob Have I Loved*. New York: HarperCollins.

Paulsen, Gary. 1988. *The Island*. New York: Dell.

Rose, Dan. 1987. "Knowing Ourselves." In *Black American Street Life: South Philadelphia, 1969–71*, 1–29. Philadelphia: University of Pennsylvania Press.

Rowe, John Carles. 1990. "Structure." In *Critical Terms for Literary Study*, eds. Frank Lentricchia and Thomas McLaughlin, 23–49. Chicago: University of Chicago Press.

Sebestyn, Ouida. 1987. *The Girl in the Box*. New York: Dell.

Thomas, Joyce Carol. 1982. *Marked by Fire*. New York: Avon.

Five

Deconstruction
Unraveling *The Giver*

The deconstructive critic seeks to find, by this process of retracing, the element in the system studied which is alogical, the thread in the text in question which will unravel it all.

J. Hillis Miller,
"Stevens' Rock"

An Introduction to Deconstruction

Deconstruction/Not Destruction

Some of the anxiety about *deconstruction* results from a misconception about the meaning of the term. It does not mean, as it is sometimes construed, to "dismantle" or to "destroy," as though it were "a fancier form of 'destruction.'" As a way of reading, it does not aim to obliterate the meaning of a text but to open up a text so that meaning multiplies indefinitely through a process in which we resist complacency in our readings. In this resistance, we practice the inquiry that theory demands, rigorously questioning our positions and our statements about texts (Lynn 1994, 90).

Reacting to the misunderstanding of *deconstruction* as *destruction*, critic Barbara Johnson offers a clear statement of what deconstruction aims to do and the methods by which we employ this way of reading:

> *Deconstruction* is not synonymous with *destruction*. . . . The deconstruction of a text does not proceed by random doubt or arbitrary subversion, but by the careful teasing out of warring forces of signification within the text itself. (Johnson 1985, 5)

As Johnson suggests, deconstruction is a careful approach to the language of the text, but it must be done in the playful spirit of "teasing out" relationships in the language of the text. It is important "to approach deconstruction with anything but a scholar's sober and almost worshipful respect for knowledge and truth. Deconstruction offers a playful alternative to traditional scholarship" (Murfin 1994, 420).

How does deconstruction as a way of reading relate to the literary theories presented in previous chapters? For starters, there can be no one "correct" reading of a text as the formalists claim. The archetypal critics' claim that one schema can organize all literature cannot be substantiated. And despite what structuralists contend, no single sign system can unify the text or the world. Instead, deconstructionists believe, we must learn to live in the uncertainty of multiple interpretations, to accept what deconstructionists call the *undecidability* of the text. This is a powerful notion that can liberate our thinking about our ways of reading and about the ways in which we look at our world as it is constructed in language.

Deconstructionists do not reject all the notions of the theories that preceded theirs. On the contrary, deconstruction shares and modifies ideas from earlier theories. It shares the method of close reading with formalism. In one sense, a deconstructive reading is "like an extension" of a formalist reading. To read deconstructively, we work against a norm or an accepted way of reading and interpreting, beginning with the assumption that a text is logical and coherent and proceeding through our reading to expose incoherence in the text. That is, we identify the unity that appears to be in the text, and then we divide and dispel it (Lynn 1994, 94). In its idea that readers cannot resolve all of the ambiguities, paradoxes, and tensions in a text, deconstruction challenges the formalist notion that a text has a stable meaning. The impossibility of simple resolutions opens up the possibilities of multiple interpretations.

Deconstruction emerged in response to structuralism. It is, therefore, a poststructuralist theory, and many critics use the terms *deconstruction* and *poststructuralism* interchangeably. In opposition to the structuralist contention that meaning is possible because of the differences that exist between binary opposites, Jacques Derrida, the French philosopher whose name is synonymous with deconstruction, has contended that such simple oppositions are impossible. The meaning associated with a sign cannot be counted on as permanent, Derrida said; meaning is always shifting, being transformed by the relation of one sign to another (Bressler 1994, 75). Therefore, nothing like a unified text or a single correct reading is possible. All readers produce different readings based on the ways in which they interpret the language relationships in a text, in which they explore what deconstructionists call the "play" of language.

Deconstruction in Practice

Although deconstruction is difficult to define, we can understand it better when we see it in action as an interpretive practice (Atkins and Johnson 1985, 2). For traditional readers, learning how to practice deconstruction as a reading strategy means changing our concept of textuality. Formalists define a text as a fixed entity, a completed structure, a work of art. In the poststructuralist perspective, *textuality* refers to the text as a working space, a place of play:

> We know that a text consists not of a line of words . . . but of a multidimensional space in which are married and contested several writings, none of which is original: the text is a fabric of quotations, resulting from a thousand sources of culture. (Barthes 1992, 1132)

As readers using deconstructive strategies, we work within this complex space of multiple writing where "everything is to be *disentangled* but nothing *deciphered.*" As we read and interpret, we sort out (disentangle) the different strands from which a text is woven, but we cannot declare with certainty (decipher) that any one of them or even all of them together can constitute a meaning for the text. "Structure can be followed" or " 'threaded' (as we say of a run in a stocking) in all its reprises, all its stages, but there is no end to it, no bottom" (Barthes 1992, 1132). *Reprises* is the key word in our reading of *The Giver*. And we will follow the repetition of the word *release* in the novel to suggest meanings based on its recurrence.

Roland Barthes' essay "From Work to Text" (1979) provides an excellent introduction to the deconstructive approach. Its title suggests the shift from the formalists' focus on the autonomous text as a finished work of art to the poststructuralist fascination with the shifting meanings in the weave of the written text. Barthes states six propositions about textuality, three of which are especially useful in our reading of Lowry's *The Giver*.

First, a text is a "methodological field," a place in which to work with language; most important, Barthes stresses, "*the Text is experienced only in an activity, a production*" (Barthes 1979, 74–75). This activity is the process of reading, and the production is the result of that reading, our interpretation.

Second, "the Text is plural," *plural* signifying more than the obvious multiple meanings. Barthes' plurality is "irreducible":

> The Text's plurality does not depend on the ambiguity of its contents, but rather on what should be called the stereographic plurality of the signifiers that weave it (etymologically the text is a cloth; *textus*, from which text derives, means "woven"). (Barthes 1979, 76)

This complex stereographic image is an unusual one for the act of interpreting a text. A stereograph is a picture composed of a pair of stereoscopic images; when viewed through a stereoscope (a pair of special spectacles), the image becomes three-dimensional. Barthes also refers to the text as stereophonic, meaning that its fabric is also woven of the echoes of other texts. This makes the text *intertextual*, a key term in poststructural thinking. *Intertextuality* means that the text is woven of what Barthes calls "quotations without quotation marks" (Barthes 1981, 39); these quotations are not synonymous with allusions in a text.

Third, the notion of "play" determines how the text operates and how we read it. Barthes explains that "The text itself *plays*" in the same sense that a door hinge offers a door an element of "play," some leeway in its movement. The reader also "*plays* the Text in the musical sense of the term" (Barthes 1979, 79). The "Text" in this concept is a musical score: "It asks the reader for an active collaboration" (Barthes 1979, 80). *Collaboration* suggests the interplay that goes on between text and reader, and, to extend the metaphor, a collaboration that necessarily results in a different musical interpretation for each performer (reader) based on the performance (interpretive) skills that each player brings to and learns from the text.

The Giver: The Text Playing/Playing the Text

To demonstrate the undecidability of meaning as a function of how *The Giver* "plays" and how we might "play" the novel as readers, we trace the thread that seems to hold the text together but which actually starts unraveling the text from the first pages. The word *release* is that single strand, what one critic calls the "element in the system studied which is alogical, the thread in the text in question which will unravel it all" (Miller 1991, 126).

The Giver: An Introduction

The action opens in what appears to be a futuristic utopian world governed by the principle of Sameness. Pain, war, and human suffering apparently do not exist, and life is controlled by The Book of Rules. Citizens are valued by their work and their ability to contribute to communal life. Devotion to the principle of Sameness, however, does not obliterate difference; in fact, difference gives the ruling powers a standard by which they assign members of the community to their life's work. Age is the most significant determining factor of difference, and difference in the very young and very old results in what the inhabitants believe to be "release," a peaceful departure from the life of the community. This turns out to be only one meaning of *release*, and the increasing ambiguity of the word provides the basis for our deconstructive reading.

The central characters in the novel are the aging Giver and twelve-year-old Jonas, chosen to be the Receiver of cultural memory, both its pleasures and its pains. What the Giver gives and the Receiver receives, however, is privileged knowledge unknown to all other members of the community. Theirs are honored positions, and they share the knowledge of a past society full of opposites such as war/peace and hot/cold, of life differentiated by colors, emotions, feelings, and choices. Their knowledge is a well-kept secret, potentially destructive of the constructed life of the supposedly "ideal" world they inhabit. After Jonas accepts his position as the Receiver, he begins to realize that this perceived utopian world is actually a dystopic nightmare. The turning point in the novel comes when he makes a choice between these two worlds, deciding on his own release. An overview of the novel will help contextualize our interpretation of it.

Chapter Overviews

Chapter 1: Language and Feeling. The novel opens with an emphasis on language as Jonas attempts to choose the right word to express a feeling and as his "groupmate" Asher gets a lesson in language precision. At the end of the day, in a family ritual, Jonas and his sister Lily report their feelings, which their parents logically explain away. Jonas' parents are named only by their functions as Father and Mother, and their occupations represent reversals of traditional gender roles—he a Nurturer, she a Worker in the Department of Justice.

Chapters 2–5: Education for Sameness. In the community's highly standardized educational system, schoolchildren attend a yearly Ceremony that acknowledges their growth and rewards them with a distinction in dress and the assignment of greater responsibility. An infant named Gabriel, who does not fit the established behavior code, is granted a one-year reprieve from release if he can be nurtured into conformity by Jonas' father.

All the language of the community is functional; Jonas' fellow students are not *classmates* or *friends* but *"groupmates,"* an indication of a communal language that erases individualism. Similarly, when Jonas reports a dream about his attraction to Fiona, a young female groupmate, his mother explains that these are his "first Stirrings" (Lowry 1993, 37) and that he must be treated with pills so that they do not recur.

Chapters 6–8: The Ceremonies of Maturation. The yearly celebrations culminate in the Ceremony of Twelves and reveal the community's standard procedures for constructing Sameness. Newborns remain nameless until the Ceremony of Ones when they are placed with a family that has requested a child. Mothers do not give birth to their children; this work is assigned to Birthmothers. Distinguishing characteristics of subsequent ages include dream-telling, learning precision in language, and interdependence (Threes); front-buttoned jackets, the "first very visible sign of growing up" (Sevens); and the first bicycle, the "proverbial emblem" that signals the move "away from the protective family unit" for Nines (41–42).

At twelve years of age, Jonas is named the Receiver of Memory (Chapter 8), the most important of all the assignments, because he has been observed to possess the "Capacity to See Beyond" (63).

Chapters 9–16: In Training. Jonas' new position alienates him from his groupmates. His training rules stipulate that he may question anybody and expect to get answers and that he may lie. In his daily training with the Giver, Jonas begins to receive the whole world's memories, including knowledge of pleasure and pain. As he confronts ambiguities in the memories, he changes, stops reporting dreams to his family because he is "not ready to tell a lie, not willing to tell the truth." In a dream of snow and sledding, he senses "a destination: a *something*—he could not grasp what" (88). When he has a Seeing Beyond experience in which Fiona's hair changes, the Giver explains that he is beginning to see the color red because the concept of Sameness has not yet been mastered by the community's geneticists.

As his memory develops, Jonas questions what lies beyond the community's boundaries; and when he asks for more complex feelings, he suffers the pain of a broken leg and receives preliminary knowledge of hunger and warfare. Although his impulse is to change things, he finds himself locked in by his duty to the collective memory. He makes an illegal decision to transmit pleasant memories to Gabriel who, still not conforming to behavior standards, continues to cry throughout the night. The memories work, and the infant calms down.

Jonas receives the vivid memory of war, happy memories of a birthday party celebrating individuality, and, best of all, a festive winter holiday memory.

Chapter 17–20: The Desire for Change. Jonas' initial sense that he is powerless to effect change gives way to a revolutionary idea as he and the Giver contemplate the possibilities of a life in which all the citizens of the community share the burden of the collective memory. They decide to deceive the community into thinking that Jonas has been lost in the river while he actually escapes to Elsewhere. Without a Receiver, the community will be forced to deal with its memories.

Chapters 21–24: The Escape and Beyond. The carefully wrought plan falls apart when Jonas spends a night with the Giver and Gabriel misbehaves. Returning home to learn that Gabriel will be released the following morning, Jonas decides to flee with the baby. In a night journey, they escape into a landscape that grows desolate. They survive on memories of food and warmth as the nights grow cold and snow surrounds them. Jonas finds a sled, and they begin a rapid descent down a hill as we slide out of the pages of *The Giver*.

Precision of Language/Unraveling Release

The first words of *The Giver* introduce a world where language is critical and where the word *release* is a powerful term. The novel opens one December morning with Jonas on his way to school and in a linguistic dilemma. Describing himself as frightened, he thinks, "No. Wrong word" (1). If he has chosen the *wrong* word, then there must be a *right* word, and we immediately perceive the possibility of an either/or dimension of language use. Words are supposed to be carefully controlled in Jonas' world. Jonas rejects the word *frightened* because he has had an experience that has enabled him to specifically define that word. Remembering that *frightened* describes a sickening feeling that something terrible is about to happen, he recalls the experience that defines *frightened* for him. His recollection introduces the concept of release into the novel.

Release as Negative. Jonas remembers an experience that happend about a year ago when a Pilot-in-Training misread navigational instructions and flew so close that he "frightened" the entire community. Jonas' recollection ends with a reminder of the punishment for such a misreading. He recalls that, regarding the Pilot, the Speaker of the community announced that "NEEDLESS TO SAY, HE WILL BE RELEASED." *Release* is first defined in the novel in this specific context: "For a contributing citizen to be released from the community was a final decision, a terrible punishment, and overwhelming statement of failure" (2). In this definition, the word *release* signifies the ultimate punishment for a wrongful action. The word is not to be used lightly; children who use it when they are playing are scolded. The word *misread* also signals the kind of world we are entering. A misuse of language, a misreading, can lead to release, as in the case of the pilot. Rejecting *eager* and *excited*, Jonas finally chooses *apprehensive* as the "right" word for his feeling.

Release as Positive. At the end of the first day of the novel, we learn of two occasions in which *release* apparently does not mean punishment—the release of the elderly in a celebration of life and the release of a newborn child. Jonas visits the House of the Old where he hears about the release ceremony for Roberto, one of the elderly. After the "telling of his life," a toast, the chanting of an anthem, and Roberto's good-bye speech, the others bid Roberto farewell (32). Although this ritual seems benign, we do not learn exactly what happens to the released elderly citizen after this celebration.

About a week later, we learn to distinguish the release ceremony of the elderly from two other ceremonies, the Ceremony of Loss and the Murmur-of-Replacement Ceremony. In the first of these ceremonies, language erases identity; in the second, it creates identity. A child named Caleb has fallen into the river and has been lost, despite the fact that the whole community is charged with being watchful and protective of all children. The lost child is spoken out of existence in the Ceremony of Loss, his name murmured throughout the day in diminishing volume so that he seems to simply fade gradually from the community's consciousness. In a Murmur-of-Replacement Ceremony, the reverse occurs: The child's name is repeated softly, then with greater volume and more speed, until it is "as if the first Caleb were returning." This is the ultimate use of language to achieve standardization and deny difference. A child who replaces a lost child must have the lost child's name. When another new child is named Roberto after the elderly man in the release ceremony, however, there is no replacement ceremony because "Release was not the same as loss" (44). The meaning of the word *release* continues to expand as the novel unfolds.

Release as Choice. The concept of release is also related to the Ceremony of Twelves, but the context makes its meaning more ambiguous. Asher jokes about a Twelve who didn't like his assignment as a Sanitation Laborer and fled by swimming across the river and joining another community. This story presents a problem because we cannot be sure that other communities exist across the river. Asher points out that "if you don't fit in, you can apply for Elsewhere and be released," and he recalls a story that his mother told him about someone who applied about ten years ago: "Here today and gone tomorrow. Never seen again. Not even a Ceremony of Release" (*Giver*, 48). Here the word *release* is complicated; we assume from the story that a person who requests release receives no honored farewell.

The Giver adds another dimension to the word *release*, which further complicates its meaning. He explains to Jonas that when the previous Receiver failed, "the memories that she had received were released," that they went "Someplace out *there*" (104). The result was chaos because the members of the community had to assimilate the released memories, and they suffered throughout the experience. Later in the novel (Chapters 18 and 19), this story of release is completed, and we learn that the young woman Receiver was the Giver's daughter Rosemary, that she requested release because she could not stand the burdens of memory, and that she chose to inject herself, to commit suicide.

Release as Murder. The word *release* takes on a chilling meaning in a story of identical twins, a story that pulls hard at the fabric of the novel and contributes to its unraveling in the final scene. *Release* becomes more precise than it has been in all its previous threadings through the novel. Father explains that when identical twins are born, one is nurtured and the other is released, the choice being based on the higher birth weight. At the next birth of twins, the choice will be Father's. Jonas contemplates the nature of such a release. "Was there someone there, waiting, who would receive the tiny released twin? Would it grow up Elsewhere?" he wonders, unaware that somewhere someone looked exactly like it (115). In a culture that celebrates Sameness, we ask, why wouldn't identical twins be highly desired? Here is another illogicality, a hole in the philosophy of the community, a run in the Barthesian metaphoric stocking of the novel.

At the next training session, Jonas asks the Giver about release and learns that since all private release ceremonies are recorded, he can watch the release of the little twin. When he does, he is horrified to see his Father very carefully insert a needle into the top of the infant's forehead and empty the syringe. While his Father talks quietly, the infant squirms, wails, and jerks his arms and legs about until he falls silent. Now Jonas realizes that release can mean murder: "*My Father killed it!*" (150). In a final coldly perfunctory move, Jonas' Father places the infant in a carton, says, "Bye-bye little guy" and pushes the carton down a chute similar to the trash chutes at Jonas' school (151). In this darkest moment of the novel, Jonas feels "ripped" and "clawed" inside. The release of the twin calls into question all the release ceremonies in the community; but more important, it opens up a huge question about the meaning of life and death in Jonas' world.

Escape as Release. After the trauma of this "release," Jonas and the Giver carefully plan Jonas' escape. He will appear to be lost in the river, but he will actually journey to Elsewhere as the Giver remains to help the community assimilate the painful memories of the past that Jonas has received. As a final gesture, the Giver wants to transmit one more memory—music—through Jonas' Capacity to Hear Beyond. This moment figures prominently in the final scene of the novel, contributing another factor to the undecidability of this text. Jonas is emphatic in his refusal of music: "I want you to keep that, to have with you, when I'm gone" (157). Later, we will consider the ramifications of this refusal as far as the novel's meanings are concerned.

The carefully wrought plan falls apart that evening. Father announces "in his sweet, sing-song voice" that Gabriel will be *released*: "It's bye-bye to you, Gabe" (*Giver*, 165), an echo of his words during the murder of the twin. Gabriel's release comes because he has cried all night in the Nurturing Center; a year's reprieve has not standardized his behavior. To save the child from release, Jonas escapes with Gabriel into the night, stealing his father's bicycle and some food. Crossing the bridge, he rides through outlying communities (they do exist) and enters a desolate landscape. He and Gabriel establish a pattern of travel by night and sleep by day until they no longer hear search planes overhead. They journey in a world without human inhabitants, but the barren landscape begins to change, unfolding with waterfalls, wildlife, and wildflowers. Such beauties are, however, juxtaposed to Jonas' desperate fear of starvation; he struggles to find food, even resorting to re-creating meals out of his memory, which is now beginning to fade because all his received memories are returning to the community.

Jonas begins to doubt the escape. Having longed for choice and gotten it, he thinks that he may have made the wrong decision in leaving. He still sees the world as the simple choice between right or wrong that he had when he considered the word *frightened* on the first morning of the novel, but as readers we can see that the world he perceived is falling apart. The refreshing rain that he has experienced only in memories now becomes real, but it makes them wet and cold; and Gabriel, weakened by hunger, begins to cry. The novel appears to be moving toward a hopeless ending.

As his bicycle comes to an abrupt halt in a mound of snow at the bottom of a hill, Jonas' memories continue to fade; but resolute in his love for Gabriel, Jonas determines to survive by remembering warmth as he starts to climb the hill.

Unraveling Release. In its final scene, the text unravels in ambiguity. As Jonas climbs the hill, his vision is blurred in the swirling, freezing snow. At the top of the hill, the sled of his first memory transmission materializes. His heart surging with hope but his body freezing, he and Gabriel climb onto the sled and begin the descent. (For a formalist, the appearance of this sled would affirm the novel's unity and bring the story full circle, connecting Jonas' memory of a sled with the reality of this sled's appearance, resolving the tension between dystopic Sameness [Death] and utopian Difference [Life].)

Jonas starts to lose consciousness as the scene unfolds in a moment of unreality. The two boys speed "in a straight line through an incision that seemed to lead to the final destination, the place that he [Jonas] always felt was waiting, the Elsewhere that held their future and their past" (179). Jonas is too weak to guide the sled, so the straight line seems unrealistic in the context of the scene. (A formalist might interpret this straight line as an indication of the correctness of Jonas' decision to escape the nightmarish community.) The word *incision* in the description seems to be another figure of the text's unraveling because it denotes a surgical procedure, a wound. Will this ride downward be the ultimate wound, the release into the unknown? to death?

The major word in the description, however, is *seemed*, meaning "to give an impression of," a word that stands in diametric contrast to the two words *final destination*. Furthermore, this place is only a function of intuition, not knowledge, and Jonas associates it with Elsewhere, a place in the novel that has been highly ambiguous. This ambiguity is heightened now by Jonas' feeling that it holds both past and future.

Through his blurred vision, Jonas sees a scene reminiscent of the festive holiday memory, the best of the Giver's transmissions, but some details of his vision are ambiguous. First, the sled is hurling them *downward*, a word fraught with negative connotations of defeat and depression. For example, a descent into a maelstrom would perhaps clarify the straight line in which they travel. Maelstroms often violently suck objects into themselves. Another reading might be that this is the descent into the underworld, the world of Death, accomplished here in the gradual losing of consciousness through freezing. Second, Jonas sees colored lights twinkling; and even though he is losing consciousness, he *knows* that they are shining someplace where families create memories and keep them, where they celebrate love. What is such knowledge based upon? Memory? Certainly not on experience. Can he trust memory any more? Hasn't it faded earlier in the journey?

And what of the meaning of *love*? When Jonas had received the first memory of love, he had gone home and asked his parents if they loved him, to which his father had replied, "Precision of language, *please!*" Jonas' mother chastised him for using a "very generalized word, so meaningless that it's become almost obsolete" (127). (A formalist might interpret the word *love* in this final scene to represent the salvation of human feelings from obsolescence, the negation of the mother's explanation.)

Since the last two paragraphs of the novel demand very close reading in opening up the power of multiple meanings in *The Giver*, they are quoted here in their entirety:

Downward, downward, faster and faster. Suddenly he was aware with certainty and joy that below, ahead, they were waiting for him; and that they were waiting, too, for the baby. For the first time, he heard something that he knew to be music. He heard people singing.

Behind him, across vast distances of space and time, from the place he had left, he thought he heard music, too. But perhaps it was only an echo. (179–80)

(An archetypal critic would read this scene as the hero's return, not only as hero but actually carrying the figure of his rebirth, a son, another generation to carry on the heroic tradition. The music ahead of him and behind him would become in such a reading the fusion of the old world (the nightmare world) and the new world (the dream world) realized as a consequence of the hero's newly acquired knowledge. Such a reading would situate the novel in the unified structure of mythic and heroic quest narratives.)

The final paragraphs of *The Giver* open up the novel to any number of interpretations. For example, if Jonas is "aware with certainty and joy" that someone awaits them, and that the something he hears is music, then why is he not equally sure that he hears the music of another time and another place? What would explain such music? Has the Giver remembered music to ease the pain of all the memories that Jonas has placed on the community? "But perhaps it was only an echo." Perhaps not. An echo is only a *trace* of something already heard, and Jonas has never heard music; he emphatically refused music in his last meeting with the Giver. Even this trace of music is another form of the unweaving of the novel: Perhaps this last scene is no more than a figment of Jonas' imagination, his last attempt to hold onto something pleasant before he and the baby freeze to death. This is one way to read the ending: Jonas sleds into the frozen world of death, into Nowhere, since Elsewhere may not exist except as a construction of the language system of his former community, an imprecision of language to perpetuate Sameness and to diminish the knowledge of what the word *release* means.

Reading Without Closure

I hope to have demonstrated here a deconstructive reading of *The Giver*, in the sense that such a reading "implies that a text signifies in more than one way, that it can signify something more, something less, or something other than it claims to, or that it signifies in different degrees of explicitness, effectiveness, or coherence" (Johnson

1985, 141). If this reading seems inconclusive, then I have achieved my purpose. If it makes you stop and think about the possibility of reading without closure, then I am glad. I would be happiest to know that it had sent you to play texts on your own, to unravel the threads of your reading of other young adult novels.

Joining the Conversation

Before suggesting other young adult novels that might be read from a deconstructive perspective, I want to reiterate the idea that we can apply different interpretive strategies to the same novel by outlining another approach to *The Giver*. This approach grows out of Lowry's dedication: "For all the children / To whom we entrust the future." If we take this statement as an indication of her intent, we can read the novel as a form of the archetypal monomyth, the quest of the hero. Jonas' journey outward from the community occurs as a consequence of the hero's vision of another world, a world Elsewhere to which he travels so that he can gain the knowledge—or in this case, release the knowledge—that will save his world.

An Archetypal Reading

Joseph Campbell has said that the monomyth can handle any one portion of the quest story while excluding others, and *The Giver* dwells almost exclusively on the early stages of the myth. The call to adventure is clear: Although the conditions under which Jonas receives knowledge at first frustrate his desire to effect change in his community, his relationship with the Giver continually opens up a vision of a world beyond. The Giver functions as the monomythic hero's helper, the aging mentor who prepares him for the quest, as Oogruk prepares Russel in Paulsen's *Dogsong*. *The Giver* reaches its climax after the first threshold crossing, and we see only some of the tests and trials that confront Jonas as hero. Nevertheless, we are already convinced, in this reading, of the transformational power of his journey: Although he may not return, his departure itself necessitates a new orientation, a new way of life, for his community because the citizenry will be forced to deal with the memories he has released by his escape. We can believe that The Giver has the power to help the citizenry cope with the dynamic world that those memories will create.

Locating this monomyth more specifically in a literary tradition, we can interpret the novel as a form of the Christian myth in which Jesus saves his people by sacrificing his own life. In this reading, Jonas becomes a Christ figure, and the child Gabriel might suggest a watchful angel, a supernatural companion who accompanies Christ into the white world of death (the final snowy landscape of the novel).

In this mythic interpretation, names in the novel take on powerful and symbolic meanings. Jonas, for example, is the Greek form of the name *Jonah* (Kolatch 1980, 153), the figure in the Old Testament "whom Jesus accepted as a prototype of himself" (Frye 1968, 190). Jonas' location in the community of Somewhere is not unlike Jonah's stay in the belly of the big fish in the biblical narrative. The community becomes a form of the fish as leviathan—leviathan symbolizing "the whole fallen world of sin and death and tyranny" (190), from which the Messiah *releases* humankind by killing the monster. Seen in this way, life inside the community of Sameness is a symbolic form of death from which the hero escapes, his departure saving the community from its hellish dystopic existence.

Rosemary—the name of the Giver's daughter—is particularly symbolic in the context of this archetypal reading. The name fuses *Mary*, the name of the mother of Christ, and *Rose*, the multifoliate image with which Dante represents the community of believers in *Divine Comedy*. *Rosemary* is also appropriate for a character in *The Giver* because the name comes from the Hebrew word *Miriam*, meaning "sea of bitterness, sorrow" (Kolatch 1980, 423). I don't want to push this reading too far, but Rosemary's voluntary release makes it possible for Jonas to become the Receiver of Memory. In this sense, Rosemary becomes a symbolic mother who gives "birth" to the son who will save the world.

The apple in the novel recalls the Garden of Eden and the fall from innocence; the fruit that Jonas tosses to Asher is as much an agent of transformation as the fruit in the Garden of Eden. The movement out of the community is a journey away from a constructed innocence into the world of experience.

Finally, the Giver may represent a God figure, willing to sacrifice his metaphoric son for the larger good and for a future with promise and hope—the kind of future we might suppose that Lowry means in the words of her dedication.

The Deconstructive Dialogue

Texts that foreground language and its uses invite deconstructive inquiry; and readers might, to enjoy this way of reading, need a particular turn of mind that some theories of reading do not require. Teachers and students can begin to engage the play of language, the "teasing out of warring forces of signification" (Johnson 1985, 5), by taking a look at the way in which stories get told in these young adult novels: Paul Zindel's *The Pigman* (1968) and *A Begonia for Miss Applebaum* (1989) and Robert Cormier's *After the First Death* (1979).

One way to understand how to approach these novels deconstructively is to put deconstruction in the context of formalism. Whereas formalism looks for a "perfect, seamless art object existing in a timeless space outside the changing course of human events, deconstruction looks for the seams—the ways in which language fails to smooth over contradictions and gaps in logic" (Tyson 1991, 230).

The Pigman. "The Oath" that opens Paul Zindel's *The Pigman* is a perfect invitation to deconstructive inquiry as the two narrators of the novel sign their names to a statement in which they assert that they "have decided to record the facts, and only the facts about our experiences with Mr. Angelo Pignati." They will, they assure us, devote themselves to "the truth and nothing but the truth until this memorial epic is finished, So Help Us God!" (Zindel 1968, iii). They throw us right into the deconstructive enterprise where "a literary text is dynamic: it is a site of cultural production in which multiple unstable meanings vie for dominance" (Tyson 1991, 230). Their use of the language of courtroom testimony opens up the uncertainty of what will follow because even in a courtroom a jury or a judge must construct a version of reality from the testimony presented. The discrepancy in the ways in which John and Lorraine read and report the world begin in the first two chapters of the novel when John, beginning the story at school, explains that Lorraine is "panting to get at the typewriter now" (5), to which Lorraine replies, "I should never have let John write the first chapter because he always has to twist things subliminally." Lorraine explains that strange things have happened to John and her recently and that they feel they "should write them down while they're fresh in our minds" and "before John and I mature and repress the whole thing" (6). This particular version of reality, then, seems available only in the intensity of adolescent experience and in the immediacy of this moment. Discrepancies pile up as Lorraine and John tell the story. Lorraine says, "John told you about Dennis and Norton, but I don't think he got across how really disturbed those two boys are" (19). It is clear as we read that we will not get anything like a unified story. John tells us later, "I don't happen to buy all of Lorraine's stuff about omens. She talks about me distorting, but look at her. I mean, she thinks she can get away with her subliminal twists by calling them omens, but she doesn't fool me." In an intriguing confession from a writer sworn to tell "the truth and nothing but the truth," John acknowledges that "the only difference between her [Lorraine's] fibs and mine are that hers are eerie—she's got a gift for saying things that make you anxious" (54). At the end of the novel, in John's final narration, he affirms the deconstructive view of the world: "Our life would be what we made of it—nothing more, nothing less" (149).

The Pigman is the story of a life constructed by words; and as evidence of the impossibility of a stable reading of the novel, one young female adult reader wrote to Zindel to say, "When I finished reading *The Pigman* it pulled a part of me out and I want to finish this letter before that part of me goes back in." The reader affirms that she is a multiple construction as she concludes, "I am too young to understand how anyone writes a book as perceptive as yours but it had a part of almost everyone I know in it, and I can't be sure which one was me" (Zindel 1968, 154). The "truth" is that the reader is a fabric woven of all her experiences and interactions with others, including the characters in Zindel's novel. As a writer, Zindel affirms that the novel is a tissue of other texts—texts construed in its broadest sense. For example, he got the idea of creating a character who collected pigs from an actor whom he met in Houston, Texas; the story of the boatmen in the novel came from playwright Edward Albee who said that he first heard the story in Greece (154). These are the poststructural intertexts, the quotations without quotation marks that are woven into the novel.

A Begonia for Miss Applebaum. Zindel's *A Begonia for Miss Applebaum* opens with an invitation to deconstruction in much the same way that *The Pigman* does: "Something terrible has happened. There are no lies in this book and nothing phony," write Henry and Zelda who sign their names to a note that says "TO ANY KID WHO READS THIS." The issue of truth becomes deconstructively complicated when they continue: "We have to tell the whole story because we thought what we were doing was right. Well, maybe it wasn't. Maybe we were very wrong. We still don't know" (Zindel 1989, iii). The issue of their ability to tell the whole story arises in Chapter 2 when Zelda writes: "I am cranky about a lot of things Henry wrote in the first chapter. There is simply no way I can make you understand what happened to us concerning Miss Applebaum unless you know more accurate things about us than Henry has told you" (7). Similarities to *The Pigman*'s narrative techniques are clear as the novel progresses. Henry opens a chapter by telling us that he needs to amplify the information Zelda provided about Central Park: "I'm drawing a map so I can introduce more of a reality factor. Reality factors have always been my job when Zelda *sublimates* and tries to paint anything better than it really is" (60). We may interpret this deconstructively to mean that reality is a social construction, and we may also note that Henry's map is just another form of text, perhaps more accurate than Zelda's language, perhaps not. The seams in the narrative are made clear later in the novel when Henry explains, "I don't blame Zelda for having to skip around a little in recording the events that happened." In a perfect deconstructive move he explains that "as long as I'm able to fill in the gaps, we'll manage to get all the truth down. It'll just be a little rearranged according to what our brains will let us talk about" (149). "What our brains will let us talk about" is another way of saying that we construct the world in language. It is, of course, impossible to "get all the truth down."

After the First Death. Robert Cormier's *After the First Death* is a rich landscape for working deconstructively and exposing the seams of this narrative of psychological warfare. Patty Campbell describes the novel as a "a fairly complex structure with built-in puzzles and trapdoors" where two main narrative streams construct the story, namely, "the first person ruminations that are presumably the voice of Ben and later the general, and the events on the bus told in the third person from the alternating perspective of Miro and Kate (and—very briefly—Raymond and one other child)" (Campbell 1989, 74). Given these multiple narrators, the novel's seams are exposed and open to investigation.

The novel foregrounds the power of language in the construction of reality, as Artkin, the leader of the terrorist group explains to Miro Shantas, one of the young terrorists: "After the terror must come the politics, the talking, the words. At the proper time, the words carry more power than bombs, Miro. So while we still use bombs, there comes a time when we must use words" (Cormier 1977, 111). In contrast to this kind of reference to language, when we look into the mind of Raymond we see reality constructed simply, from the child's perspective: "Raymond was a good boy. He always did what his mother told him to do." He recalls that "his mother smelled sweet, like perfume. His father smelled like the outdoors." He registers his captivity in a childlike way: "Now in the bus, Raymond did not fidget. He was afraid of the men in the masks" (106–07).

The novel is full of references to the different kinds of language that create reality. Kate sees the terrorists unmasked; and realizing that she may be killed, she uses language to arouse Miro's sexuality. In the process, however, she feels "cheap and soiled and treacherous, knowing she was using the words to awaken him to her, using them the way a prostitute would use her body to arouse a man." She realizes that Miro is a construction of terrorist culture: "Who had made him a monster? This world, his world. Who was guilty, then: the monster or the world that created it?" (171). Later, she realizes how "innocent he was in the most terrible sense of innocence: the innocence of a monster" (218). The juxtaposition of *innocence* and *monster* opens up more seams in the world that the novel constructs.

During the negotiations between the terrorists and Inner Delta, a monitor speaks "code words" that Miro cannot understand; the voice of the monitor is "a robot voice" that is "impersonal, as if it issued from a machine and not a person" (175); such a voice seems appropriate in a world where humans can behave as inhumanely as these terrorists do.

Protesting the impending death of the child Raymond, Kate discovers that the language she has known is inadequate to express her feelings: "The words were strangled somewhere inside of her and the sound that came from her lips was a sound she had never heard before, as if she had suddenly found a new vocabulary, a new language, a language of despair and futility" (182). In this moment, the fabric of her world tears open, exposing the world of a bitter experience. Later, when Miro tortures Ben, language is an issue again: "The boy made a mewing sound like a small animal seeking to please its master but not knowing the master's language" (206). This scene represents the power of language to dominate, and, ultimately, to destroy.

The novel appears to unravel near the end in the dialogue that occurs between Ben and his father. In the spirit of the uncertainty that surrounds a deconstructive reading, Patty Campbell suggests three interpretations for this part of the novel: (1) Ben's father is in a mental institution after his son's death, and his guilt causes him to re-create Ben in his mind; (2) the only voice we hear is General Marchand's, and he is in a mental hospital recalling his days at Castleton Academy where the typing in the novel appears to take place; (3) this section is entirely Ben's voice (Campbell 1989, 75–76). Campbell offers plenty of material for deconstructive work with this complex novel. What she says that we miss here is "the perfect click of recognition" (75–76), or, we might say, the formalist completed and unified structure.

Finally, another deconstructive approach to *After the First Death* might resemble our analysis of *The Giver* in which the binary oppositions of positive/negative and pleasure/pain are inverted in the changing meanings of the word *release*. Here I'll simply point the direction for such a reading. The principle binary opposition in Cormier's novel is good/evil, and at the beginning of the novel it appears that good is clearly represented by Inner Delta while evil is represented by the terrorists. In this deconstructive reading, the positive associations with Inner Delta are turned upside down when General Marchand sacrifices his son in order to defeat the terrorists. A deconstructive reading would trace this reversal as it occurs in the narrative.

A Final Note

I like what J. Hillis Miller (1982) says about the way he reads because I enjoy reading this way, too: "I try to attend to the threads of the tapestry of words . . . rather than simply the picture the novel makes when viewed from a distance" (3). Attending to the threads is one of the joys of reading in the deconstructive way.

Works Cited

Atkins, G. Douglas, and Michael L. Johnson. 1985. Introduction to *Writing and Reading Differently: Deconstruction and the Teaching of Composition and Literature*, eds. G. Douglas Atkins and Michael L. Johnson, 1–14. Lawrence: University of Kansas Press.

Barthes, Roland. 1979. "From Work to Text." In *Textual Strategies: Perspectives in Post-Structuralist Criticism*, ed. Josue V. Harari, 73–81. Ithaca: Cornell University Press.

———. 1981. "Theory of the Text." Trans. Ian McLeod. In *Untying the Text: A Post-Structuralist Reader*, ed. Robert Young, 39. London: Routledge. Quoted in Jeremy Hawthorn, *A Concise Glossary of Contemporary Literary Theory*, 100. London: Edward Arnold, 1994.

———. 1992. "The Death of the Author." Trans. Stephen Heath. In *Critical Theory Since Plato*, ed. Hazard Adams, 1130–33. New York: Harcourt Brace Jovanovich.

Bressler, Charles. 1994. "Deconstruction." In *Literary Criticism: An Introduction to Theory and Practice*, 71–86. Englewood Cliffs: Prentice Hall.

Campbell, Patty. 1989. "*After the First Death*." In *Presenting Robert Cormier*, 72–145. New York: Twayne.

Cormier, Robert. 1979. *After the First Death*. New York: Dell.

Dante. *Divine Comedy*. Trans. Allen Mandelbaum. Berkeley: University of California Press. 1980.

Frye, Northrop. 1968. "Archetypal Criticism: Theory of Myths." In *Anatomy of Criticism*, 131–239. New York: Atheneum.

Johnson, Barbara. 1985. "Teaching Deconstructively." In *Writing and Reading Differently: Deconstruction and the Teaching of Composition and Literature*, eds. G. Douglas Atkins and Michael L. Johnson, 140–48. Lawrence: University of Kansas Press.

———. 1980. *The Critical Difference: Essays in the Contemporary Rhetoric of Reading*. Baltimore: Johns Hopkins University Press, 1980.

Kolatch, Alfred J. 1980. *The Dictionary of First Names*. New York: Perigee.

Lowry, Lois. 1993. *The Giver*. New York: Bantam Doubleday Dell.

Lynn, Steven. 1994. "Opening Up the Text: Deconstructive Criticism." In *Texts and Contexts: Writing About Literature and Critical Theory*, 87–112. New York: HarperCollins.

Miller, J. Hillis. 1982. "Two Forms of Repetition." In *Fiction and Repetition: Seven English Novels*, 1–21. Cambridge: Harvard University Press.

———. 1991. "Stevens' Rock and Criticism as Cure, II." In *Theory Now and*

Then, ed. J. Hillis Miller, 117–31. Durham: Duke University Press.

Murfin, Ross C. 1994. "Deconstruction and *The House of Mirth*." In *The House of Mirth by Edith Wharton*, ed. Shari Benstock, 419–31. *Case Studies in Contemporary Criticism*. Boston: St. Martin's.

Paulsen, Gary. 1985. *Dogsong*. New York: Puffin.

Tyson, Lois. 1991. "Teaching Deconstruction: Theory and Practice in the Undergraduate Classroom." In *Practicing Theory in Introductory College Literature Courses*, eds. James M. Cahalan and David B. Downing, 227–38. Urbana, IL: National Council of Teachers of English.

Zindel, Paul. 1989. *A Begonia for Miss Applebaum*. New York: Bantam.

———. 1968. *The Pigman*. New York: Bantam.

Six

Reader-Response
Identity Themes in *Fallen Angels*

*Perhaps an even better analogy for the reenactment of the text is
the musical performance. The text of a poem or a novel or a drama
is like a musical score. . . . In the literary reading, even the key-
board on which the performer plays is—himself.*

Louise Rosenblatt
The Reader, the Text, the Poem (1978)

Reader-Response Theories

An Overview

Our readings of Walter Dean Myers' *Fallen Angels* (1988) will be
guided by critical inquiries that are collectively referred to as reader-
response theory. You may be familiar with some versions of this theory, or you may be practicing it in your classroom, especially if you
have been influenced by the work of Louise Rosenblatt.

Susan Suleiman (1990) describes the variety of reader-response
approaches. The theory, she says, is "not a single widely trodden path
but a multiplicity of crisscrossing, often divergent tracks that cover a
vast area of critical landscape in a pattern whose complexity dismays
the brave and confounds the faint of heart" (6). Attempting to map
"the principal tracks in the landscape," she distinguishes six approaches
to the field:

1. rhetorical
2. semiotic and structuralist
3. phenomenological
4. subjective and psychoanalytic

5. sociological and historical

6. hermeneutic.

It is not my purpose to explain how these approaches differ, but Suleiman maintains that in practice they overlap and that their vitality depends on the fact that they give many dimensions to analysis and make a wide range of interpretations possible (Suleiman 1980, 6–7).

In *Interpretive Conventions* (1982), Steven Mailloux describes the present state of reader-response theory as "metacritical chaos," to which he proposes to bring order. He categorizes the wide range of these theories as "affective, phenomenological, subjective, transactive, transactional, structural, deconstructive, rhetorical, psychological, speech act and other criticisms" (19). To bring some order to the field, Mailloux limits his discussion to the five reader-response critics who have, in his opinion, had the most influence in the United States: Norman Holland, David Bleich, Wolfgang Iser, Jonathan Culler, and Stanley Fish. To distinguish their theoretical approaches, Mailloux constructs a schema in which he progresses historically from the earliest reader-response theorists to the most recent. Early approaches explored reader subjectivity in psychological models (Holland and Bleich). Later, the focus shifted to the concept of intersubjectivity through a phenomenological model (Iser and Fish's early work). Most recently, structuralist and poststructuralist response theories are represented by the social models of Culler and Fish. In this chapter, we will read *Fallen Angels* from the critical approaches of the theorists who stand at each extreme of Mailloux's schema: Norman Holland and Stanley Fish.

In developing his own version of response theory, Mailloux proposes an idea that will serve as a working metaphor for this chapter. He suggests that reader-response is a "rhetoric of entanglement," a way of reading in which the reader makes a series of sequential responses to the text, responses that enable the reader to build an interpretation (Mailloux 1982, 90). He also describes his theory of "interpretive conventions" as "communal procedures for making intelligible the world, behavior, communication, and literary texts" (149). His metaphor of entanglement works for both of my approaches to *Fallen Angels*: A highly subjective response is a way of getting intimately entangled with a text, and the idea of interpretive conventions weaves me into the intricate threadings, the "communal procedures" of the community of English teachers.

Characteristics of the Theory

Despite the wide range of differing approaches and the bewildering array of names, most contemporary reader-response theories, which developed from the early 1960s to the late 1980s, share the following characteristics (Leitch 1988, 212):

1. They focus on the reader rather than on the autonomous text.

2. They believe that interpretation emerges from the reader's transaction or interaction with the text, not from a set of rules or presuppositions about the text (e.g., formalism's insistence on textual unity).

3. They insist that a text is anything but unified; on the contrary, a text is discontinuous, filled with gaps or moments that have been left unwritten and that the reader fills in while "making" the text.

4. They use the word *text* to signify an event unfolding in time, an event in which meaning occurs during the process of reading. The text is a possibility, a weaving that readers co-create in the process of living through a reading.

5. They contend that reading is not a completely free activity; it is constrained by our attitude that knowledge is either (a) preexistent and received by us or (b) made by us in an act of social construction, that is, we produce it within a community of learners who share some of our basic concerns and experiences in human life.

6. They describe readers in a variety of ways: informed, ideal, implied, actual, and virtual; some readers are called *superreaders*, while others are referred to as *literents*.

7. They do not concern themselves with the question of historical influences on the work or with the ideas of aesthetics. Aesthetics values a work as a completed object, something *out there* for our admiration and evaluation. Reader-response theories investigate what is *in here*—inside the experience of the person who is reading.

8. More than any other critical theory, they have been concerned with pedagogy, locating both text and reader in the classroom. Reading is a process, they believe, to be observed and studied in the actual labor of readers, not an idea to be theorized only in an abstract, philosophical way.

Reading Subjectively

Louise Rosenblatt and Transactional Theory

The work of Louise Rosenblatt, a pioneer in reader-response theory, offers a good introduction to the basic principles guiding our reading of Walter Dean Myers' *Fallen Angels*. Rosenblatt first expounded her theory in *Literature as Exploration* (1938) where she explained that each reader produces a "unique experience" as a result of reading because each reader brings his or her "personality traits, memories of past events, present needs and preoccupations" as well as his or her psychological and physical conditions to the act of reading (Rosenblatt 1976, 37). In *The Reader, the Text, and the Poem* (1978), Rosenblatt set out to present, as she said, a "matured and more developed theory of the literary work of art and the implication for criticism" (xii). In her second book (1978), she rejects the critical extremes that (1) view the reader as a tabula rasa (blank slate) who receives the imprint of the poem or (2) view the text as empty, awaiting the content brought by the reader (1–5). Reading is a temporal event, one that unfolds through time, and the reader's response is conditioned by this temporality. Rosenblatt uses the word *text* to designate "a set or series of signs interpretable as linguistic symbols," and her word *poem* is a generic term for all literary forms (12).

In considering the poem as an "event," Rosenblatt (1978) draws two conclusions about the reader and the text: (1) the text is a stimulus, activating the reader's past experiences with literature and with life; (2) the text functions as a blueprint, a guide through which the reader selects, rejects, and orders responses during the reading (11). She describes the transactional process in which " 'the poem' comes into being in the live circuit set up between the reader and the 'text' " (14). In other words, the reader brings the poem into being. While this process is clearly not objective, it is not wholly subjective because "the physical signs of the text" enable the reader "to reach through himself and the verbal symbols to something sensed as outside and beyond his personal world" (21). The transaction between reader and text breaks the boundary between inner and outer worlds and constructs a new world.

In *Response and Analysis: Teaching Literature in Junior and Senior High School* (1991), Robert Probst draws heavily on Rosenblatt's theory and offers suggestions for its practice in the classroom. Because Rosenblatt's work has received so much attention in its relationship to the classroom, here we will explore another approach to a transactional reading of Myers' novel.

Norman Holland and the Identity Theme

Norman Holland provides a version of transactional theory and a strategy for performing it in his essay "UNITY IDENTITY TEXT SELF" (1975). The title is derived from the key words of the sentence "*Identity* is the *unity* I find in a *self* if I look at it as though it were a *text*" (121). Explicating this sentence helps us understand how to apply Holland's reader-response approach. Holland shares his concept of text with the formalists: *Text* refers simply to "the words on the page" (118). *Unity*, however, signifies something more complex for Holland than the organic unity that formalists sought in the work. Holland's unity designates a point at which a reader arrives after having explored the themes in a text; during this exploration, the reader selects certain thematic details and distills them into a central theme. *Unity* is further complicated by the psychology of the *self*, by which Holland means "the real total person of an individual," which includes both body and mind (120–21). *Identity* also presents psychological complications because it emerges from an "infinite sequence of bodily and behavioral transformations during the whole life of an individual" (Lichenstein 1961, quoted in Holland 1975, 120).

Holland pulls these ideas together in a musical simile very close to Rosenblatt's in this chapter's epigraph. We can "conceive of the individual as living out variations on an identity theme much as a musician might play out an infinity of variations on a single melody" (Holland 1975, 120). Our basic identity, then, is the single melody of Holland's simile; but at any given time, for example, when we are reading a novel, our identity can be varied, transformed by the way in which we identify with some person in the fictional world. Thus, we can each have a different response to a text, and some of us, sharing similar identity themes, can feel connected to each other through the text. In this way, we can understand what Holland means when he says that "*interpretation is a function of identity*" (123).

Given these ideas, how do we interpret a text? Holland symbolizes his three-stage interpretive process (d-f-t) with the acronym DEFT, which stands for the sequence "defense," "fantasy," and "transformation." He makes it clear that this process is not a tidy sequence of steps completed in order: "Obviously," he says, "they all go on together" (Holland 1975, 124).

The DE in the acronym refers to the way in which the text becomes uniquely our own. As we read, we re-create the text, shaping it with our own identity by passing it through a network of defense (DE) mechanisms with which we respond to our world, adapt to it, cope with it. The F represents fantasy. The text contains fantasies; and as we read, we create our own fantasies that suit our identity, that give us pleasure. To use Holland's musical analogy, the fantasies in the F stage of the process are variations on our identity theme. In the T, or transformative, stage, we complete the re-creation of our identity by transforming the raw fantasies of the second stage into a coherent experience. In other words, we put the text together at a larger level, either intellectual or aesthetic. We can accomplish this coherence in a number of ways: for example, by comparing our experiences to the experiences of others who have read the same text or by bringing other knowledge to bear on the reading experience. We can also respond critically by treating the text as "an encoded message to be decoded" (Holland 1975, 126). One way to apply Holland's DEFT approach to *Fallen Angels* is to read it as a metaphor for the warring self.

Reading *Fallen Angels*/Reading the Self

Fallen Angels juxtaposes two worlds: the world of home in the United States and the world of war in Vietnam. As we read the novel, we find ourselves experiencing these two worlds through a third world—the mind of Richie Perry, the central character, the figure with whom most readers identify in the novel.

September 15, 1967. Anchorage, Alaska. Richie Perry, a seventeen-year-old Harlem high school graduate who has chosen for financial reasons to join the army rather than to go to college, is being transported to the war. Although he is supposed to be excused from duty as a result of an injury, the personnel file containing this information is misplaced, and he is sent on to Vietnam. The novel narrates the year in which he struggles to stay alive so that he can return home.

Travelling in memory, I see myself in relation to the opening scene of Myers' novel. My September 1967 takes place in a different landscape. I have chosen to go to college and am deferred from the Vietnam War. A student at the College of William and Mary, I have declared my major—English—and I elect courses in Romantic and Victorian English poetry as well as aesthetics. I also choose to study American history from the Civil War to the present, although my experience has taught me that my classmates and I will never make it to the present: We will linger in the Civil War and the First World War, and suddenly the Second World War will be but a blur as we rush to the end of the semester. We are living during the Cold War and the Vietnam War, but they seem to be on the other side of the world. We are safe but anxious in the hallowed halls of ivy.

Richie comes to life in a world of developing camaraderie. We meet a succession of people who will populate his world for a year, most important among them his friend Harold Gates, known as Peewee. There is Lieutenant Carroll from Kansas; Johnson from Savannah, Georgia; Captain Stewart, the company commander; and Lobel, a Jewish soldier who keeps talking to us about the movies. Only a few women appear in the story, among them Judy Duncan from Irving, Texas. Everyone is from somewhere, and we never forget that they all want to make it home again.

Back home there are a few more important people, especially Richie's mother and his little brother Kenny. And there is Mrs. Liebow, Richie's last English teacher at Stuyvesant High School in Harlem, one of the few people who has given him a vision of himself, discussed his identity with him.

Other than the people in the novel, I respond most to the letters that Richie writes. This is one of the ways in which I, and many of you perhaps, identify with Richie. We are people with language. We own it, and we cannot exist without it. It constructs us, and we construct the world with it. Because he has a way with words, Richie is chosen, soon after his tour of duty begins, to write letters of notification to the families of the dead. Throughout the novel he also writes letters to his mother and brother. These two kinds of letters organize the novel; they trace the fate of innocence from the first letter Richie writes (when Lieutenant Carroll is killed) to the horrific one he wishes he could write at the end of the novel.

In the first polite letter, he reports that Lieutenant Carroll died bravely and honorably and that all the guys in his squad appreciated his leadership. "I am sorry," he concludes, "to write to you under these circumstances" (131). Near the end of the novel he imagines writing a very different letter, and the two letters symbolize the transformation that takes place in his identity during the war. After a devastating experience in which the bodies of fallen comrades are burned so that the enemy cannot mutilate them, Richie imagines a bitter letter that would communicate to a mother what had actually happened to her son:

> We lost your son, ma'am. Somewhere in the forests he lies, perhaps behind some rock, some tree? We burned his body, ma'am. In a rite hurried by fear and panic, we burned what was left of him and ran for our lives. Yes, and we're sorry. (256)

Fallen Angels tells the story of sorrow that shatters the psyche, that winds through a year relieved only in the final scene when on the wings of a silver plane, the Freedom Bird, Richie and Peewee, hand in hand, "are headed back to the World" (309).

The Identity Theme

The identity theme in *Fallen Angels* describes most of us at certain times in our lives: It is the theme of becoming, the theme that emerges through our rites of passage, linking us but at the same time making us unique in the details of our separate coming-of-age stories. This identity theme emerges from what we do and how we think, from the ways in which the mind works, how it wars with itself as we struggle between adolescence and adulthood, fighting our unique battles. The theme is simultaneously about victory and defeat, about the dream that we will achieve greatness or the fear that we will disintegrate. It is about defending our position, saving the mind from fragmentation so that in the process of becoming, we are not destroyed. When Richie recalls the image of a Viet Cong whom he killed, he thinks that the enemy soldier has ceased to be a human being: "He was a thing, a trophy." Then he wonders about his own future: "I wondered if I could become a trophy" (84–85). Here Richie asks the big question of our shared identity theme: Will I become the hero or the victim of my own life?

Framing Identity. The development of the identity theme in Richie's life began in high school. Two recollections in the novel illustrate what Holland calls variations or transformations of Richie's identity theme. The first variation is described in a conversation that Richie had with his English teacher Mrs. Liebow. Once, when he was fifteen, she told him that she saw a doubleness in him, that he was too much an observer and too little a participant in life. She suggested that he change. Vietnam transforms him. His participation and powers of observation allow us to experience the war as we do in *Fallen Angels*. Richie can "see," articulate what others cannot, take pictures in language and hand them to us.

In Vietnam, Richie recalls what it meant to be an observer back in Harlem: "There was always a way to frame things, to put them into a romantic setting, that made you feel good" (35). This framing image contributes to what Holland calls adaptation and transformation. For example, after the death of Lieutenant Carroll, Richie frames the experience, and it is clear that his identity has been transformed as a result of it:

> Lieutenant Carroll was inside of me, he was part of me. Part of me was dead with him. . . . I just had these pictures of him walking along on his patrol or sitting in the mess area, looking into his coffee cup. It was what I was building in my mind, a series of pictures of things I had seen, of guys I had seen. I found myself trying to push them from my mind, but they seemed more and more a part of me. (137)

This imagery is complex. First, to use the language of poststructuralism, Carroll has been woven into the fabric of Richie's life; he is an *intertext*, a term I shall deal with later in this chapter. The rim of the coffee cup is another framing image; and from what we learn about Carroll, we can imagine that he is daydreaming about his wife and children. Finally, the pictures are like part of a movie that Richie is filming in his mind, a movie of all these men and their relationships, of events in his life that will change forever the person that he can be. These pictures culminate in the final scene of the novel. Richie and Peewee are headed home, and the final image completes Holland's transformation of identity. As the Freedom Bird glides toward California, Richie slips into a memory. He is back in Vietnam, on a patrol that is extraordinary and symbolic, the final clip in his war film. He locates himself in a central position; he is the unity that links the living and the dead. As he walks the boonies, past rice paddies, he brings up the rear behind the living—Monaco, Peewee, Walowick, Lobel, Brunner, and Johnson. When he turns around, he sees the dead marching behind him, among them Lieutenant Carroll. This is where he stands as a man, a youth headed home toward the living but transformed forever by the dead. In this final picture, Richie's identity theme is mine, and yours, I would guess. Ahead of us others lead; behind us march the dead, heroes and victims in wars real and imagined.

Becoming Somebody. Recalling his conversation with Mrs. Liebow, Richie describes a variation of his identity that occurred when he played basketball in high school: "I was somebody else there: Mr. In-Your-Face, jiving and driving, looping and hooping, staying clean and being mean, the inside rover till the game was over" (35). Part of the process of becoming somebody is constantly struggling with the question "Who am I?" It seems that during the painful years of adolescence we become a number of somebodys. We model ourselves after people we admire or think that we admire, and then we decide that such a person is not who we are, so we try someone else. Perhaps we try to fit into sports as a member of the team or into the a social group that appeals to us. That works, too—it feels good to be part of something larger than we are. But there's still the matter of who we are as individuals. Richie's description of himself on the basketball court is full of musical rhythms and rhymes that symbolize the joy of moments of positive identity; but they are, at last, only part of a game that is diversionary: Such games are among the variations on the single melody that sings us through life.

The question "Who am I?" continues to trouble Richie during the war, and he defines himself in relation to Johnson, a soldier from Savannah, Georgia, who is so black that "even the whites of his eyes were dark" (29). Richie admires Johnson's knowledge, experience, and savvy. Johnson knows how to survive in the war; to Richie, the war makes Johnson "a certain somebody" (113). In the war, Richie becomes aware that survival might mean becoming "somebody else," somebody other than the "Mr. In-Your-Face" he has been. His description of himself as "jiving and driving" and his admiration for

Johnson illustrate what Holland calls "the millions of ego choices that constitute the visible human . . . ever changing and different, yet ever continuous with what went before" (121). Constructing a self to survive the war becomes one of the variations of Richie's identity theme. He starts to realize that he must kill the Congs before they kill him, and he knows that this means "being some other person" than he was when he got to Vietnam: "Maybe that was what I had to be. Somebody else" (216).

The gruesome imagery of defacement when Richie kills his first Viet Cong graphically defines the "somebody else" that war demands. Almost out of control, Richie empties a clip of ammunition into the soldier's face. When he finishes, there is no face, just "an angry mass of red flesh" (181). The enemy is defaced, but so is Richie; he remembers looking down at the slain Viet Cong and "feeling my own face torn apart" (182). Is Richie the hero or victim in this scene? Our individual responses to this moment constitute a variation on our identity theme, on our idea of what makes a hero.

Fantasy: Variations on Heroism. The war offers some variations on the theme of being a hero in which idealism may represent the pleasurable fantasy that Holland includes in the DEFT process. What kind of hero do we expect in war? What kind of hero can a person become? Is it possible to realize the ideal in the realities of the Vietnamese landscape or in the everyday world we inhabit?

One variation on heroism in *Fallen Angels* emerges from the action of being a good soldier. When Richie tries to write his brother Kenny about the war, he tries to identify himself through this variation: "Being a good soldier meant doing your job" and "it meant killing the enemy." Recalling that he had thought about being a writer before the war because his teachers had said he "used words well," he cannot be dishonest in his language. "Writing that I had done a good job killing just didn't work," he thinks (190). He cannot make Kenny think that he is a good soldier in this sense, because he has already killed the enemy, defaced a man and himself, and he knows that this is not heroism.

A chaplain who comes to talk to the company offers an idealistic variation on the heroic theme. He tells the soldiers that they are defending freedom for both Americans and the South Vietnamese, praising their "acts of heroism and courage" as celebrations of life for which "all America thanks you" (215). This is the patriotic ideal, heroism for the fatherland, bravery for others, the ultimate altruism in the struggle for the victory of Good, the vanquishing of Evil.

Later, when Richie tells Lobel that he has not written to tell Kenny how the war really is, Lobel upholds the heroic ideal from the popular culture: Tell Kenny, he advises, that the war is "just like the way things are in the movies." Richie fears that Kenny will romanticize the war, but Lobel simplifies the whole concept of what a hero is: "You know, to a kid if you kill somebody and the somebody is supposed to be a bad guy, you're a hero" (268). Now the notes of heroic variations play in and out of each other: Being somebody and killing somebody may be variations on the same theme, but the person who gets killed is also "somebody." When one identity is gained, another is lost.

Lobel's simple dichotomy of Good and Bad may, however, be necessary for Holland's kind of fantasy. We fantasize a heroism that defeats Evil. Such a fantasy is essential to the Great American Hero that the chaplain constructs and to the John Waynes that the movies make, but it does not play out in the character of Richie in the novel, nor, I wager, does it play out in most of our lives. Most of the time the struggle is too complicated for simple formulas, no matter how glorious the story or how real the heroes may look before us on the screen.

Unity. According to Holland's version of reader-response theory, when we finish reading a novel, we put it together, make something coherent out of the temporal experience of having lived through the text. One way in which we accomplish this is to bring our knowledge to bear on the text, to evaluate it. Richie works at answering the question "Who am I?" throughout the novel by juxtaposing his knowledge of himself before the war with images of himself during the war. Recalling that at seventeen he had been a kid, he realizes that the war is transformative: All the killing and dying around him, he says, "was making me look at myself again, hoping to find something more than the kid I was." He identifies the variations that have been part of his identity, and he thinks about himself becoming a man, achieving a version of Holland's unity: "Maybe I could sift through the kid's stuff, the basketball, the Harlem streets, and find the man I could be" (187). Later, he questions who he has become in the war: "Who the hell were these people? These soldiers? Was I really one of them? If I was, could I ever be anything else again?" (295–96). He has played out one of Holland's identity variations, but he doubts that he can remain the man whom war has constructed. Finding the person who we *can* be—this is one of the quests of human life, a quest that is a function of all the games that we play, the streets we cross, and the wars we survive, both the physical ones and the psychological ones.

The Poem of the Mind. *Fallen Angels* is a "poem" in Louise Rosenblatt's meaning: "'Poem' presupposes a reader actively involved with a text and refers to what he makes of his responses to that particular set of verbal symbols" (Rosenblatt 1978, 12). Reading *Fallen Angels* from a reader-response approach, I recall Wallace Steven's "On Modern Poetry" in which he declares that "The poem of the mind is the act of finding / What will suffice" (Stevens 1990, 239–40). Stevens' poem can be taken as a metaphor for the reading process as it has changed from formalism where "the scene was set" and where the mind/reader "repeated what / Was in the script." Newer literary theories have demanded new practices because "the theatre was changed" and "Its past was a souvenir." Reading modern poetry or reading from a new perspective means that the mind "has to be living, to learn the speech of the place." Interpretation cannot, in this sense, count on the familiar ways of reading, of understanding language and how it has always worked. Instead, "It has / To construct a new stage" and "It has to be on that stage." This new stage can be the metaphoric modern classroom where reading and interpreting literature is a performance, an event in time.

Reading/Responding in an Interpretive Community

Another version of reader-response theory locates us in the world we share as English teachers, the world we construct out of the ways in which we have been taught to read. Because we English teachers share common reading practices and a common canon, we belong to interpretive communities; these communities are the central concept of Stanley Fish's social reader-response theory.

Fish explains this concept in his essay "Interpreting the Variorum" (1976) in which he attacks formalist ways of reading that originate from the belief that the text is self-sufficient and that meaning is embedded in it. As you know, formalist approaches ignore the act of reading as an event taking place in the time in which the text is experienced, lived through. In the reading procedures that Fish proposes, readers' activities receive the most attention. He regards the work of reading not as a way to arrive at textual meaning but as an activity "*having* meaning" in itself (172). As we read, he says, we are not guided by specific procedures or methodologies; instead, we read in a "moving field of concerns" and interpretive strategies that we share with other readers who belong to our interpretive community. We make assumptions and revise them; we make judgments and regret them as we read on; we arrive at conclusions and then abandon them, ask questions, supply answers, solve puzzles in the text.

According to Fish (1976), interpretation, or "text making," does not happen randomly; rather, it results from "the fragile but real consolidation of interpretive communities that allows us to talk to one another," to engage in conversation about texts as a result of interpretive strategies that are neither natural nor universal but learned (182–83). In this context, the ways in which we read are products of all the talking that has gone on in the English classrooms, or interpretive communities, in which we learned to read. In our teaching, we construct such communities and continue to learn in them.

Fish (1976) defines a reader in an interpretive community as the "intended reader." This term does not apply to the reader whose single goal is to comprehend the author's purpose or to the reader who simply registers a response to a text and then talks freely about it—perhaps, for example, associating the text with personal experiences. Instead, Fish's intended reader is educated and is in command of linguistic competencies (174). In other words, Fish's reader knows *how* to read. The reader's response to a text occurs as a function of these how-tos that the reader shares with the other members of the interpretive community.

Intertextuality and the Interpretive Community

As readers, Fish explains, we are "predisposed to perform certain acts" as we experience the text. We "find" themes because we are looking for them. We "confer significances," for example, on "flowers, streams, shepherds, pagan deities," and we "mark out formal units." Such acts make up a "set of interpretive strategies" that, when they are executed, "become the large act of reading." Interpretive strategies are not reserved until we have finished reading a text; they are actually "the shape of the reading," and they make the text rather than arise from it (Fish 1976, 179–80).

As an English teacher, I belong to an interpretive community whose members are always exploring how their experiences with a particular text are related to their experiences with other texts that they know and have taught. They are also interested in how students relate texts to each other (Beach 1993, 37). Their interest is in what the poststructuralists call intertextuality. The term *intertextuality* is defined quite differently in various theoretical contexts, but for our purposes, we will use this definition:

> Any text is a new tissue of past citations. Bits of code, formulae, rhythmic models, fragments of social languages, etc. pass into the text and are redistributed within it, for there is always language before and around the text. Intertextuality, the condition of any text whatsoever, cannot, of course, be reduced to a problem of sources or influences; the intertext is a general field of anonymous formulae

whose origin can scarcely be located; of unconscious or automatic
quotations, given without quotation marks. (Barthes 1981, 39)

In their second reader-response to *Fallen Angels* as members of an
interpretive community, English teachers will recognize their own
quotations "without quotation marks" based on all the texts they
have read and taught. Here I will suggest a few such intertexts that I
find in *Fallen Angels*.

Camaraderie: The Intertext of Love. For those of us who have
studied classical literatures, the unfolding relationship between Richie
and his comrades in *Fallen Angels* echoes ancient war stories about the
bonds between soldiers. At the end of the novel, Richie defines the
relationships that have developed during the war: "I had never been
in love before. Maybe this was what it was like, the way I felt for
Monaco and Peewee and Johnson and the rest of my squad. I hoped
this was what it was like" (301). The word *love* in this passage recalls
the story of Nisus and Euryalus in Vergil's *Aeneid*: "One love united
them, and side by side / They entered combat" (9. 245–50). Together
they volunteer to reconnoiter to find Aeneas, to go out on a patrol not
unlike those in *Fallen Angels*.

Coming upon an enemy camp, Nisus and Euryalus slaughter the
Romans but are caught in the act and killed. Euryalus falls like "a
bright flower cut by a passing plow" or a poppy that "bows its
head . . . / When overborne by a passing rain" (9. 617–20). In these
images, Vergil portrays the innocence of soldiers who fall in the war,
soldiers not unlike those who fall in Myers' novel. "Fortunate, both!"
Vergil writes: "If in the least my songs / Avail, no future day will ever
take you / Out of the record of remembering Time" (9. 633–35).

The phrase "remembering Time" recalls a story in Tim O'Brien's
The Things They Carried (1990) that serves as an intertext for my reading of *Fallen Angels*. The narrator of O'Brien's story, "Spin," says:

> Forty-three years old, and the war occurred half a lifetime ago, and
> yet the remembering makes it now. And sometimes remembering
> will lead to a story, which makes it forever. That's what stories are
> for. Stories are for joining the past to the future. . . . Stories are for
> eternity, when memory is erased, when there is nothing to remem-
> ber except the story. (40)

Myers' novel is a text in which we live through Richie's experiences
so that "the memory makes it now." To use Vergil's phrase, the novel
is another "record of remembering Time," another story joining past
and future in the same way that intertextuality connects our past
reading and teaching with the new texts we read and teach.

Other Intertexts. All readers in the community of English teachers will create their own intertextual links to *Fallen Angels*, everything from the familiar war novels, *The Red Badge of Courage* and *All Quiet on the Western Front*, for example, to memorable poems such as Thomas Hardy's "The Man He Killed" and the poems of World War I, Siegfried Sassoon's familiar "Suicide in the Trenches" among them. The letters that Richie writes in the novel recall to me Walt Whitman's "Come Up from the Fields Father" where, one autumn in Ohio, a daughter calls her family together to read an ominous letter, to realize that "the only son is dead" (Whitman 1973, 31).

There are, of course, other kinds of intertexts. Myers' cinemagraphic descriptions of war violence and Lobel's constant references to the movies suggest *Platoon* (1986), perhaps the most graphic of all the Vietnam war films, as an intertext. There is, too, that unforgettable picture of the naked child fleeing My Lai. Modern technology has recorded and preserved the Vietnam War more than it has any other war before it. All those photographs and news stories provide intertexts, quotations without quotation marks.

In a reader-response approach, the most important response is our personal one, and several intertexts appear for me in one of the most electrifying moments in *Fallen Angels*, a moment that occurs in cinemagraphic detail.

On a rainy Tuesday morning that "promised to be the worst day of the war," some South Vietnamese soldiers catch a woman and two children near the edge of the paddies; without an interpreter, the soldiers can't communicate with the woman and children, so they let the three go. Feeling sorry for the children, Peewee wants to give them a gift; and using a handful of grass, he quickly starts making a doll. Richie watches as American soldiers follow the woman to the edge of camp where she hands one of the children to a soldier whose "arms and legs" are "flung apart from the impact of the blast." The child, mined, explodes in the soldier's arms. An horrific scene ensues. Other soldiers fall to the ground, "as if the very idea of a kid exploding in your arms had its own powers, its own killing force." The woman flees across the paddy, and Richie sees her "fold backward" as rifle fire tears her apart, her body moving in one direction, her legs moving in another. The other child, standing knee deep in the water, is gunned down. Peewee walks away, leaving the doll he had made "facedown in the endless mud." The scene ends: "It was raining again" (230–31).

As a member of an interpretive community first trained in formalist reading techniques, I see this scene as complete, framed and wrapped in rain. It seems both a linear movement through time and space and a completed circle, a frozen moment of experience.

When the scene is over, I see the child, shattered. I see the fallen soldiers. I see the mother and the other child, shot dead in the rice paddy.

It is a moment when I stop reading because I must try to absorb what I have seen. In the silence and through the rain I hear music, a song that has played through my head many times, a song that I have taught as poetry, a protest song that becomes, after this reading, a song for fallen angels, Pete Seeger's ballad, "Where Have All the Flowers Gone?" Seeger's song asks a series of questions about the whereabouts of young soldiers who have gone to war. The answers to these questions focus on the terrible costs of war—lost loves and lost lives—and the lessons of war, lessons that never, ironically, seem to be learned.

As a teacher of poetry I hear another song of protest as the child explodes before my face. I think about the Vietnamese mother in this scene and about other mothers. I know there are "enemy" mothers who did not blow up their children (Are those actually *her* children? I ask). I hear a poet, asking questions that provide a chilling intertext for the electrifying moment in the rice paddies.

In "What Were They Like?" (1971), Denise Levertov asks us to re-envision the Vietnam War from the perspective of the ancient culture of Vietnam (517). The speaker in the first half of Levertov's poem asks six questions about this Asian culture:

1. Did the people use stone lanterns?
2. Did they celebrate spring in the opening of flower buds?
3. Did they laugh?
4. Did they wear ornaments made of silver, jade, ivory, and bone?
5. Did they celebrate their history in grand storytelling?
6. What was their speech like? Was it like singing?

In the second half of the poem, a polite voice replies (its bitterly ironic language often playing on the words of the questioner):

1. Their hearts, once light, became hard as stone.
2. They no longer delighted in the opening of spring buds because their children were dead.
3. Burned mouths find laughter bitter.
4. Once joyful ornaments became insignificant among all the charred bones of the dead.
5. Once bombs had smashed the peaceful watery mirrors of the rice paddies, screaming replaced the ancient stories.
6. Speech, once songlike, has fallen silent.

The poem, too, falls silent in the ironies of Levertov's response to the effects of war on the innocent and on an ancient culture.

The Poem of the Act of the Mind

In reader-response approaches, we create the text, the "poem," in a performance, an event acted out on the stages of our minds. Such a response is not always easy to describe because "response to literature takes place in the black box of the mind," and it is "difficult to look inside and see what's going on" (Probst 1991, 655). In this chapter, I have tried to play out variations on my own identity as well as to suggest how many of us share in these variations: Who are we? What makes heroes? What bonds us together? Can we hang on to home once we leave it? To create the text of *Fallen Angels*, I have collaborated with Richie and with Walter Dean Myers. Louise Rosenblatt, Norman Holland, and Stanley Fish and their theories have provided me with ways of reading and interpreting the novel. Vergil, Tim O'Brien, Wallace Stevens, Walt Whitman, Pete Seeger, and Denise Levertov have provided intertexts, "quotations without quotation marks," that have helped me make the reading uniquely my own while also connecting me to English teachers who, like me, weave the text into the rich tapestry of their reading and teaching experiences.

Joining the Reader-Response Conversation

Virginia Monseau's "Students and Teachers as a Community of Readers" (1992) provides helpful insights into what a reader-response approach to young adult texts looks like in the English classroom. She says that young adult literature can help teachers build interpretive communities with their students, and she engages specific theoretical perspectives that we have examined in this chapter. In discussing Rosenblatt's idea that reading as an active process improves students' social understanding, Monseau emphasizes the role that theory can play in the classroom and in the world beyond. Monseau's article includes transcriptions of classroom conversations that provide insight into the way in which several teachers work with students in reader-response approaches to young adult fiction. She also refers to reader-response theorist David Bleich in her discussion of criteria for selecting young adult novels that include the physical, psychological, and social preoccupations of adolescents. Monseau's theorizing of young adult literature in her community of readers also reflects the reading theory of Wolfgang Iser, which will form the basis of our reading of

Budge Wilson's "The Leaving" in the next chapter. Iser's image of the text as a mirror, Monseau says, allows different students to see themselves reflected in the same young adult novel. This article makes a fine introduction to Monseau's *Responding to Young Adult Literature* (1996) in which she explores how reader-response approaches to young adult literature can encourage students to read widely and how the knowledge that English teachers gain from their students' responses can transform their teaching.

Monseau has done some collaborative work with Sharon Stringer in the exploration of the relationship between psychology and the young adult novel in English and psychology classes at their university. In the Fall 1994 issue of the *ALAN Review*, their work appears in successive articles that create a conversation about Robert Cormier's *After the First Death*. Stringer's "The Psychological Changes of Adolescence" (1994) examines the question "How does the search for identity mold a person's 'strength of character'?" Stringer offers a number of psychological theories as she discusses Cormier's *The Chocolate War* (1974), *I Am the Cheese* (1977), and *The Bumblebee Flies Anyway* (1983). In "Studying Cormier's Protagonists: Achieving Power Through Young Adult Literature" (1994), Monseau delves more deeply into the Cormier novels from the perspective of high school students and their identity crises. She concludes with specific suggestions of how classroom teachers might organize their instruction to help adolescent readers begin to understand that their "emotional autonomy" depends on "inner strength" and that such strength will help them face the difficulties of the hard work of growing up (33).

The reader-response approach works well with young adult fiction that deals with the difficulties that adolescents face as they leave childhood and begin the uneven transformative process of becoming adults. In addition to the Cormier novels discussed in the Stringer and Monseau articles, we might add Cormier's *Fade* (1988) and *We All Fall Down* (1991). Chris Crutcher's novels are also excellent for reader-response approaches, including *Running Loose* (1983), *Stotan!* (1986), *Crazy Horse Electric Game* (1987), *Chinese Handcuffs* (1989), and *Ironman* (1995).

Nilsen and Donelson (1993) and Arthur (Charlie) Reed (1994) devote considerable attention to realistic fiction in their textbooks on young adult literature. Although Reed offers more extensive categorization of the concerns of such novels, the two textbooks agree that adolescents face problems in the following categories: identity; physical appearance; relationships with family, friends, and society; race, ethnicity, and class; sexuality; substance abuse; suicide; illness, and death. A brief sampling of young adult novels which explore some of these issues and which work well with reader-response approaches include the following:

Physical appearance: Robert Lipsyte, *One Fat Summer*
Family relationships: Sue Ellen Bridgers, *Notes for Another Life*
Race: Mildred Taylor, *Roll of Thunder, Hear My Cry*
Ethnicity: Linda Crew, *Children of the River*
Sexuality: Isabelle Holland, *The Man Without a Face*
Suicide: Susan Beth Pfeffer, *About David*
Death: Robert Newton Peck, *A Day No Pigs Would Die*

Works Cited

Barthes, Roland. 1979. "From Work to Text." In *Textual Strategies: Perspectives in Post-Structuralist Criticism*, ed. Josue Harari, 73–81. Ithaca, NY: Cornell University Press.

———. 1981. "Theory of the Text." In *Untying the Text: A Post-Structuralist Reader*, trans. Ian McLeod, ed. Robert Young, 31–47. London: Routledge.

———. 1992. "The Death of the Author." Trans. Stephen Heath. In *Critical Theory Since Plato*, ed. Hazard Adams, 1130–33. New York: Harcourt Brace Jovanovich.

Beach, Richard. 1993. "Psychological Theories of Response." In *A Teacher's Introduction to Reader-Response Theories*, 71–101. Urbana IL: National Council of Teachers of English.

Bridgers, Sue Ellen. 1981. *Notes for Another Life*. New York: Bantam.

Cormier, Robert. 1974. *The Chocolate War*. New York: Dell.

Cormier, Robert. 1977. *I Am the Cheese*. New York: Dell.

———. 1983. *The Bumblebee Flies Anyway*. New York: Dell.

———. 1988. *Fade*. New York: Dell.

———. 1991. *We All Fall Down*. New York: Dell.

Crane, Stephen. 1982. *The Red Badge of Courage*. New York: Norton.

Crew, Linda. 1989. *Children of the River*. New York: Delacorte.

Crutcher, Chris. 1983. *Running Loose*. New York: Dell.

———. 1986. *Stotan!* New York: Dell.

———. 1987. *Crazy Horse Electric Game*. New York: Dell.

———. 1989. *Chinese Handcuffs*. New York: Greenwillow.

———. 1995. *Ironman*. New York: Greenwillow.

Fish, Stanley. 1976. "Interpreting the Variorum." *Critical Inquiry* 2 (Spring): 465–85. Reprinted in Jane P. Tompkins, ed., *Reader-Response Criticism: From Formalism to Post-Structuralism*, Baltimore: Johns Hopkins University Press, 1980, 164–84.

Hardy, Thomas. 1902. "The Man He Killed." In *The Bedford Introduction to Literature*, ed. Michael Meyer, 960. Boston: St. Martin's.

Holland, Norman N. 1975. "UNITY IDENTITY TEXT SELF." *PMLA* 90: 813–22. Reprinted in Jane P. Tompkins, ed., *Reader-Response Criticism: From Formalism to Post-Structuralism*, Baltimore: Johns Hopkins University Press, 1980, 118–33.

Holland, Isabelle. 1972. *The Man Without a Face*. New York: HarperCollins.

Leitch, Vincent. 1988. "Reader-Response Criticism." In *American Literary Criticism from the Thirties to the Eighties*, 30–80. New York: Columbia University Press.

Levertov, Denise. 1971. "What Were They Like?" In *The Voice That Is Great Within Us: American Poetry of the Twentieth Century*, ed. Hayden Carruth, 517. New York: Bantam.

Lichtenstein, Heinz. 1961. "Identity and Sexuality: A Study of Their Interrelationship in Man." Quoted in Norman Holland, "UNITY IDENTITY TEXT SELF," *PMLA* 90 (1975): 813–22.

Lipsyte, Robert. 1977. *One Fat Summer*. New York: Harper and Row.

Mailloux, Steven. 1982. *Interpretive Conventions: The Reader in the Study of American Fiction*. Ithaca, NY: Cornell University Press.

Monseau, Virginia R. 1992. "Students and Teachers as a Community of Readers." In *Reading Their World: The Young Adult Novel in the Classroom*, eds. Virginia R. Monseau and Gary Salvner, 85–98. Portsmouth, NH: Boynton/Cook.

———. 1994. "Studying Cormier's Protagonists: Achieving Power Through Young Adult Literature." *ALAN Review* 22 (Fall): 31–33.

———. 1996. *Responding to Young Adult Literature*. Portsmouth, NH: Boynton/Cook.

Myers, Walter Dean. 1988. *Fallen Angels*. New York: Scholastic.

Nilsen, Alleen Pace, and Kenneth L. Donelson. 1993. *Literature for Today's Young Adults*. 4th ed. New York: HarperCollins.

O'Brien, Tim. 1990. "Spin." In *The Things They Carried*, 33–40. New York: Penguin.

Peck, Robert Newton. 1972. *A Day No Pigs Would Die*. New York: Dell.

Pfeffer, Susan. 1980. *About David*. New York: Dell.

Platoon. 1986. Directed by Oliver Stone. 120 minutes. Hemdale Film Corp. Videocassette.

Probst, Robert. 1991. "Response to Literature." In *Handbook of Research on Teaching the English Language Arts*, eds. James Flood et. al., 633–63. New York: Macmillan.

Reed, Arthea J. S. 1994. *Reaching Adolescents: The Young Adult Book and the School*. New York: Merrill.

Remarque, Erich Maria. 1929. *All Quiet on the Western Front*. Trans. A. W. Wheen. Reprint, New York: Little, Brown.

Rosenblatt, Louise. 1976. *Literature as Exploration*. 4th ed. New York: Modern Language Association.

————. 1978. *The Reader, the Text, the Poem: A Transactional Theory of the Literary Work*. Carbondale: Southern Illinois University Press.

Sassoon, Siegfried. 1918. "Suicide in the Trenches." In *Collected Poems: 1908–1956*. London: Faber and Faber. 1961.

Seeger, Pete. 1995. "Where Have All the Flowers Gone?" In *In Cross-Roads: Classic Themes in Young Adult Literature*, 144–45. Glenview IL: Scott, Foresman.

Stevens, Wallace. 1990. "Of Modern Poetry." In *The Collected Poems of Wallace Stevens*, 239–40. New York: Vintage.

Stringer, Sharon. 1994. "The Psychological Changes in Adolescence." *ALAN Review*. 22 (Fall): 27–29.

Suleiman, Susan and Inge Crossman, eds. 1980. Introduction to *The Reader in the Text: Essays on Audience and Interpretation*, 3–45. Princeton: Princeton University Press.

Taylor, Mildred. 1976. *Roll of Thunder, Hear My Cry*. New York: Bantam.

Vergil. 1983. *Aeneid*. Trans. Robert Fitzgerald. New York: Vintage.

Whitman, Walt. 1973. "Come Up from the Fields Father." In *Leaves of Grass*, eds. Sculley Bradley and Harold Blodgett, 302–03. New York: Norton.

Seven

Feminism
Mother/Daughter Transformations
in "The Leaving"

First, a story.

> Once upon a time, and a very sad time it was, though it wasn't in
> my time, nor in your time, nor in any real time, there was a man
> who told secrets to other men. And the man was a Critic King and
> the other men were his vassals. And no woman ever heard the
> secrets. And no woman ever read the books which the secrets were
> about. But the king had a daughter. And one day, the daughter read
> the books and heard the secrets. And the daughter saw that the
> secrets were not real secrets and the books were not real books. And
> she was very angry. So she talked to other women. Through nights
> and days and dreams and waking the women talked together. And
> the king and his vassals grew old and died. The women looked at
> each other's golden faces and heard each other's golden voices. And
> they lived long together in the land, whole again, which they called
> Feminist Criticism. (Humm 1994, 1)

Maggie Humm opens her survey of feminist criticism from the 1960s
to the 1990s with this fairy tale, and I begin with it here to point out
some key ideas that we will investigate in our overview of feminist
literary theory and criticism. First, the matter of power. Humm's fairy
tale deconstructs (and finally destroys) that bastion of all fairy tales:
the patriarchally constructed world. This is the world where men rule,
singly and collectively, and where they decide the shape of their
daughters' futures. Power is always a function of masculinity, which,
in the fairy tale, is the most important given in the universe. Feminists, as Humm's story shows, have the power to change this patriarchal world and even to build a new one.

116

Second, the matter of language. The male inhabitants of the fairy tale own language to such an extent that women do not have access to it and to the books that contain the knowledge created by language. This is a world ruled by male-dominated theory, a world where women are *kept* in two senses of the word. First, they are kept, controlled by men. Second, they are marginalized intellectually, kept out of the mainstream of knowing. In other words, they have no epistemology: They do not know how they know except as men tell them.

Gender finally leads to a quiet revolution in the Critic Kingdom when the king's daughter gains access to the men's books and their language. She begins to see that everything in the kingdom really is a social construction; she sees through the ruse, the secrecy, of male language. She discovers that these men have made their world and the women in it, too. Her subsequent anger leads her to share her new knowledge with other women. The conversations of these women help them create a community, and their talking and thinking result in a new world order. One of the objectives of feminist theory and criticism is to bring about change, to make a new world in which women speak and write with their own powerful language.

An Introduction to Feminist Ways of Reading

The Feminist Quilt

Humm tells us that the women critics in her story engage in conversation; their existence is collaborative. This is true in the world of feminism, too, where theorists and critics do not share a "single large critical system" and where they do not agree on one way of reading that comes from "a single authority figure or from a body of sacred texts." There is no Critic Queen comparable to Humm's Critic King, no "Mother of Us All," no "single system of thought" that provides feminists their basic ideas. Instead, they derive their tools of literary analysis from the broad spectrum of literary theory (Showalter 1985, 4).

To describe the diversity of feminist work, Cheryl B. Torsney (1989) uses the metaphor of a "critical quilt of plurality, strong and varied, pieced in community" (180). Since the 1960s, these quilt pieces have included perspectives as diverse, Maggie Humm (1994) tells us, as myth criticism, psychoanalytic criticism, Marxist-socialist-feminist criticism, French feminist criticism, black feminism, lesbian criticism, poststructural/deconstruction/postmodern criticism, and Third World feminist criticism (1–32). What is noticeably missing from Humm's list is reader-response criticism, in which she sees certain dangers. Most reader-response approaches, she contends, carry with them "the implicit assumption of a 'free' reader set apart from external realities," a reader "engaged in individualistic self-development," a reader "without children or supermarket shopping" (6–7). I disagree—and so does Patricino Schweickart in her illuminating essay "Reading Ourselves: Toward a Feminist Theory of Reading" (1991). We will read and interpret Budge Wilson's "The Leaving" from a reader-response perspective suggested by Schweickart's essay.

Reading Differently: Men in Feminism

As a man giving a feminist reading, I reflect the perspective of a leading feminist critic who states that men can "learn to apprehend the meanings encoded in texts by and about women—just as women have learned to become sensitive readers of Shakespeare, Milton, Hemingway, and Miller." This kind of "relearned reading" is a necessary part of the act of *re-vision* that "constitutes the key to an ongoing literary history." The promise of this new way of reading is that it can "offer us all a potential enhancing of our capacity to read the world, our literary texts, and even one another, anew" (Kolodny 1985, 59).

Elaine Showalter (1985) agrees that "feminist concerns can bring a new energy and vitality to literary studies, for men as well as women" (4). She concludes that women in the 1990s are demanding "a new universal literary history and criticism that combines the literary experiences of both women and men, a complete revolution in the understanding of our literary heritage" (10). In *Speaking of Gender* (1989), Showalter describes the movement toward gender studies as a "new phase" of feminist criticism (2).

Feminist Inquiry

Reading from the feminist perspective offers opportunities to inquire into issues that were unexplored or ignored in patriarchally constructed ways of reading. These areas include the following:

1. The reconstruction of a distinct history and literary tradition for women

2. The relationship of women's writing to the traditional male canon and the formation of an alternate canon

3. Black feminist criticism

4. Representations of women in literature, the visual arts, and in popular culture

5. The debate over gender: biologically determined or socially constructed?

6. The traditions and culture of lesbians

7. What it means to read from gendered perspectives

8. Women's writing, both its nature and the conditions of its production

9. Autobiography and "life writing"

10. The question of difference

11. Questions related to the existence or the possibility of a specific female language and the possibility of a distinctly female way of knowing, a female epistemology (Walker 1993, 39)

The fourth perspective will inform our reading of how the mother and daughter are portrayed in the male-dominated world of "The Leaving."

One critic suggests that we can begin a feminist inquiry by asking a series of general questions about a text. What, we might ask, is the gender of the author? Can we tell what the author's attitude is toward women and their place in society? What effect might the author's culture have on the life depicted in the text? Who narrates the story? a male or a female? What roles do women play in the world of the text? Are they major characters or do they fill only minor roles? Do we see women treated stereotypically? What do the male characters think of the women characters? How do the women speak? Is their language different from the language of men? (Bressler 1994, 109).

A more specific, integrated approach to feminist criticism requires that we develop a consciousness of the female experience and offers us a way of reading that will help us do that. This approach, *gynocriticism*, is an alternative to traditional androcentric reading models. Our interpretation of literary texts focuses on four areas: (1) images of women's bodies as they are presented in the text, (2) the language of women and the ways in which it differs from the language of men, (3) the psyches of women, and (4) the culture that shapes women, their ideas and their language (Showalter 1986, 243–70). Our reading of "The Leaving" reflects three of these areas as we consider the language, psyche, and environment of the mother and daughter in the story. Specifically, we will examine what Maggie Humm calls "techniques of signification, such as the mirroring of mothers and daughters or textual moments of mother/daughter empathy, which are undervalued in traditional criticism" (Humm 1994, 8). Mother/daughter empathy leads to the transformation that takes place in the Nova Scotian world of Wilson's story.

Feminist Reading and Reader-Response

Interweaving feminism and reader-response theory creates a new way of reading, as Patricino Schweickart tells us in "Reading Ourselves: Toward a Feminist Theory of Reading" (1991). She reviews three problems of reader-response theory that, according to Jonathan Culler, have preoccupied its practitioners. First, the matter of control: Does the reader control the text, as Norman Holland and Stanley Fish contend, or does the text control the reader's response, as Wolfgang Iser and others contend? Second, as far as the subject (reader) and object (text) relationship is concerned, who supplies what? What is already there, inside the text? What does the reader bring to the text? Third, what about the endings? Do readers come away with meanings, or do they feel that reading is actually impossible, that the meaning of texts is undecidable? (Schweickart 1991, 529–30).

According to Schweickart, changes occur when feminist criticism enters the reader-response conversation. Gender and politics, both suppressed in other reader-response models, become prominent as "the activities of reading and writing" become "an important arena of political struggle, a crucial component of the project of interpreting the world in order to change it" (Schweickart 1991, 532). The word *change* is crucial here. Schweickart stresses the point that feminist criticism is not just a way of interpreting literature. It is, instead, a "mode of *praxis*," and the point of such praxis is *"to change the world."* In the act of reading, "literature is realized as *praxis*. Literature acts on the world by acting on its readers" (531). *Praxis*, a Greek word meaning "action" or "practice," is derived from the word *prassein*, which means literally "to pass through." Schweickart's implication, then, is that reading not only is an activity in which we pass through a text but also is an activity in which the text passes through us and then affects the way in which we act as we pass through the world.

Schweickart (1991) describes the relationship between reader and writer as an "intersubjective construction":

> The reader encounters not simply a text, but a "subjectified object": the "heart and mind" of another woman. She comes into close contact with an interiority—a power, a creativity, a suffering, a vision—that is *not* identical with her own. (542)

Schweickart's stress on the word *not* indicates that not all women share the same experiences but that all readers set up their own intersubjective relationship with the writer of the text they read.

What about the larger community outside the intersubjective relationship that reading establishes between writer and reader? What about the interpretive community of Stanley Fish, for example? Sch-weickart (1991) suggests that the feminist reading process addresses this community as well: "To read a text and then to write about it is to seek to connect not only with the author of the original text, but also with a community of readers" (545). In our reading of "The Leaving" we will attempt to connect with the author's "interiority," to understand the "vision" that Budge Wilson offers in the worlds she creates in her short stories. We will do this by practicing Wolfgang Iser's reading approach.

Iser's Theory: Reading the Gaps

Iser's reader-response theory differs from the approaches we used for reading Walter Dean Myers' *Fallen Angels* in Chapter 6. There we read from two extremes of reader-response criticism—Norman Holland's highly subjective transactional model and Stanley Fish's poststructural interpretive community model. We will read "The Leaving" from Iser's intersubjective or phenomenological perspective. Intersubjectivity here refers to a relationship between text and reader in which the meanings of the text are not received meanings, as, for example, in a formalist reading. Instead, the meaning of the text results from the reader's *interaction* with the text. The reader actively internalizes the text so that the reader's view of the work "becomes, in part, a view of himself: the work has been structured into the reader and is no longer a merely objective fact" (Hawthorn 1994, 99). In this way of reading, the reader enjoys a much more creative role than is possible from other theoretical perspectives.

A key concept in Iser's model for the reading process is signified by the word *gaps*, or, in its fancier, theoretical form, *indeterminacies*. In his theory, Iser asserts that a text only takes on a life when it is "realized" or "concretized" in the activity of reading. In other words, the text does not exist until a reader brings it into being by interact-ing with the words on the page. This interaction is a creative process, and it also involves words that are not written on the page. Iser says that a text is not completely written, that it contains gaps. These are moments that are left open, spaces in which things are left unsaid, places (also called blanks) where the flow of the narrative is inter-rupted in some way. Such blank spaces engage our imaginations so that "whenever the flow is interrupted," we are given the opportunity "to bring into play our own faculty for establishing connections—for filling in the gaps left by the text itself" (Iser 1974, 55). We are always, Iser says, looking forward and looking backward, so that "during the process of reading, there is an active interweaving of anticipation and retrospection." "Activating the reader's imagination" is part of the writer's work, Iser says, and "no author worth his salt will ever attempt to set the *whole* picture before his reader's eyes" (57). Wilson has not set the whole picture before us in her story, and reading "The Leaving" engages us actively as we pass through the story and fill in the empty spaces she has left there. In giving an example of gaps, Iser points to the authorial intrusions in nineteenth-century fiction, places where the author stands back from the story and addresses the reader, as, for example, Dickens and Thackeray do. There are, of course, many kinds of gaps, some more subtle than others; Wilson's most obvious gaps are literally blank spaces on the page that separate the eight sections of her story. Whatever the nature of such gaps, Iser believes, the indeterminacies they create are "fundamental preconditions for reader participation" (Iser 1971, 14).

Reading and Interpreting "The Leaving": An Overview

> For we think back through our mothers if we are women.
> Virginia Woolf

The lead title, "The Leaving," of Budge Wilson's short story collection is a metaphor for the relationships between the women characters in most of the nine stories in the volume. Each narrator experiences a leaving as part of the difficult process of growing up. A brief description of the stories in the order in which they appear in the book will indicate the richness of the collection.

"The Metaphor" explores the death of a favorite English teacher and the question of mothering framed in a young girl's use of figurative language. For a detailed reading of this story, see my "English Teachers, Mothers, and Metaphors" (1996). "Lysandra's Poem" is about the loss of a friend, while "My Mother and I" investigates the loss of a father who, though long believed to be a hero, turns out to be quite ordinary. "Mr. Manuel Jenkins" involves a bittersweet infatuation of a young girl and her mother for a transient who, in the end, must leave their world. The title story, located at the center of the collection, is a coming-of-age story for both a young girl and her mother who "leave" the concepts of self constructed for them by the men in their family. "Waiting" offers portraits of two sisters, one the extroverted star of the family and the other a kind of "lady in waiting" who blossoms into a young woman at the end of this story, leaving behind the pallid image of herself that has always stood in sharp contrast to her sister's colorful life. The emotional conflicts in the hauntingly beautiful "My Cousin Clarette" grow out of the jealousy that a young girl, who considers herself plain, feels for her cousin, whom she describes as "a shot of pure crimson in our comfortable beige life" (154). The leaving occurs years later when the jealous young girl witnesses Clarette's suicide as her cousin steps into the path of an oncoming train.

"Be-ers and Do-ers" is the one story that disappoints me in this collection because I cannot believe in the pedantic and grating language of the mother. Ironically, this is the only story in which Wilson deals with a mother/son relationship; most stories in the collection focus on relationships between females: mothers and daughters, sisters, and friends. In "Be-ers and Do-ers," Albert's mother has been disappointed with her son all his life because, like his father, he has been content to "be." The boy's sister is the narrator. The climactic moment of the story occurs when there is a fire just after Christmas, and the narrator tells us how eighteen-year-old Albert saves his family from disaster. As he stands before his mother with his hands blistering from burns, his mother tells him, "And *that* . . . is what I've been looking for, all your life. Some sort of a sign that you were one hundred percent alive" (185). As it turns out, he isn't alive by her standards, and the rest of his life seems to be spent just "being."

"The Pen Pal," the last story in the collection, deals with a young girl's desire to share the secrets of her changing body as she reaches puberty. Lacking a strong relationship with her mother, she writes intimate letters to a distant pen pal named Hilary, whom she supposes to be a girl. Hilary writes only one letter (which we do not see), but it contains the news that Hilary, to the narrator's humiliation, is a boy. The story's epistolary form makes it unique in the collection.

"The Leaving" and Other Stories is, in my opinion, a unified structure in which the stories are arranged in pairs around the title story. In terms of gynocriticism's four foci, a number of these stories will reward close study. "The Metaphor" and "Lysandra's Poem" both deal with the figurative uses of language and with young women who write themselves into being. "My Mother and Father" and "Mr. Manuel Jenkins" both are commentaries on male/female relationships and the limitations and possibilities that such relationships offer to female characters. "The Leaving" brings all of these subjects—language, relationships, the process of becoming—into focus in one amazing story. The next pair, "Waiting" and "My Cousin Clarette" investigate female relationships that result from the contrast between the fate of a plain girl and that of her vivacious counterpart. The last two stories, "Be-ers and Do-ers" and "The Pen Pal," inquire into the dynamics between males and females, again in the context of the coming-of-age theme.

Some of the most powerful stories in the collection deal with the ways in which the female characters use language to understand themselves and to construct their world. In the title story, the young female narrator comes to some sense of her identity as a woman because, as Woolf (1929) says, she thinks back through her mother.

"The Leaving": Tracing the "Continuous Thread of Revelation"

The title story provides the most positive example of a mother/ daughter relationship in the collection. Set in Nova Scotia, "The Leaving" covers a ten-year span in the life of its narrator, from her first awareness of what it means to be a woman until she is a university student thinking back through her mother and telling this story. The story grows out of her recollection of a three-day trip that she took with her mother. She was twelve at the time; and now, as an adult, she interprets the trip not only as her own coming-of-age story but as her mother's as well. The most important element in the story is the strong bond that develops between mother and daughter as a consequence of the trip. Both of their lives are changed because they learn to think differently, to see the world differently. As a result, they create positive futures for themselves and for each other. The mother's construction of her life after the trip also changes and transforms the male-dominated world of her family. The twenty-two-year-old narrator tells the story in eight sections. As we move through these eight sections and the blank spaces between them, our reading process will reflect Wolfgang Iser's reader-response theory.

Quilting "The Leaving"

As we read the gaps in the story, you might keep in mind a quilting metaphor from Mary Catherine Bateson's Composing a Life (1989). Bateson describes the process of deciding how to live as a woman in a changing world:

> There are no singular models, but only resources for creative imagi-nation. . . . [Y]ou cannot put together a life willy-nilly from odds and ends. Even a crazy quilt, the various pieces, wherever they come from, have to be trimmed and shaped and arranged so they fit together, then sewn firmly to last through time and keep out the cold. Most quilts are more ambitious: they involve the imposition of a new pattern. But even crazy quilts are sewn against a backing; the basic sense of continuity allows improvisation. Composing a life involves an openness to possibilities and the capacity to put them together in a way that is structurally sound. (62–63)

Reading creatively, we can imagine ourselves watching the central characters in the story piece together their lives, sewing the creative quilts of their selfhood. The tracing action of this interpretation results, then, from the ways in which we thread together the sections of the story, the individual quilt pieces, as we read.

Section One. The unnamed narrator recalls being awakened at 3 A.M., her mother standing beside her bed and telling her to get ready to go with her. Thinking back on that moment, she describes a world where children had few or no rights: "If your father wanted you to shovel snow or fetch eggs, he told you, and you did it. He didn't ask. He told. Same with Ma" (104–05). This first section ends in a dialogue in which the narrator questions why she has been chosen to go; her mother replies "Because yer the smartest. And because yer a woman." In the final sentence of this section, the narrator tells us, "I was twelve years old that spring" (105).

Gap One. I fill in this first space on the page by thinking about how this story emerges out of darkness. The sparse language of the last sentence echoes in my ear, and it seems to fit the world of the story. I do not know the narrator's name, and I know nothing about her mother's appearance, but I anticipate that details will follow. I am focused on the mother/daughter relationship, surprised that Ma considers the young girl to be a woman. What does *woman* mean in this world? I wonder. I read *spring* as rebirth, and I read *twelve* as the narrator's impending birth into adolescence. Both words, in conjunction with the title, suggest the trip as metaphor. Considering 3 A.M. to be a carefully calculated departure hour (part of Ma's "creative imagination"), I wonder where the men are. Sleeping soundly, probably, before they get up and start telling these women what to do.

Section Two. This section focuses on Ma, but I learn a great deal about the daughter from the language of her storytelling. Now she describes her mother's physical appearance: tall, slender, her face strong and handsome, her mouth set in a straight line, her chin good and firm. Her eyes are "veiled," and I start making connections with veils as cultural symbols of modesty and separation from the world. The narrator interprets her mother's veiled eyes to mean that she has "shut herself off from her surroundings," that she's thinking private thoughts or maybe not thinking at all (105). The set mouth and veiled eyes appeal to my imagination; I begin to see a face. Learning that sometimes Ma's eyes "come alive with concern and love" and at other times she retreats "behind her frozen face," I become curious about the conditions of her life. Her daughter tells me that her clothes are "baggy," "shabby," "faded," and "graceless" (106). I think about how much Budge Wilson has packed into the language of this story, but also about how much has been left unwritten, how actively the story is engaging my imagination.

The remainder of the section provides details of the departure: Ma's careful planning, the six-mile walk into town. Wondering what motivates the leaving, I hear Ma say, "I plans t' do some thinkin," (108). The narrator has pulled me inside the story. I am walking down the mountain now in the narrator's memory, curious and expectant, as she recalls how the frost lent "a silver magic to the bushes and the rough ground," how the moonlight gave "a still dignity to the shabby houses" along the road (108). I am learning to respect the power of her adult imagination to bathe the starkness of her remembered world in nuance and color, to remember the poetry in it.

Annapolis is the first stop on the journey; Ma has arranged a stopover at a friend's empty house until the train arrives. I wonder with the daughter, What's our destination? How long will we stay? Ma replies, "Dunno. Till it's time" (109).

Gap Two. "Till it's time for what?" I ask. I am still puzzled. What's the girl's name? How has her mother arranged this stopover in Annapolis? I imagine that she has a limited number of friends and acquaintances in town; the farm seems isolated in the mountains. How far away is the destination? I try to imagine Ma's life before her marriage. How does she see the world? Why are we leaving with such urgency? What's happened?

Other trips in my reading become intertexts as I think about what this leaving could mean—trips that were symbolic, "wholes unto themselves":

> They were stories. Not only in form, but in their taking on direction, movement, development, change. They changed something in my life: each trip made its particular revelation, though I could not have found words for it. (Welty 1984, 75)

The trip I am taking with Wilson's two women is a metanarrative, a story about telling a story. It is that kind of circular event in which we travel back into the landscape of memory as our imagination helps us make sense of where we have been, both literally and figuratively. It is story as "revelation," as the storyteller lifts the veil from our eyes.

Section Three. The narrator now interprets one meaning of the trip, telling us that the long walk (six miles) into town "had shunted me straight from childhood into adolescence" (109). I notice Wilson's pacing as a storyteller as I move quickly through this short section, about one third the length of section two. I begin thinking about two central matters in the story: (1) the developing relationship between mother and daughter and (2) the role that the men in the family play in that relationship. Although my references to "the narrator" and "her mother" may seem a bit tedious, I will not name them until they name themselves, a naming that is central to a feminist reading of this story.

During the train ride from Annapolis to Halifax, the narrator's two biggest concerns are money and the men left at home; the narrator's mother refuses to tell her where the money for the trip came from. As Ma sleeps, the girl thinks of her father and her brothers at home. As she asks herself a series of questions, I begin to fill in the other gaps in the story, to construct life on the mountain. She wonders how the men will take care of themselves, cook their food, make their beds; and who, she thinks, will they "complain to after a hard day?" (111). The men, I understand, are the center of the home; they are waited upon, and they see housework as woman's work. The mother and daughter seem to exist only to provide comfort for these men. I wonder: To whom do the women complain after a hard day's work? I imagine a world where the women, like the children whom the narrator describes in the first section, do as they are told, and where they have few choices.

The narrator's remaining questions are equally revealing: Who, she wonders will take care of daily routines? gather the eggs, get the mail, bring in the water and wood? wash and mend the men's clothes? bandage their cuts? The picture is clear: Women are servants in the narrator's house. The narrator is conditioned to her subservient role in the family; she concludes this part of the story with a sentence that convinces me: "It was inconceivable to me that they could survive for long without us" (111).

Gap Three. With the narrator's vivid picture of the male/female relationships at home, I begin to construct the years of Ma's life that have led to the leaving. Her life has no doubt worn her down; she has resolved not to continue as the angel in the house, the quiet woman who waits on men and makes few demands. I anticipate that "The Leaving" will involve a return, that the strength the narrator senses in her mother will bring about change.

Section Four. Mother and daughter arrive in Halifax, the Nova Scotian capital, spend two days there, and decide to return home. They spend the first day exploring the city where the bridge to Dartmouth "lifted its enormous metal wings into the sky" (112). This image of flight combines with other images of freedom in this section, and I begin to interpret the trip as a flight to freedom. As they stand on the bridge looking at the ships below that are headed, they imagine, to

Europe, Africa, and the far north, Ma begins to talk, and her daughter remembers the feeling she had at that moment, as if her mother were "trying to tell me something important, but didn't want to say things right out." "They're goin' somewheres," her mother says (112). Maybe, I respond, Ma feels that her life has come to a standstill. The destinations that the ships represent and the freedom to travel to other worlds obviously fascinate her, and this trip is perhaps her first effort at "goin' somewheres."

When they visit Dalhousie University, the relationship between mother and daughter unfolds more clearly as another image of freedom emerges. Ma's reason for bringing her daughter on this trip is implied in her remarks about education: "If yer as smart as the teacher claims," she said, "maybe you'll come here some day t' learn." When the daughter questions where the money will come from, her mother replies, "They's ways" (112–13). Ma has a vision, I begin to think, for her daughter's future: She will not remain a servant in the master's house. The daughter's intelligence will be the wings on which she takes flight, her language the ticket to freedom.

As they walk through the city on a dazzling May day, window shopping and visiting the Public Gardens, the daughter asks her mother why all the people whom they encounter seem so happy. Her mother replies that it may be more than the brilliant weather: "Maybe some of them's free," she says (114). The images of freedom (the bridge as a bird, the ships in the harbor) reach a high point at this moment. Part of the story veil is lifted, and we better understand the impetus for the leaving: a moment of freedom from the responsibilities and cares of housekeeping.

During a visit to the public library on the second day, Ma sees a copy of Betty Friedan's *The Feminine Mystique* (1963) and surprises us with the news that she has read it. We learn that she has had only a fifth-grade education, but she can read: "Y' reads slow, but y' knows how" (114). She responds to her daughter's curiosity about the book by explaining that she found it in a box delivered to them by the Salvation Army. She spent the last year reading Friedan's book, which she describes as if it were a person: "She was a real troublin' book. But she was good," and she has learned the most important lesson, perhaps, of her life: "Found I weren't alone" (115). The revelation seems to ease some tension in the story, and the narrator remembers that her mother's mouth, usually set and straight, relaxed, became "soft and cheerful." When Ma reveals that the egg money has financed the trip, the news sends "a thrill of fear" running through her daughter who wonders "what Pa would do." Her fear is consistent with what we know of the power that her father and brothers have over her and her mother's lives. Her conscious fear manifests itself that night in her unconscious, in "strange and troubled dreams" (116).

Gap Four. Obviously, my major anticipation has to do with what effect Ma's discovery of herself as a member of the larger community of women will have on life at home. I anticipate how differently mother and daughter will handle this new knowledge, and I remember that the girl is only twelve, her life very much conditioned by her responses to the men in the house. Only now, it seems, is her life becoming conditioned by her mother as a person with potential authority in the world.

Section Five. Only thirteen lines long, this section announces the end of the trip as the narrator registers change in her mother's demeanor. The narrator senses both hope and "an odd fierce dignity" (117). From a feminist perspective, Ma now seems ready to act, to put her ideas into practice and to change her world and her daughter's future.

Gap Five. Questions fire off in my mind. Will Ma be able to stand up to Pa? What will the brothers do? What will the daughter do? Does she have sufficient strength to support her mother if the need arises? I imagine a confrontation in the kitchen where the ceiling is low; I feel stifled there. The place is a wreck because the men have ignored it. I think about how short that last section was, how Wilson paces the story, builds suspense as she moves toward a resolution.

Section Six. A bus trip home. The long climb up the mountain. Ma's mouth "back in its taut line," her eyes "troubled." With these images, the daughter tells us that she "could feel a difference" in her mother, a "new dogged strength in the set of her face." Just as I wonder if the daughter has her own reserve of strength, she tells me, by way of comparison with her mother: "There was no strength in me, except such as I derived from her" (117).

Once we're inside the kitchen, Pa seems "to fill the entire room" (118). I am not surprised. This is *his* house. In a voice "low and threatening," he demands an explanation: "Where you bin, woman?" (119). His first words tell the story I have imagined. To him Ma is nameless; she is a woman, and her work is to please him, to satisfy him. His remark reminds the narrator of a life full of "woman" commands:

> "How come my supper's not ready, woman?" "Move smart, woman! I'm pressed fer time!" "Shut up them damn kids, woman!" "Move them buckets, woman! They're in my way!" "This food ain't fit t' eat, woman. Take it away!" (119)

When Ma tries to respond to his question, he tells her, "Shut yer mouth, woman, and git my supper" (119).

What happens next is the most crucial moment in "The Leaving":

> She moved to the center of the room and faced him. "My name," she began, and faltered. She cleared her throat and ran her tongue over her lower lip. "My name," she repeated, this time more steadily, "is Elizabeth." (119)

For perhaps the first time in her life, Ma locates herself in the center and not on the margins of experience. Leaving has given her the power to stand alone, and she has the courage and the ability to name herself, to construct herself, to find, in the intimacy of her name, the freedom to release herself from the oppressive language and the domination of her husband. Although he mocks her by repeating her sentence, he leaves; and as she instructs her daughter to help her and to "Act smart there, Sylvie," she names the narrator for the first time. Regarding Wilson's construction of "The Leaving," this double naming is central to the events that follow in the remaining sections. In the environment of her former world, Elizabeth begins to improvise, to quilt (in Bateson's metaphor) a new life for herself and for her daughter.

As section six concludes, Elizabeth enacts one of the political aims of feminism—to change the world. Although she at first concedes that it is too late to change her sons, she asks one of them to carry in the water, even though, as Sylvie notes, "water carrying was woman's work" (122). The son obliges, silently, and she thanks him, Sylvie tells us, "in a speech as unusual as her other one" (122). It is clear that this has been a world of one-way communication: man to woman. Elizabeth has begun to change that in her courageous action and in her assertive language.

Sections Seven and Eight. The power of language effects change in the house. Elizabeth stands up to her husband, but she does not nag. Sylvie figuratively constructs the difference between nagging and her mother's subsequent responses to her husband. "Nagging," she explains, "is like a constant blow with a small blunt instrument." While it is annoying, it is seldom effective in changing anything. When Elizabeth speaks up, however, her instrument is "a shining steel knife with a polished cutting edge,"—a "weapon" to convince Pa that if he pushes her too far, she will react (123).

Other changes occur. Pa begins to call Elizabeth by her name. Then she gets a room of her own, an attic storeroom that she converts, with her sons' help, into "her own place—her escape," from which she always emerges, Sylvie remembers "softer, gentler, more still" (123–24). Sylvie eventually goes to Dalhousie University, where she tells this story to us. On her last trip home, she recalls, her father spoke to Elizabeth "as though she were more of a person and less of a thing," and she acknowledges that her mother and father love each other "with a kind of love that is difficult for my generation to understand or define" (124–25).

In section eight, Sylvie reflects on the story in a particularly feminist frame of mind. She does not try to tie up the events of her life into one neat bundle or to explain every detail. When she reflects on why things happened as they did, her "thinking slides away" and her "vision blurs." She is content to dwell in an uncertainty that is often very hard for men to comprehend. She is certain that the Friedan book and the act of leaving "do not explain everything": "Maybe my mother was ready to move into and out of herself anyway; and no one can know exactly what went on in her thoughts before and after she left" (125). The in/out and before/after imagery makes me think of the way in which Sylvie has told their story, moving in and out of memory and time, quilting together the events before and after the leaving, crafting the finished story.

Elizabeth has first learned that she belongs to the community of women in Friedan's book. In an appropriate ending to the story that she tells, Sylvie writes over her mother's language as she resists closure in her interpretation of the leaving: "But of that strange three-day departure, I can say, as Ma did of her book, "She was a real troublin' trip. But she was good" (125). In an image that is the opposite of male linearity, Sylvie circles back into her story, her repetition of her mother's words not only a return to the experience but an affirmation that the story does not end.

The Thread of Revelation

Reading this final sentence, I realize that I have traced a circular design that describes the event of reading "The Leaving." Elizabeth read a text, and Elizabeth's life became a text for Sylvie's growing up, and Elizabeth and Sylvie became a text for Sylvie's story, and Sylvie's story is the text of Wilson's story, and Wilson's story is my text for understanding more about the feminine worldview. "The Leaving" is a way of thinking back through our mothers in a storytelling that becomes what Eudora Welty (1984) calls "the continuous thread of revelation" (75). This story helps me to know subjectively, to read intersubjectively, to read as a man reading a woman. This is reading as revelation.

Joining the Conversation

First, I invite careful feminist readings of each of the other stories in Budge Wilson's collection. They repay close study. In addition, the novels from earlier chapters are excellent choices for joining the conversation on feminism and gender issues. For example, the role of Grandma Sarah and the Killburn's grandmother in family and cultural history would make a fascinating study in *M.C. Higgins, the Great* in addition to the emphasis we placed on the roles of Banina and Lurhetta in M.C.'s growing awareness of the complexities of the world. Although we considered the powerful role of Nancy in *Dogsong*, an intriguing study might be made of the portrayal of other women in the novel, particularly Russel's mother and her abandonment of her son, the mother in the dream sequences, and the references to women in the poems and stories that introduce the chapters in Part 1 of the novel. *The Moves Make the Man* presents an opportunity to study the juxtaposition of Bix Rivers' mentally and physically broken mother with Jerome Foxworthy's strong mama, who, though injured (broken) in a horrible accident, regains her health and whose power holds the family together. *The Giver* might be placed in conversation with *Moves* because this dystopic nightmare subverts the nurturing image of mothers that forms the powerful connecting thread in Jerome Foxworthy's life.

Patricia P. Kelly (1992) helps us join the conversation in "Gender Issues and the Young Adult Novel," in which she discusses novels that present mother/daughter relationships. She cites Margaret Mahy's *The Catalogue of the Universe* (1986) as an example of a positive relationship and Sue Ellen Bridgers' *Notes for Another Life* (1981) as an example of a negative one. In her essay, Kelly examines a number of gender categories, including a girl's relationship to her body, to other girls, and to her father and mother. She offers practical suggestions for investigating romance novels as well as novels that deal with boy/girl and boy/boy relationships. She concludes with a discussion of Robert O'Brien's *Z for Zachariah* (1974) and Bridgers' *Permanent Connections* (1982) as examples of young adult novels with good gender role models.

In "Reading from a Female Perspective: Pairing *A Doll's House* and *Permanent Connections*" (1993), Kelly discusses her theoretical approach in declaring that she wants to demonstrate how "some principles of feminist criticism" may be applied to the study of literature without getting "embroiled in a variety of personal definitions of feminism that readers might have" (127). She offers practical advice for theorizing about a young adult novel from a feminist perspective, and she details her approach in a series of sequential lessons that may serve as models for work with students in our classrooms. First, she contextualizes the notion of reading from a female perspective by using Marge Piercy's poem "A Work of Artifice." The poem raises feminist issues with which Kelly opens up the world of Ibsen's play. Kelly suggests teaching *A Doll's*

House and *Permanent Connections* in succession, again offering specific suggestions for her approach. To give students further practice in "feminist literary-critical activities," Kelly (1992) offers students opportunities to look at "feminist issues across literature" (135–37). Kelly's reading suggestions are helpful to those who are new to the field of young adult literature. Her suggestions include, among others, Norma Fox Mazer's *Someone to Love* (1983), Virginia Hamilton's *A Little Love* (1984), and Susan Terris' *Nell's Quilt* (1987). Regarding feminist theory, Kelly suggests that the study of a novel in which there are few female characters offers insight into the portrayal of women in a world in which men are the central characters. She suggests Chris Crutcher's *Stotan!* (1986), a novel that includes the story of a battered woman. One intriguing character in the novel is a man who can coach a swimming team to victory but who cannot be successful in his marriage.

In "Must Boys Be Boys and Girls Be Girls? Exploring Gender Through Reading Young Adult Literature" (1992), Lois Stover investigates the value of young adult literature in a society where men's and women's roles are being "redefined, abandoned, and reexamined" as we explore gender, gendered selves, and the relationships between self and others (94). Her references offer choices in young adult literature as well as critical studies. She discusses her work in London on Gene Kemp's *The Turbulent Term of Tyke Tyler*, a novel with non-gender-specific pronouns, and she points us toward young adult novels through which we can analyze the portrayal of female characters. For example, Katherine Paterson's *Jacob Have I Loved* (1980) (see Chapter 10), Richard Pecks' *Remembering the Good Times* (1985), and Ouida Sebestyn's *The Girl in the Box* (1989) all portray strong female characters, who, however, play roles within the societal structures of family and career that reflect traditional gender relationships. Stover mentions Nicki Marr in M. E. Kerr's *Night Kites* (1986) (see Chapter 9) as a character who "continually revels in her own unconventionalism and delights in disturbing others through her nontraditional behavior" (97). In its use of alternating male and female first-person narrators, M. E. Kerr's *I'll Love You When You're More Like Me* (1987) provides an intriguing opportunity to consider how men and women read the world. In a section entitled "Using the Novels Once You Find Them: Discussion Topics Related to Gender Issues," Stover offers practical advice on finding and selecting young adult novels that deal with gender issues, and she suggests specific approaches to these texts. She includes a chart that lists discussion topics with sources for background information for the teacher, for example, Carol Gilligan's *In a Different Voice: Psychological Theory and Development* (1982), Erik Erikson's *Identity,*

Youth and Crisis (1968), and Belenky, Clinchy, Goldberger, and Tarule's *Women's Ways of Knowing* (1986).

In her discussion of coming-of-age novels, Reed (1994) offers teachers direction in selecting young adult novels that deal with the maturation of girls. She follows the rites-of-passage sequence of separation from childhood, transition (the journey), and incorporation of the young adult into the adult community; this same sequence informed our reading of *Dogsong* (Chapter 3). Noting that young adult novels deal with the problems of physical maturation in girls more than in boys, Reed names Judy Blume's *Are You There God? It's Me, Margaret* (1970) as a cutting-edge book for separation from the childhood stage. Representative novels of the transitional stage include Jean Craighead George's *Julie of the Wolves* (1972), Suzanne Fisher Staples' *Shabanu, Daughter of the Wind* (1989), Bruce Brooks' *Midnight Hour Encores* (1986), Katherine Paterson's *Jacob Have I Loved* (1980), Cynthia Voigt's *Homecoming* (1981) and *Dicey's Song* (1982), Sue Ellen Bridgers' *Home Before Dark* (1976), and Robin McKinley's *The Blue Sword* (1982) and *The Hero and the Crown* (1985). Among these, *Julie of the Wolves*, *Jacob Have I Loved*, and McKinley's novels serve as examples of the female character's incorporation into the adult community (Reed 1994, 90–117).

One final suggestion. George's *Julie of the Wolves* makes a splendid counterpoint to Paulsen's *Dogsong* in its focus on the relationship between traditional Eskimo culture and the encroachment of white culture, the tactics necessary for survival in the Arctic tundra, the reverence for animals and their role in the food chain, and the coming-of-age of a young Eskimo split between two worlds, the old ways and the world of technology. In George's novel, the central character's split existence is symbolized by the character's two names: (the American) Julie and (the Eskimo) Miyax. Each novel is divided into three parts, the last of which is the return to civilization following the transformation that occurs during the Arctic journey. These two outstanding novels will allow students to consider the ways in which female and male young adults deal with the problems of survival and continuity and the role that survival and continuity play in the preservation of culture.

Works Cited

Bateson, Mary Catherine. 1989. "Opening to the World." In *Composing a Life*, 57–74. New York: Plume.

Belenky, Mary F., Blyth M. Clinchy, Nancy R. Goldberger, and Jill M. Tarule. 1986. *Women's Ways of Knowing*. New York: Basic.

Blume, Judy. 1970. *Are You There, God? It's Me, Margaret.* New York: Bradbury.

Bressler, Charles E. 1994. "Feminism." In *Literary Criticism: An Introduction to Theory and Practice*, 102–13. Englewood Cliffs, NJ: Prentice Hall.

Bridgers, Sue Ellen. 1976. *Home Before Dark.* New York: Bantam.

————. 1981. *Notes for Another Life.* New York: Bantam.

————. 1982. *Permanent Connections.* New York: Harper and Row.

Brooks, Bruce. 1984. *The Moves Make the Man.* New York: Harper and Row.

————. 1986. *Midnight Hour Encores.* New York: Harper and Row.

Crutcher, Chris. 1986. *Stotan!* New York: Dell.

Erickson, Eric. 1968. *Identity, Youth, and Crisis.* New York: Bantam.

Friedan, Betty. 1963. *The Feminine Mystique.* New York: Dell.

George, Jean C. 1972. *Julie of the Wolves.* New York: Harper and Row.

Gilligan, Carol. 1982. *In a Different Voice: Psychological Theory and Women's Development.* Cambridge: Harvard University Press.

Hamilton, Virginia. 1974. *M.C. Higgins, the Great.* New York: Macmillan.

————. 1984. *A Little Love.* New York: Berkeley.

Hawthorn, Jeremy. 1994. "Intersubjectivity." In *A Concise Glossary of Contemporary Literary Theory*, 2d. ed., 99. London: Edward Arnold.

Humm, Maggie. 1994. "Feminist Criticism: The 1960s to the 1990s." In *A Reader's Guide to Contemporary Feminist Criticism*, 1–32. New York: Harvester Wheatsheaf.

Ibsen, Henrik. 1965. *A Doll's House.* In *Four Major Plays.* New York: Signet.

Iser, Wolfgang. 1971. "Indeterminancy and the Reader's Response to Prose Fiction." In *Aspects of Narrative*, ed. J. Hillis Miller, 1–45. New York: Columbia University Press.

————. 1974. "The Reading Process: A Phenomenological Approach." In *The Implied Reader: Patterns in Communication in Prose Fiction from Bunyan to Beckett*, 274–94. Baltimore: Johns Hopkins University Press. Reprinted in Jane P. Tompkins, ed., *Reader-Response Criticism: From Formalism to Post-Structuralism.* (Baltimore: Johns Hopkins University Press, 1980), 50–69.

Kelly, Patricia P. 1992. "Gender Issues and the Young Adult Novel. In *Reading Their World: The Young Adult Novel in the Classroom*, eds. Virginia R. Monseau and Gary M. Salvner, 154–67. Portsmouth, NH: Boynton/Cook.

————. 1993. "Reading from a Female Perspective: Pairing *A Doll's House* with *Permanent Connections.*" In *Adolescent Literature as a Complement to the Classics*, ed. Joan F. Kaywell, 127–42. Norwood, MA: Christopher-Gordon.

Kemp, Gene. 1980. *The Turbulent Times of Tyke Tyler.* London: Faber and Faber.

Kerr, M. E. 1986. *Night Kites.* New York: HarperKeyPoint.

————. 1987. *I'll Love You When You're More Like Me.* New York: Harper and Row.

Kolodny, Annette. 1985. "A Map for Rereading: Gender and the Interpretation of Literary Texts." In *The New Feminist Criticism: Essays on Women, Literature, and Theory*, ed. Elaine Showalter, 46–62. New York: Pantheon.

Lowry, Lois. 1993. *The Giver*. New York: Bantam.

Mahy, Margaret. 1986. *The Catalogue of the Universe*. New York: Atheneum.

Mazer, Norma Fox. 1983. *Someone to Love*. New York: Dell-Laurel Leaf.

McKinley, Robin. 1982. *The Blue Sword*. New York: Greenwillow.

———. 1985. *The Hero and the Crown*. New York: Greenwillow.

Moore, John Noell. 1996. "English Teachers, Mothers, and Metaphors." *ALAN
Review* 23:3 (Spring): 41–44.

Nilsen, Alleen Pace, and Kenneth Donelson. 1993. *Literature for Today's Young
Adults*. 4th ed. Glenview, IL: Scott Foresman.

O'Brien, Robert. 1974. *Z for Zachariah*. New York: Macmillan.

Paterson, Katherine. 1980. *Jacob Have I Loved*. New York: HarperCollins.

Paulsen, Gary. 1985. *Dogsong*. New York: Puffin.

Peck, Richard. 1985. *Remembering the Good Times*. New York: Dell.

Reed, Arthea J. S. 1994. "Coming-of-Age Novels." In *Reaching Adolescents: The
Young Adult Novel and the School*, 90–117. New York: Macmillan.

Schweickart, Patrocino. 1991. "Reading Ourselves: Toward a Feminist Theory
of Reading." In *Feminisms: An Anthology of Literary Theory and Criticism*, ed.
Robyn R. Warhol and Diane Price Herndl, 525–50. New Brunswick, NJ:
Rutgers University Press.

Sebestyn, Ouida. 1989. *The Girl in the Box*. New York: Bantam.

Showalter, Elaine. 1985. "The Feminist Critical Revolution." In *The New Feminist Criticism: Essays on Women, Literature, and Theory*, ed. Elaine Showalter, 3–17. New York: Pantheon.

———. 1986. "Feminist Criticism in the Wilderness." In *The New Feminist
Criticism* , ed. Elaine Showalter, 243–70. New York: Pantheon.

———. 1989. "The Rise of Gender." In *Speaking of Gender*, ed. Elaine Showalter, 1–13. New York: Routledge.

Staples, Suzanne Fisher. 1989. *Shabanu: Daughter of the Wind*. New York:
Knopf.

Stover, Lois. 1992. "Must Boys Be Boys and Must Girls Be Girls?: Exploring
Gender Through Reading Young Adult Literature." In *Gender Issues in the
Teaching of English*, eds. Nancy Mellin McCracken and Bruce C. Appleby,
93–110. Portsmouth, NH: Boynton/Cook.

Terris, Susan. 1987. *Nell's Quilt*. New York: Farrar, Straus, and Giroux.

Torsney, Cheryl B. 1989. "The Critical Quilt: Alternative Authority in Feminist Criticism." In *Contemporary Literary Theory*, eds. G. Douglas Atkins and
Laura Morrow, 180-99. Amherst: University of Massachussetts Press.

Voigt, Cynthia. 1981. *Homecoming*. New York: Atheneum.

————. 1982. *Dicey's Song*. New York: Atheneum.

Walker, Victoria. 1993. "Feminist Criticism, Anglo-American." In *Encyclopedia of Contemporary Literary Theory: Approaches, Scholars, Terms*, ed. Irena R. Makaryk, 39–44. Toronto: University of Toronto Press.

Welty, Eudora. 1984. "Learning to See." In *One Writer's Beginnings*, 42–75. New York: Warner.

Wilson, Budge. 1990. *The Leaving and Other Stories*. New York: Philomel.

Woolf, Virginia. 1929. *A Room of One's Own*. Harcourt Brace Jovanovich.

Eight

Black Aesthetics

Signifyin(g) in *A Lesson Before Dying*

It is a peculiar sensation, this double-consciousness, this sense of always looking at one's self through the eyes of others. . . . One ever feels this twoness,—an American, a Negro; two souls, two thoughts, two unreconciled strivings; two warring ideals in one dark body.
W.E.B. Dubois

The Black Literary Tradition

Houston S. Baker Jr., the eminent African American scholar, says that we need two essential pieces of information if we are to understand the black literary tradition. First, the black American is a social construction, or as Richard Wright explains it, "The word Negro in America means something not racial or biological, but something purely social, something made in the United States" (Wright 1964, 80). Second, Baker (1971) says that the black American must be understood in a "sociohistorical framework" (2). Historically, black Americans have felt a dual identity, the "twoness" that Dubois describes in the epigraph. This "double-consciousness" is at the heart of Ernest Gaines' *A Lesson Before Dying*, a novel in which two black males construct themselves as men in a post-Reconstruction patriarchal South that continues to insist on their "twoness."

Background Information

The historical development of modern black literary criticism in the United States provides a necessary context for reading Gaines' novel.

138

First, one of the major events in the development of the tradition was the Black Arts movement in the 1960s; then the phrase "Black is beautiful" came to include the recognition of cultural artifacts that had shaped and were shaping a literary tradition despite the oppression of African Americans throughout American history. These artifacts included the slave narrative as an American literary form, spirituals as powerfully coded forms of communication, and the power of the African American vernacular in the linguistic practices of this country. Second, these recognitions began to counter the domination of white literature as the defining form of "American" literature. These recognitions set into motion the process of critiquing racial stereotypes that had characterized the presence of African Americans in the popular culture. These stereotypes included familiar characters such as the Black mammy, Aunt Jemima, Black Sambo, and Jim Crow, as well as prevailing ethnic notions that blacks were savage, ugly, inferior, and incapable of sophisticated writing. Third, literary works formally unrecognized were recovered and scrutinized as important statements of the presence of African Americans in the literary traditions of the United States. These works made their way into school curricula. People who had formerly thought of "black" literature in the stereotypes of *Little Black Sambo* and the Uncle Remus stories began to discover the worlds created by "lost" writers such as Zora Neale Hurston. The poetry of Langston Hughes began to appear in anthologies, and serious study engaged indigenous forms such as Frederick Douglass' *Narrative of the Life of Frederick Douglass, an American Slave* (1845). The Black Arts movement and its political parallel, the Black Power movement, began to shape a new cultural history for the United States (Fowler 1994, Notes).

A Theoretical Context

In the context of literary theories presented in the preceding chapters, early work in African American criticism occurred as a reaction to the formalists' way of reading and to their claim about the universality of meaning. Leading black theoreticians, among them Larry Neal and Amira Baraka, worked out of the principles of social realism. Black art, they said, was directly related to black life. It imitated it. Therefore, the only way to read African American literature was "broadly cultural and richly contextualized." Art, these earlier leaders asserted, did not exist for art's sake, as the formalists claimed. It was not universal. It was particular to a people and its culture. One of the results of this thinking was that during the 1960s black history was first introduced into school curricula to contextualize the black experience for both blacks and whites (Gates 1992, 291).

A reaction to this social realism of the 1960s brought about change in the 1970s. Black literature replaced history as the predominant area for critical analysis as leading critics emphasized texts as acts of language. After 1975, scholars demonstrated that the "blackness" of a text resided in its "practical uses of language," and they used both formalist and structuralist strategies to guide their readings. At the same time, black women's studies emerged and gave new energy to the field (Gates 1992, 292).

Changes that occurred in the 1980s may be seen as a combination of the work of the two previous decades. In the "new black aesthetic movement" of the 1980s, scholars "began to re-theorize social—and textual—boundaries" as they employed poststructural theories and investigated the "black, expressive, vernacular culture." They employed close reading practices that inquired into both the literary text and the "social text" (Gates, 1992, 292). Our reading of *A Lesson Before Dying* will demonstrate from the poststructural perspective that investigates intertextualities in the novel.

An Introduction to Black Literary Theory and Criticism

First, a matter of semantics. I use the nonhyphenated phrase "African American" to represent the black tradition in American literature. When I cite others who use other designations, I remain faithful to their language.

Second, a clarification. While not a novel written specifically for young adults, *A Lesson Before Dying*, will, I believe, find its place alongside Gaines' *The Autobiography of Miss Jane Pittman* and *A Gathering of Old Men* on many of the lists of the best novels for young adults. It is one of the most powerful novels I have read in the last four or five years, and I especially recommend it for use in classes of mature readers. One of its major themes is freedom and the way in which its African American characters achieve different kinds of freedom despite the oppression of the dominant culture. Our reading of *A Lesson Before Dying* will demonstrate how Gaines' characters use language as power to negotiate their circumstances and, in some cases, overcome the control of their masters.

Guiding Questions

Now, on to theory. In his essay "Criticism in the Jungle," African American scholar Henry Louis Gates Jr. asks some specific text-oriented questions that help us shape an inquiry into the power of language in the African American literary tradition and in *A Lesson Before Dying*.

Among the six questions that Gates asks, three are especially useful to us in the reading of young adult fiction. The first two questions provide a framework for the third. The first asks, "How do we read black texts?" The second is related and asks if Western methods of explication can be " 'translated' into the black idiom?" The third question is the most important to our reading of *A Lesson Before Dying*. Gates argues that every black text is "two-toned" or "double-voiced," and he asks "How do we explicate the signifyin(g) black difference that makes black literature 'black'?" (Gates 1971, 3). Gates offers, I believe, a practical point of entry into black criticism for readers unfamiliar with African American literature and its criticism.

Question 1: How do we read black texts?. Gates describes his way of reading as eclectic because he draws on the reading practices of critics who are outside the black literary tradition. Although he uses some principles of theories presented in previous chapters of this book, he also explains that his use is improvisatory, not unlike playing jazz. Gates believes, as I do, that theory is enabling, inviting; it helps us work with texts, and we are not obliged to read out of only one frame of reference (Gates 1971, 4).

Recalling his own education in theory, Gates (1987) creates a useful metaphor that also reflects this book's perspective on how theory serves us:

> Literary theory functioned in my education as a prism, which I could turn to refract different spectral patterns of language use in a text, as one does daylight. Turn the prism this way, and one pattern of color emerges; turn it that way, and another pattern configures. (xvii)

As a prism, literary theory illuminates the texts we read. This illumination, I contend, is one of the primary values of having a working knowledge of the wide range of strategies that contemporary theories offer us. In applying our working knowledge (turning the prism), theory allows us to shine different lights through a text. Not every theoretical strategy, of course, illuminates every text. Contemporary literary theories challenge the traditional claim that a "single universal poetics" is "applicable to all humanity" (Leitch 1992, 83), and Gates clearly agrees with this idea. Theories of criticism are not "universal procedures similar, say, to surgical techniques" (Gates 1987, xv). The difference in the image of the prism and surgical techniques is telling: The prism is more artistic in the bands of colors it emits, and literature seen through it is more apt to be a more imaginative creation. The surgery image suggests the familiar dissection of literary

texts of which critics have often been accused. My students have
sometimes lamented what they perceived to be such surgery, telling
me that it destroyed the experience of reading. The developments in
contemporary literary theories in the second half of the twentieth
century have reflected the insufficiency of such surgical work in
understanding texts.

**Question 2: Can the methods of explication developed in
Western criticism be "translated" into the black idiom?**
"Theory," Gates (1971) contends, "like words in a poem, does not
'translate' in a one-to-one relationship of reference." He says that
critics of black literature use "any 'tool' which helps us to elucidate,
which enables us to see more clearly, the complexities of figuration
peculiar to our literary traditions" (4). A number of his key words are
instructive of his approach to reading and our application of it to
Gaines' novel. First, in his analogy between theory and the language
of a poem, Gates implies the freedom that modern theory gives us to
negotiate, to play with language in a context where words are not
fixed entities. Instead, words are capable of a plurality of meanings;
analysis opens up texts rather than rigidly defining their meanings.
Second, Gates refers to "the critic of black literature," a phrase that
does not privilege any reader of the tradition but includes all critics.
Third, "the complexities of figuration" are at the heart of Gates' reading, *figuration* here meaning the ways in which a word stands for
something other than itself, as, for example, in a metaphor or simile.

In his phrase "our literary traditions," Gates emphasizes the importance of the critic's awareness of context by pointing out that the
African American writer as the producer of texts occupies spaces "in at
least two traditions: a European or American literary tradition, and one
of the several related but distinct traditions." Therefore, the "heritage"
of each black text written in a Western language is "two-toned or
double-voiced": "Its visual tones are white and black, and its aural
tones are standard and vernacular" (Gates 1971, 4). As far as ways of
reading are concerned, this image of doubleness enriches the black text,
conceptualizing rather than obliterating the "many-strandedness of
black literatures," which are defined by their "hybridity" (Leitch 1992,
89). In discussing *A Lesson Before Dying*, we will trace the weave of these
double strands and demonstrate how they "figure" Gaines' text.

**Question 3: "If every black canonical text is . . . 'two-toned' or
'double-voiced,' how do we explicate the signifyin(g) black difference that makes black literature 'black'?"** The most specific in
relation to practical ways of reading, this question motivates answers

that provide strategies for analyzing African American texts. Gates (1971) explains the importance of this question:

> For a critic of black literature to be unaware of the black tradition of figuration and its bearing upon a discrete black text is as serious a flaw as for that critic to be unaware of the texts in the Western tradition which the black text echoes, revises and extends. (6)

Critical attention, he contends, must focus on the "most repressed" element in the black tradition: "the language of the black text" (6). Language and the forms that it takes in shaping narrative are the loci of our critical inquiry in this chapter.

How do we proceed? Gates tells us that "black literature is a verbal art like other verbal arts"; and working out of structuralist theories of the text, he tells us that the text is "a world, a system of signs" that reflects the worldview, the consciousness of its writer. When we read a black text, then, we must be conscious of its blackness and the ways in which blackness is signified:

> We urgently need to direct our attention to the nature of black figurative language, to the nature of black narrative forms. . . . [W]e must begin to understand the nature of intertextuality, that is, the nonthematic manner by which texts—poems and novels—respond to other texts. (Gates 1987, 40–41).

In our close reading of *A Lesson Before Dying*, we will pay attention to all three of these issues: (1) to *black figurative language* as a form of signifyin(g); and (2) to *black narrative forms* as part of (3) the *intertextuality* of the novel. We will focus on two intertextual structures: on autobiography as a variation of slave narratives, and on spirituals as coded communication in the world of American slaves.

Signifyin(g) in the Black Tradition

To focus on the repressed language of the black text, Gates has developed a "theory of reading that arises from Afro-American culture" (Gates 1984, 286). He calls his approach "critical signification," and he derives it from "the black rhetorical strategy called signifyin(g)." Gates' punctuation of the word "signifyin(g)" appears to enact the double-voicedness of the black literary tradition. The *g* in parenthesis signifies the proper spelling in standard English, while the word without the *g* indicates its pronunciation in the black vernacular.

Gates defines "signifyin(g)" as a concept that is "entirely textual or linguistic." In this practice, "a second statement or figure repeats, or tropes, or reverses the first" (Gates 1987, 49). This linguistic skill, the ability to say one thing and mean another, has been basic to the survival of blacks in Western cultures that have oppressed them. Gates contends that the ability to read these significations, to decipher their complex codes, is a fundamental "metaphorical literacy." It is, he declares, "just about the blackest aspect of the black tradition" (Gates 1971, 6). The reader wishing to approach black literature critically, it is clear, must be able to read the significations of the black text in order to understand its meanings.

Other critics' ideas about signifyin(g) are helpful as we read and interpret *A Lesson Before Dying*. These ideas include Roger Abraham's notion that signifying occurs through body language, especially in the use of the hands and the eyes, and Claudia Mitchell-Kernan's concept that signifying reverses or undermines pretense, pretending to be informative while it is actually persuasive (Gates 1984, 288–89).

An Introduction to *A Lesson Before Dying*

Set in Louisiana in the late 1940s, the novel opens in October and ends in April. It presents a dichotomized black-and-white world that echoes life in the pre–Civil War South. The plantation house of the wealthy Henri Pichot looms above the poor dwellings of the black people who live in the Quarter, among them the aging friends Tante Lou and Miss Emma. The church, at the center of life in the Quarter, doubles as the school. In nearby Bayonne, the action takes place in the courthouse and in a tiny cell and visiting room of the jail where Miss Emma's godson Jefferson awaits execution for a murder he did not commit. Like the plantation, Bayonne is segregated—whites uptown and blacks in the back of town at The Rainbow Club, a favorite gathering place.

The lives of the two key figures in the novel, Grant Wiggins and Jefferson, are woven together in an intense and intricate relationship. Each man suffers forms of imprisonment that are both literal and metaphoric. Jefferson's imprisonment in the Bayonne jail serves as a metaphor for the racial injustice of the slavery system and the continuing oppression of that system almost a century after the Emancipation Proclamation. Grant, although "freed" by the advantage of a university education, feels literally entrapped as the teacher in the Quarter. His mind is a metaphoric prison because he lacks the strength of will to free himself; he also feels trapped in the cycle of poverty and ignorance that the white culture perpetuates.

Grant tells the story in the first person. The first sentence of Chapter 1 locates him in a paradox that is symbolic not only of his position in the novel but also of the lives of blacks in a predominantly white world: "I was not there, yet I was there" (3). This sentence reflects the way in which he tells the story: He reports from his own observations, and he tells what other people have told him. In his first sentence, he refers to the trial in which Jefferson is convicted and sentenced to death by electrocution. In the course of the novel, Grant becomes a metaphorical attorney for the defense in Jefferson's second "trial" in the execution room, but he is also absent from that one.

"Signifyin(g)" Rhetoric

The novel opens on a Friday afternoon in late October and tells the story of the trial, including the conflicting versions of the murder of a white store owner as presented by Jefferson and by the prosecutor. It introduces the key image of the hog which is woven throughout the novel. The image appears to signify on Claude McKay's sonnet "If We Must Die" in which the image of black men being slaughtered like hogs constitutes the most ignoble of deaths. The speakers in the sonnet are determined to die nobly; though presssed against a wall, they assert that they will fight to the death, that they will die standing. The poem juxtaposes the two contrary images that characterize Jefferson in the novel—a hog and a man—animal and human. One of Miss Emma's major concerns is that Jefferson will walk like a man to his death, and the novel is filled with images of standing, images that signify literal standing as well as "standing for." McKay's poem provides us a sociocultural dimension for these images in the novel.

Attempting to gain sympathy for Jefferson near the end of the trial, his lawyer denigrates him as a "cornered animal" who struck the store owner in fear, without thinking, "a trait inherited from his ancestors in the deepest jungle of blackest Africa." He tells the jury that Jefferson is "a thing" that does "your" work—holding a plow handle, loading cotton bales, digging ditches, chopping wood, and pulling corn (Gaines 1993, 7–8). He emphasizes Jefferson's illiteracy as he implies that the accused cannot name the months of the year or tell whether Christmas comes before or after July Fourth. He saves the ultimate degradation until the end as he makes his final plea for justice. There will be no justice in taking Jefferson's life, he says: "Why I would just as soon put a hog in the electric chair as this" (8). This description robs Jefferson of his status as a human being; it devastates him to such an extent that he believes the attorney's words are true. In poststructural terms, he becomes a social construction of what he perceives to be a more powerful man with a more powerful language. The novel proceeds out of this moment to investigate how a man reduced to an animal can reconstruct himself as a man. Appropriately, at the end of the novel, Jefferson's own words, written in his diary, effect his reconstruction. He discovers that he has the power to declare himself a man and in so doing to erase the name "Hog."

Signifyin(g) in the Kitchen 1

Powerful scenes in which we observe signifyin(g) practices occur in the kitchens of Emma, Tante Lou, and Henri Pichot. Chapter 2 builds on the image of the hog with two signifyin(g) sentences that set into motion the narrative threads that weave Grant and Jefferson together. The first sentence is "He don't have to do it." The second is "You the teacher" (13), a sentence that is spoken to Grant by a number of characters in the novel, each time signifyin(g) his responsibility as an educated black man to speak for the uneducated people in the Quarter.

On the Monday after Jefferson is sentenced to death, Tante Lou and Miss Emma inform Grant of his role in Jefferson's salvation. Gaines establishes the power and stability of these two women in the images with which he introduces them into the story; they sit in Tante Lou's' kitchen, waiting for Grant to come home from school, "like boulders, their bodies, their minds, immovable" (14). They issue Grant an imperative that will change him just as they want him to change Jefferson.

Miss Emma states her case: She doesn't want the white men to "kill no hog"; she wants Jefferson to walk like a man to the electric chair—"on his own two feet" (13). The scene that follows illustrates Roger Abrahams' idea that "signifyin(g)" can "denote speaking with hands and eyes," encompassing a wide range of gestures and expressions (Gates 1984, 288). Images of eyes occur almost constantly throughout *A Lesson Before Dying*, and they signify in the manner of Abraham's definition. After Miss Emma's declaration, Grant realizes that the two women are communicating to him by their looks and that they expect him to be able to read their intent; both stare at him as though he were "supposed to figure out the rest of it" (13). When he understands and begins to protest, Emma says "He don't have to do it," but that is exactly the opposite of what she means with respect to Gates' definition that "signifyin(g)" includes "the ability to say one thing and mean another" (Gates 1971, 6). When she repeats the sentence "He don't have to do it," Grant realizes what she is signifyin(g): that he *does* have to do it.

Miss Emma's signifyin(g) continues when she explains why Grant must be the person who visits Jefferson at the jail: "You the teacher" (13). Her sentence illustrates Mitchell-Kernan's conception of signifyin(g) wherein "what pretends to be informative may intend to be persuasive." Under the conditions of this kind of signification, "the hearer is constrained to attend to all potential meaning carrying symbolic systems—the total universe of discourse" (Gates 1984, 289). Grant is caught in the double-voiced universe of discourse. He knows how to read the language of his culture; but trained as he is in the language of the university, he also knows how to read the language of the white culture. Miss Emma's apparently simple statement of fact says one thing and means another. It says, literally, "You are a teacher in the local school." But it signifies much more. Grant (and we) interpret it to mean a number of things. On one level of signification, it translates into power: "You live in both the white world and the black world, and because you can speak the language, you can negotiate meaning between the two. You know how to communicate. You can reach Jefferson when no one else can. You have the gift of language." On a much deeper level, the sentence signifies obligation: "You owe your former student the dignity of his manhood. You owe the elderly in this community the peace of mind that will come with the transformation of Jefferson from hog to man. You owe black people the freedom from oppression that your education, in some measure, enables you to possess. You do not have a choice."

Signifyin(g) in the Kitchen 2

The trip to Pichot's house and the events that occur there are chronicled in Chapter 3, which is full of signifyin(g) language. Pichot is entertaining friends in the library, but he comes when Miss Emma asks for him. After explaining that she does not want Jefferson to die a hog, she asks Pichot to speak to the sheriff and secure permission for Grant to talk to Jefferson for her. She declares her purpose: She wants the teacher to make Jefferson know that "he's not a hog, he's a man" (20–21).

In the conversation that follows, Miss Emma signifies in Mitchell-Kernan's sense that language "can also be employed to reverse or undermine pretense or even one's opinion about one's own status" (Gates 1984, 289). When Pichot does not respond to her statement about what she wants, she tells him, "I done done a lot for this family and this place," and she reminds Sheriff Guidry that his wife, Pichot's sister, also knows what she has done in her years of loyal service to the family (22). Her insistence signifies Pichot's obligation: We may interpret her language to mean, "I have served you well for a long time, and now you owe me something in return. I expect you to deliver it. Although I may seem to be at your mercy, we both know that I have power. I can negotiate because of what I have done for you."

Signifyin(g) at the Jail

Chapters 9, 10, and 11 detail the series of visits to the jail. At first Miss Emma accompanies Grant, but the visits are disappointing: Jefferson will not talk, and he refuses most of the food that she brings. Food and eating are powerful signifiers in the novel. After a while, Miss Emma weakens and decides that she cannot continue the visits, so Grant goes alone. On one visit, a scene of high drama picks up and continues the thread of animal imagery in the story.

In one horrific moment, Jefferson becomes the hog that he has been named. He asks if Grant has brought some corn, because that is what humans feed hogs. Then he defines himself in relation to humans: "Youmans don't stay in no stall like this. I'm a old hog they fattening up to kill" (83). Kneeling on the floor beside the bag of food that Miss Emma has sent, he sticks his head into the bag and eats the food; he does not use his hands, and he makes the sounds of a hog. Trying desperately to reach Jefferson, Grant implores him to respond to him, because if he does not, the white men will have succeeded in turning him into an animal. Despite Grant's plea, Jefferson remains unresponsive.

Signifyin(g) Structures

Critical signification in Gates' theory of reading has another dimension in which a text can itself be "a signifying structure, a structure of intertextual revisions." In the African American tradition, Gates explains, authors often revise at least two earlier texts, usually from different literary periods or from other generations. For example, Ralph Ellison's *Invisible Man* (1952) signifies on (or revises) a number of texts, among them Richard Wright's *Native Son* (1940) and *Black Boy* (1945) as well as W.E.B. Dubois' *The Souls of Black Folk* (1903). Why do authors create such signifyin(g) structures? Gates answers that such readings and critiques of other black texts are "an act of rhetorical self-definition" and that the African American "literary tradition exists because of these precisely chartable formal literary relationships, relationships of signifying" (Gates 1984, 290).

In *A Lesson Before Dying*, we can trace the weave of two signifyin(g) structures: the slave narrative and spirituals. These represent "the earliest and most significant forms of oral and written literature created by blacks during slavery" and out of which "the fabric of tradition in Afro-American literature is woven." Spirituals blended elements of both Protestant Christianity and African religions. Their coded language critiqued the plantation system and "the slave's search for freedom in *this* world." Slave narratives, which were both individually autobiographical and communal, created "a heroic fugitive character unlike any other in American literature" (Dixon 1985, 298). In his novel, Gaines repeats the language of the spirituals and

uses it to signify the theme of freedom. He revises the autobiographical narrative as a diary that records the transformation of a dejected
man into a hero.

Signifyin(g) Structure 1: Spirituals

The spiritual as an intertextual signifying structure first appears in the
novel when Grant hears Miss Eloise, a neighbor, singing her "Termi-
nation song" (Chapter 13). It is a tradition in the local church that on
every third Sunday members stand up and sing a favorite hymn, after
which they tell other members of the congregation where they are
"determined to spend eternity" (97). Miss Eloise's song is the spiritual
"Were You There When They Crucified My Lord?" The repeating pattern of the spiritual asks a series of questions about witnessing the
sacrifice of Christ on Good Friday: "Were you there when they
crucified my Lord, when they nailed him to the tree, when they laid
him in the tomb?" it asks. There are no answers to the questions. This
familiar spiritual serves a number of functions in the novel. First, it
prefigures Jefferson's references to another spiritual, "Crucifixion";
the language of "Crucifixion" becomes an important symbol in the
"lesson" that he teaches Grant Wiggins. Second, it foreshadows Jefferson's execution, which becomes a symbolic crucifixion. Third, it is a
coded commentary on the first line of the novel: "I was not there, yet
I was there." What it signifies as it circles back to that opening sentence is the literal absence of Grant at the trial as well as the literal
absence of the singer at the Crucifixion of the Lord. At a more complex
level, it signifies the *presence* of all who have witnessed injustice and
all who have suffered and died at the hands of others, a sacrifice for
which Christ is the ultimate symbol in the Christian tradition. The
implied answer to each of the spiritual's questions is "Yes, I was there
in the spirit of my faith."

When Grant visits Jefferson a few weeks before Christmas (Chapter 17), the spiritual appears as intertext in their conversation about
the electric chair. Pretending ignorance of the approaching holiday,
Jefferson asks, "That's when He was born, or that's when He died?"
His sentence signifies: He pretends not to know, but he knows. When
Grant answers "Born," Jefferson sets into motion some of the most
powerful signifyin(g) in the novel. He explains that he knows Easter
was the day when Christ was nailed to the cross, a day when Christ
"never said a mumbling word" (139). His words, from the spiritual
"Crucifixion," perhaps affirm that his Aunt Emma's religious convic-
tions have taken hold in him. "They crucified my Lord," the spiritual
begins, "An' he never said a mumblin' word." Its pattern tells the
story of heroic silence: "They nailed him to the tree, / They pierced

him in the side, / The blood came twinklin' down, / and He bow'd his head an' died," but "He never said a mumblin' word; / Not a word, not a word, not a word" (Johnson and Johnson 1989, 174). The meaning of Jefferson's signifyin(g) on "Crucifixion" is that his own silence at the time of his execution will raise him, like Christ, to an heroic level. Similarly, like Christ, his words will live after him as his diary breaks the silence of his death.

The signifyin(g) on spirituals continues when, in late February, Grant and Reverend Ambrose are summoned to Pichot's house (Chapter 20). There they receive the news that the execution will occur on the second Friday after Easter, April the eighth, sometime between noon and three o'clock. When Grant asks why they have selected that date, Sheriff Guidry offers a number of reasons, both political and religious. The state has a large Catholic population and a "sensitive few" of them would be upset if the execution took place during Lent or right before or after Easter. Another reason is that one execution has already been scheduled before Ash Wednesday, and one is all that authorities will risk so close to the holy season. Grant understands the significance of the execution date: Two weeks *after* Easter, he reasons, the sensitive ones "will have forgotten about their Savior's death" (158). Grant's thinking reveals a number of ideas central to the novel. First, the power of a "sensitive few" white people can determine the fate of a black man. Second, religion for these few is little more than an empty ritual, observed and then forgotten, a contrast to the powerful role that the church and religion play in the lives of black people, a role coded into the language of their spirituals.

In Grant's next visit to the jail (Chapter 22), Jefferson's references to "my last supper" continue the intertext of spirituals and sacrifice, and another important event occurs. During this visit, Grant offers to bring Jefferson a portable radio so that he can listen to music and so that he can have something that belongs only to him. He also offers to bring a notebook and pencil so that Jefferson can record his thoughts; Jefferson agrees to write in the notebook, which becomes one of the central symbols of the novel.

On the Thursday before Good Friday, Grant visits the jail (Chapter 28), and the "Crucifixion" intertext reappears as he and Jefferson discuss Good Friday. We realize that Jefferson is constructing himself as a man in the figure of Jesus, the Christian hero, the central figure in his Aunt Emma's religious life. Responding to the news that tomorrow is Good Friday, Jefferson reminds himself that Christ died on Good Friday and that Christ "never said a mumbling word" (221). As they discuss the approaching execution, Grant encourages Jefferson to do something for Emma, namely, "Walk like a man" (222), and Jefferson responds with a lesson about what faces him.

Echoing the spiritual "Lonesome Valley" with its image of Jesus walking into the valley of the shadow of death when "nobody else could do it for him, He had to walk it by himself," Jefferson explains that no one can go to the chair for him: "I got to go myself" (223). He sees himself in the figure of Christ: "That's how I want to go, Mr. Wiggins. Not a mumbling word" (223).

With that figuration as his context, Jefferson delivers a lesson on his place in the world and on the work that he must do. He says he is "an old stumbling nigger" who must take up the cross for all of them; "Your cross, nannan's cross, my own cross." He describes his life without his parents who "dropped me when I wasn't nothing." He recalls how he went to work as a six-year-old child, driving a water cart, pulling cotton sacks, cutting cane, swinging an ax, chopping wood. He has been able, finally, to transcend the image of the hog, and he declares, "Yes, I'm youman. . . . But nobody didn't know that 'fore now." He describes the cursings and beatings he has endured and the role he has had to play to survive in the white man's world. He played out, he says, the stereotype of the smiling Negro as happy child: "Grinned to get by" because, he thought, "that's how it was s'pose to be." He indicts his teacher, too: "You never thought I was nothing else" (224). The lesson is a revelation to Grant, who tells Jefferson that his eyes "were closed before this moment," and that he realizes now that "his eyes have been closed" all his life. In a reversal of all his earlier refusals to eat, Jefferson now offers Grant food. Like Christ, he has fed his friend spiritually, and now he offers to literally feed him. The metaphor of food in the novel reaches its highest moment of signification in this act.

Signifyin(g) Structure 2: The Slave Narrative

Jefferson's Diary: Signifyin(g) on the Slave Narrative. The notebook in which Jefferson records his thoughts while awaiting execution is perhaps the most powerful structural signification in the novel. Language has been a tool of liberation for Grant; and with the notebook, he offers Jefferson language as a tool of self-discovery and salvation. A double signification occurs. Grant narrates the novel in the form of a very elaborate and extended diary of his own experiences with the characters in the novel. The story he tells and Jefferson's diary combine as structural significations and revisions of one of the first forms of written African American literature: the slave narrative.

In American literature, "the slave narrative represents the attempt of blacks to write themselves into being" (Davis and Gates 1985, xxiii). This sentence accurately describes what happens in Jefferson's diary: He literally writes himself into being as a man. A number of clarifications are in order, however, with respect to the way in which

Gaines revises the form of the slave narrative as a "signifyin(g)" structure in his novel.

Slave narratives were autobiographical performances. In autobiography, the writer "is not a neutral and passive recorder but rather a
creative and active shaper" who does not present events in simple
chronological order but who expresses them in "patterned significance"
as present and past, present memory and past experience becoming
"present being" (Olney 1985, 149). Jefferson's diary enacts just such a
performance. In its limited language, it recounts the events of his life
and his reflections on them up until the morning of his execution;
it reconstructs him as a man just as he loses his life. Paradoxically,
however, his status as a man will be preserved in the penciled words of
his pages.

Jefferson's diary revises the narrative form on which Gaines
signifies. For example, it does not follow the "master outline" of
twelve sections that can be drawn from the great slave narratives.
These include preliminaries to the actual narrative, among them an
engraved, signed portrait and various testimonials to the narrator's
existence. These preliminaries, in other words, establish the authen-
ticity of the text. The actual narrative follows and contains a statement of being ("I was born") and various accounts of cruel masters,
exemplary slaves, barriers to slave literacy, descriptions of the material status of slaves, the patterns of their existence, attempts at escape,
the taking on of a new last name as an act of identity as a free person,
and some reflections on being a slave. These narratives almost always
recounted "the realities of the institution of slavery, almost never the
intellectual, emotional, moral growth of the narrator" (Olney 1985,
152–54). These latter concerns—reflections on slavery and the internal processes of "becoming"—constitute the very substance of Jefferson's diary, appropriate as a revision of the slave narrative since it was
written nearly 100 years after the abolition of slavery. Jefferson's
diary is not a literal description of an institution that had been abol-
ished; it is a metaphor for the possibility of triumph over the continuing and dehumanizing effects of that institution. It is thematically
related to the slave narratives. "Literacy, identity, and freedom," the
"omnipresent thematic trio of the most important slave narratives"
(Olney 1985, 158), all emerge from Jefferson's diary.

Jefferson makes forty-one episodic entries of varying lengths; the
entries are unnumbered, but I have numbered them consecutively for
easy reference. He addresses the following subjects: visits to the jail (4,
11, 14, 15, 18, 19, 25); his dreams (3, 7, 17); work stories (6); love (9,
18); the act of writing and Wiggins' response to it (1, 8, 10, 12, 25);
food (2); biblical stories (5, 21); Paul Bonin, the white deputy who

befriends him (13); crying (16, 20); and final thoughts as his death approaches (22–41). Read in sequence, the diary affirms Jefferson's ability to read his world and to construct himself as a man within it.

Jefferson's narrative begins with a metaphoric "I was born," in the sense that his diary details his birth into language, his birth as a writer. He addresses the opening entry to Grant Wiggins, explaining that he has no experience as a writer: "i aint never rote nothin but homework i aint never rote a leter in all my life" (226).

The sixth entry opens with a reflection on God's favoritism of white people: "it look like the lord just work for wite folks cause ever sens i wasn nothin but a litle bot [boy] i been on my own haulin water to the fiel . . . so i get the peple they food an they water on time" (227). Black people, he reasons, are alone in the world and they work hard all their lives just to survive while God provides white people privileges.

He reflects on the nature of love and how love is signified, whether by doing or saying: "i kno i care for nanan [Miss Emma] but i dont kno if love is care cause cuttin wood and haulin water and things like that i dont kno if thats love or jus work to do and you say thats love." He thinks about the diary: "i aint done this much thinkin and this much writin in all my lif before" (229).

In several entries, he describes the visits of Pichot and other white men to the cell, and he makes it clear that he understands their role in his oppression. He realizes that the deputy Paul is in a difficult position as he tries to befriend him while also playing his official role in front of the other white men: "paul trying to be hod [hard] when he aint . . . he is the only one rond yer kno how to talk like a youman to people." He contrasts Paul to the other white men who visit him; addressing them directly in the diary, he says that he "knows" them, this word signi-fyin(g) that he understands their motives: "i jus never say non of this befor but i know yall ever las one of yall" (230). It is clear that he is not the ignorant animal that white men think he is. His knowledge indicts his oppressors, who, ironically, even as they visit him and pretend to care about him, are betting that he will die like a hog.

On the eve of the execution, Guidry pays a visit to the cell, and Jefferson's narrative reveals the sheriff's concern with his own repu-tation. The sheriff asks Jefferson if he has treated him right during his time in jail, and Jefferson responds that he has. The sheriff's sugges-tion affirms his real concern: "and he say is you gon put that in yo table [tablet] and i say yesir an he say put that down in yo tabet i tret you good all the time you been yer" (233). Ironically, Guidry says that he will leave the light on all night so that Jefferson can continue to write. This is doubly symbolic. The sheriff has helped to negate the presence of a black man in the world, and now he wants to illuminate the darkness of his last night on earth so that Jefferson can bear witness to the sheriff's "right" treatment.

The theme of identity emerges in the final entries of the diary. Writing on the day before the execution, Jefferson reveals how close he feels to Grant Wiggins and how sad he is to learn that he will never see his teacher again. Although he has cried on Grant's last visit when he learned that his friend would not be there on the day of the execution, he has wept tears of joy, he says, because Grant has been so good to him. Nobody, he continues, has ever been that good to him and made "me think im somebody" (232). The notebook is one of the ways in which his own language has helped him understand the "somebody" that he has become.

The diary ends in a farewell to his teacher that sings in its springtime imagery: "day breakin / sun comin up," he writes; "the bird in the tre soun like a blu bird / sky blu blu mr wigin." Then he bids Grant farewell, asking him to tell the others what he has achieved: "tell them im strong tell them im a man" (234). The image of the bird foreshadows a final image of flight at the end of the novel.

Grant's Narrative. The chapter following the diary (Chapter 30) narrates nine vignettes, each a scene reported later to Grant Wiggins, scenes from which he pieces together the preparations for the execution in the final hours of Jefferson's life. This beautifully crafted chapter rewards close study in the way in which it reveals the attitude of the townspeople toward the execution and toward racial issues.

The final chapter of the novel contains the sentence that confirms my interpretation of *A Lesson Before Dying* as a contemporary double slave narrative. At noon on the day of the execution, Grant instructs his students to kneel in prayer by their desks. His thoughts echo the first sentence of the novel, as Grant questions himself: "Why wasn't I there? Why wasn't I standing beside him?" (250). In the key sentence of the novel, he declares his own identity and locates himself in the history of his race: "I know what it means to be a slave. I am a slave" (251). *A Lesson Before Dying* is his slave narrative, too, an autobiographical performance, a final realization that he, like Jefferson, has allowed himself to be constructed by white men, by their language and by their expectations of what an educated black man can do in their presence.

As Grant awaits news of the end, a yellow butterfly lights near him as he stands outside the schoolroom, and he tells himself, "It is finally over" (252). The butterfly is, perhaps, a triple signifier. First, it figures Jefferson's metamorphosis, his transformation from an ugly hog into a beautiful man. Second, it figures the flight of the soul after death, often represented in Christian symbology as a butterfly. Third, it may represent the transformation in Grant as a result of having received a lesson from the life of Jefferson—a lesson before dying.

In the final scene, Paul Bonin reports that the execution is over; he ties together many of the threads of the narrative. Of the lesson: "You're one great teacher." Of Jefferson's manhood: "I saw the transformation. I'm a witness to that" (254). His word *witness* carries us all the way back to the trial scene in the first pages of the novel, but it signifies in the larger context. In African American history, the word *witness* signifies on slaves' membership in a religious community. In a complex signification, Paul, who shares his name with the disciple who bore witness to Christ, becomes part of the spiritual community into which slaves were "initiated through the spiritual potency of personal testimony." Among the "explicit principles of character and right living" that slave communities demanded of each other was this one: "for the 'soul' to be a witness for my lord" (Dixon 1985, 301– 302). If we take Jefferson to be a figure of Christ, then Paul, although a white man, joins the fellowship of the black community as he bears witness to Jefferson's identity as a sacrificial figure.

Paul suggests the multiple lessons of the novel when he asks a symbolic question: "School is just about ready to end, huh?" (255). The school term is ending, and so is the novel. Many people have learned lessons before dying. Both Jefferson and Grant have learned a lesson, and both have been the teacher. Now Paul Bonin becomes the teacher: "Allow me to be your friend," he tells Grant, in a request that echoes Grant's own proffer of friendship to Jefferson months earlier. We realize that the friendship between Paul and Grant, born out of their shared respect for Jefferson, may be the hope for the future of the rural Louisiana world they inhabit. Paul wants Grant to bear witness to Jefferson in the Quarter: "Tell them he was the bravest man in that room today. I'm a witness. . . . Tell them so." After he leaves, the emotional impact of his own lesson sweeps over Grant, and he faces his class unmasked: "I was crying" (256). These are the double tears of sorrow and brotherhood that end these lessons.

Joining the Conversation

Joyce Carol Thomas' short story "The Young Reverend Zelma Lee Moses" (1990) provides a good introduction to the signifyin(g) practices of the African American tradition, and it also involves a lesson. As an introduction to signifyin(g) practices, it offers a number of advantages: It is short; it signifies clearly on the sermon, spiritual, and the African American folktale; and it is full of humor.

Zelma Lee is a child when she delivers her first sermon one Easter morning in the Perfect Peace Baptist Church of Sweet Earth, Oklahoma. The sermon signifies on the slave practice of call and response as Zelma Lee, a "jubilee all by herself" (110), proclaims to the congregation that something other than "just metal nails" was holding the Lord to "that old rugged cross." They sing out "Wasn't just nails" and together Zelma Lee and the congregation create a litany of the Easter story (106–107). As the story unfolds, Zelma Lee falls in love; she also gains such fame as a preacher and singer that hordes of visitors come to Sweet Earth. She sings a spiritual entitled "Lord, Just a Little Mercy's All I Need". As a musician I was captivated with the spiritual, but I could not locate it among the spirituals I knew. When I asked Joyce Carol Thomas what her source was, she replied simply, "I made it up" (Thomas 1992).

The story also signifies on the African American folktale "The People Could Fly," retold by Virginia Hamilton in *The People Could Fly: American Black Folktales* (1985). The imagery of the blackbird in the folktale figures prominently in Thomas' story. In the folktale, the people fly like blackbirds "to *Free-dom*" (Hamilton 1985, 171); Zelma Lee declares to her congregation that "on the day Christ came forth from the tomb, Church, it's been given me to fly" (Thomas 1990, 119); wise women in the church consider this an ill-advised consequence of her growing fame. Thomas' story reverses the outcome of the folktale in Zelma Lee's failure to fly, but she learns a valuable lesson about love and about freedom.

One of the best ways to introduce the African American tradition to young adult readers is through Mildred Taylor's *Roll of Thunder, Hear My Cry* (1977), which Pamela S. Carroll (1993) considers to be "the focal Southern novel for young adults" (163). Carroll suggests pairing Taylor's novel with Zora Neale Hurston's *Their Eyes Were Watching God* (1942) because both novels reflect "thematic Southern preoccupations" (163). Although she approaches these novels from the transactional model of reader-response theory (see Chapter 6), Carroll points in the direction of African American theory in her desire for students to explore what Houston Baker refers to as the sociohistorical context in this chapter. Carroll plans for students "to become aware of the history of social and physical mistreatment of African-Americans in the South" (167) as portrayed in *Roll of Thunder*. She includes segregation in churches and schools, which we also see in *A Lesson Before Dying*, as well as night riders, tar and featherings, and burnings. She offers students experience with anthropology as they uncover manifestations of African American traditions and folklore in the Hurston novel. The study of both novels will lead to the development, Carroll says, of a "position on the place of Black women writers in American literature" (168).

Roll of Thunder, Hear My Cry is set during the Great Depression in Spokane County, Mississippi. During the year that the novel spans, nine-year-old Cassie Logan, its central character, witnesses the incidents that take place in her family and community. Central to the novel is the family's identity as a function of the 400 acres of land that it has owned since Reconstruction. Contextualizing the novel with respect to Reconstruction and how it affected the lives of freed slaves presents students with the chance to connect their nation's history with this fictionalized version of it. The story of Cassie and the Logan family continues in Taylor's sequels. In *Let the Circle Be Unbroken* (1981), T.J., a friend of Cassie's brother Stacey, is put on trial for a murder that occurs at the end of *Roll of Thunder*. The novel emphasizes the strength of family love set against the racial prejudice of the community. *The Road to Memphis* (1990) continues the family saga when Cassie is seventeen and takes action to help save her friend Moe Turner after a violent altercation with whites.

Joyce Carol Thomas has written a trilogy about a poor black girl that also focuses on the role of black women in their rural and religious culture. Students can explore aspects of the black experience of Abyssinia Jackson in *Marked by Fire* (1982) and in *Bright Shadow* (1983), both set in Oklahoma. In *Water Girl* (1986) the family story continues in a California setting with a new central character named Amber.

Bruce Brooks' *The Moves Make the Man* (1984) is a good choice for exploring the African American tradition. The semiotic perspective that we took toward this novel in Chapter 4 kept us confined to the text inside the covers of the book, although we did focus on the language structures of the black vernacular, particularly in reference to Dan Rose's anthropological reading of "playing black" basketball in Philadelphia. The moves in "playing black" illustrate Gates' "signifyin(g)" practices. Another angle from which *The Moves Make the Man* might be read would include a study of segregation and integration in public schools of the South in the 1960s setting of the novel; in other words, moving outside the text helps us explore the context of the novel. Although I mention some instances of racism, such as the white basketball coach's attitude toward how Jerome plays "nigger ball," other instances might be effectively explored. One prime example occurs in the racially tense episode that occurs when Bix, his stepfather, and Jerome stop at Jeb's restaurant on their way to Duke Hospital. When Jerome senses Jeb's racist attitude and suggests he will wait in the car, the word *moves* takes on a different connotation in Jeb's remark that "any car you're in will be moving, faster the better"

(255). The Jeb who has been so friendly to Bix on earlier trips tells him to "Stick the [baseball] glove up your ass and ride it out of here, nigger lover" (256). He orders Jerome to "Get out, jigaboo," and he threatens to "shoot [his] head off" if he doesn't (256).

Virginia Hamilton's *M.C. Higgins, the Great* (1984) also offers opportunities for exploring the sociohistorical contexts, especially with respect to the history of strip-mining and the devastation that it created in the geography where Hamilton sets her coming-of-age story. Another angle might be to explore the plight of poor blacks, hill people, who tried to leave the torn countryside, starting with the picture that James K. Lewis gives M.C.; he remembers seeing urban nomads, people who tried unsuccessfully to move to Cleveland. Finding no place for themselves, he tells M.C., they were left to "roam the interstates forever, growing their gardens on the shoulders of the road" (46–47). The story of Grandma Sarah's escape from slavery is also a site for the study of African American history.

Henry Louis Gates Jr. emphasizes the importance of the African American vernacular, and John and Kay Bushman point out the possibilities of using young adult literature to teach students about black dialect. The Bushmans insist that a "description of the dialect, its characteristics, its history, and its use in America is a must to meet the needs and interests of our diverse society." Some of the novels they suggest for study include: Walter Dean Myers, *Scorpions* (1988), Alice Childress' *A Hero Ain't Nothing But a Sandwich* (1973), and *Rainbow Jordan* (1981), Ernest Gaines' *A Gathering of Old Men* (1983), and Hadley Irwin's *I Be Somebody* (1984) (Bushman and Bushman 1993, 108–10).

Many other excellent young adult novels offer students and teachers opportunities to explore the African American tradition. Some that I particularly recommend are Ouida Sebestyen's *Words by Heart* (1979), Charles Johnson's *Middle Passage* (1990), Gary Paulsen's *Nightjohn* (1993), Angela Johnson's *Toning the Sweep* (1993), Paula Fox's *The Slave Dancer* (1973), and Ernest Gaines' *The Autobiography of Miss Jane Pittman* (1971). Finally, let me recommend Walter Dean Myers' *The Glory Field* (1994), which moves through 250 years of a family's history, starting with the story of eleven-year-old Muhammad Bilal in July 1753, off the coast of Sierra Leone, West Africa, and ending with Malcolm Lewis in August 1994, in Harlem, New York. The novel is prefaced with a complete genealogical table of the Lewis family, and a genealogy accompanies each of the dated sections that structure the novel. As in Taylor's Logan saga, identity grows out of a continuing relationship with a piece of land, here a field on Curry Island, South Carolina.

Works Cited

Baker, Houston A., Jr. 1971. "Black American Literature: An Overview." In *Black Literature in America*, 2–18. New York: McGraw-Hill.

Brooks, Bruce. 1984. *The Moves Make the Man.* New York: Harper & Row.

Bushman, John H., and Kay Parks Bushman. 1993. "The Language Connection." In *Using Young Adult Literature in the English Classroom*, 101–17. New York: Macmillan.

Carroll, Pamela S. 1993. "*Their Eyes Were Watching God* and *Roll of Thunder, Hear My Cry:* Voices of African-American Southern Women." In *Adolescent Literature as a Complement to the Classics*, ed. Joan F. Kaywell, 168–83. Norwood, MA: Christopher-Gordon.

Childress, Alice. 1973. *A Hero Ain't Nothing But a Sandwich.* New York: Avon.

————. 1981. *Rainbow Jordan.* New York: Putnam.

Davis, Charles T., and Henry Louis Gates Jr., eds. 1985. Introduction to *The Slave's Narrative*, xi–xxxiv. Oxford: Oxford University Press.

Dixon, Melvin. 1985. "Singing Swords: The Literary Legacy of Slavery." In *The Slave's Narrative*, eds. Charles T. Davis and Henry Louis Gates Jr., 298–317. Oxford: Oxford University Press.

Douglass, Frederick. 1845. *Narrative of the Life of Frederick Douglass, an American Slave.* Reprinted in *Early African-American Classics*, ed. Anthony Appiah, 13–110, New York: Bantam, 1990.

DuBois, W.E.B. 1903. "Of Our Spiritual Strivings." In *The Souls of Black Folk.* Reprinted in *Early African-American Classics*, ed. Anthony Appiah, 3–11, New York: Bantam, 1990.

Fowler, Virginia C. 1994. Notes: The Novels of Toni Morrison and Gloria Naylor. Virginia Polytechnic Institute and State University, Blacksburg, Virginia.

Fox, Paula. 1973. *The Slave Dancer.* New York: Dell.

Gaines, Ernest. 1971. *The Autobiography of Miss Jane Pittman.* New York: Bantam.

————. 1983. *A Gathering of Old Men.* New York: Knopf.

————. 1993. *A Lesson Before Dying.* New York: Vintage.

Gates, Henry Louis, Jr. 1971. "Criticism in the Jungle." In *Black Literature in America*, 1–24. New York: McGraw-Hill.

————. 1984. "The Blackness of Blackness: A Critique of the Sign and the Signifying Monkey." In *Black Literature and Literary Theory*, 285–321. New York: Metheun.

————. 1987. Introduction to *Figures in Black: Words, Signs, and the Racial Self*, xv–xxxii. New York: Oxford University Press.

————. 1987. "Literary Theory and the Black Tradition." In *Figures in Black: Words, Signs, and the Racial Self*, 3–58. New York: Oxford University Press.

———. 1992. "'Ethnic and Minority' Studies." In *Introduction to Scholarship in Modern Languages and Literatures*, 2d. ed., ed. Joseph Gibaldi, 288–302. New York: Modern Language Association.

Hamilton, Virginia. 1981. *M.C. Higgins, the Great*. New York: Macmillan.

———. 1985. *The People Could Fly: African American Folktales*. New York: Knopf.

Hurston, Zora Neale. 1942. *Their Eyes Were Watching God*. New York: Harper and Row.

Irwin, Hadley. 1984. *I Be Somebody*. New York: NAL Penguin.

Johnson, Angela. 1993. *Toning the Sweep*. New York: Scholastic.

Johnson, Charles. 1990. *Middle Passage*. New York: Plume.

Johnson, James Weldon, and J. Roseman Johnson. 1989. *The Books of American Negro Spirituals*. 2 vols. New York: Da Capo, Inc.

Leitch, Vincent. 1992. "Pluralizing Poetics." In *Cultural Criticism, Literary Theory, Poststructuralism*, 84–103. New York: Columbia University Press.

McKay, Charles. 1971. "If We Must Die." In *Black Literature in America*, by Houston Baker, 2–18. New York: McGraw-Hill.

Myers, Walter Dean. 1988. *Scorpions*. New York: Harper and Row.

———. 1994. *The Glory Field*. New York: Scholastic.

Olney, James. 1985. "'I Was Born': Slave Narratives, Their Status as Autobiography and as Literature." In *The Slave's Narrative*, eds. Charles T. Davis and Henry Louis Gates Jr., 148–75. Oxford: Oxford University Press.

Paulsen, Gary. 1993. *Nightjohn*. New York: Bantam Doubleday Dell.

Sebestyen, Ouida. 1979. *Words By Heart*. New York: Bantam.

Taylor, Mildred. 1976. *Roll of Thunder, Hear My Cry*. New York: Puffin.

———. 1981. *Let the Circle Be Unbroken*. New York: Puffin.

———. 1990. *The Road to Memphis*. New York: Puffin.

Thomas, Joyce Carol. 1982. *Marked by Fire*. New York: Avon.

———. 1983. *Bright Shadow*. New York: Avon.

———. 1986. *Water Girl*. New York: Avon.

———. 1990. "Young Reverend Zelma Lee Moses." In *A Gathering of Flowers: Stories About Being Young in America*, ed. Joyce Carol Thomas, 99–134. New York: HarperKeypoint.

———. 1992. Conversation with John Noell Moore. National Council of Teachers of English Convention: ALAN Workshop. Louisville, Kentucky.

Wright, Richard. 1964. "The Literature of the Negro in the United States," *White Man, Listen!* New York: Doubleday, 80. Quoted in *Black Literature in America* by Houston A. Baker, Jr., New York: McGraw-Hill.

Nine

Cultural Studies
Social Construction and AIDS
in *Night Kites*

An Introduction to Cultural Studies

Cultural studies is one of the most recent developments in the field of literary theory; its basic concepts grow out of previous theories, particularly poststructuralism. Its ways of reading dissolve the boundaries of what we generally consider literature (Belsey 1988, 409), locating literary texts in complex webs of multidisciplinary intertexts and contexts. Because of this interdisciplinarity, theorists and practitioners use the metaphor of border crossing to describe how cultural studies redefines the word *text* by "problematizing the borders of textuality." By "foregrounding issues of political, social, racial, and sexual difference and identity" (Bathrick 1992, 320–21), cultural studies includes texts from other disciplines that have previously been considered outside the boundaries of literary analysis.

Defining Culture

The word *culture* is so difficult to define that Raymond Williams (1976), a leader in the field of cultural studies, called it "one of the two or three most complicated words in the English language (76). It is ambiguous, as are other terms that define totalizing concepts, such as *society, history, myth*, and *ideology* (Watkins 1992, 173). Culture may be defined broadly as "the descriptive sum of the 'mores and folkways' of societies". In this sense, culture is "threaded" through all human social practices, and we use the term to sum up the interrelationships of these practices (Hall 1994, 612).

James Berlin and Michael Vivion (1992) have worked out a "provisional definition" of culture for the English classroom. Culture, they say, refers to (1) "the signifying practices that represent experience in language, myth, and literature" and (2) the "relatively autonomous responses of human agents to concrete historical conditions" (viii–ix). Here they cross the borders of the literary theories presented in earlier chapters. The making of meaning in formal, archetypal, structuralist, and poststructuralist theories can be broadly included in the first part of their definition. The second part includes opportunities for more reader-oriented responses to literary texts in a broader cultural context. Cultural studies, therefore, threads together most of the principal ways of reading discussed in the preceding chapters. It pushes toward a "multiperspectivism" that challenges the idea that any one literary theory can dominate the English profession (Bathrick 1992, 325).

Cultural Studies and the English Classroom

Berlin and Vivion further define cultural studies as "the study of the ways social formations and practices are involved in the shaping of consciousness," as that shaping is both "mediated by language and situated in concrete historical conditions (ix)." Therefore, they describe English classrooms where the discipline of cultural studies is practiced as places where both students and teachers "will engage in critique" in a critical examination of the economic, social, and political conditions within which the signifying practices of culture takes place (xii). The field of cultural studies provides students with methods for discovering the semiotic codes that have produced texts and through which we interpret texts. This kind of work cuts across aesthetic, economic, political, philosophical, and scientific systems, preparing students to be "citizens in the democratic public sphere" (Berlin and Vivion 1992, xii).

Berlin and Vivion follow "the poststructuralist textual turn" wherein persons are referred to as "subjects" who are "multiple social constructions, the effects of signifying practices." In other words, there is no complete or totally developed "you" or "I"; we are constantly in the process of becoming, fluid beings moving through a fluid world. From the perspective of cultural studies, reality is also a social construction, and the signifying practices from which people make themselves and their world are "the central activity of culture" (Berlin and Vivion 1992, ix). In *Night Kites* we explore how characters are culturally constructed and how they construct themselves as a consequence of the historical conditions of their world, specifically in dealing with AIDS.

Ideology and Border Crossings

The concept of ideology is paramount in the cultural studies process because it is "enmeshed" in what we value economically, socially, and politically. What we value shapes us and includes family, school, workplace, peer group, the arts, media, and other modes that relate to the making and using of the materials within our social structure (Berlin and Vivion 1992, xi). Another way of describing these shaping forces is to consider them "social apparatuses," that is, systems of difference in sex, race, religion, education, ethnicity, and class. In addition to those just mentioned, these constructions include communication networks—television (public and cable), Hollywood films, and the literature of the popular culture, including comic books, romance novels, science fiction, and Westerns (Kavanagh 1990, 309–13). In cultural studies, all of these constructions become texts. In *Night Kites* we examine how ideology constructs self and social reality in the texts of family, peer groups, the popular culture, and disease.

How, specifically, might we cross the borders of a text in performing a cultural studies reading in the English classroom? Using the familiar text of *King Lear* as an example, one critic suggests that a cultural analysis would concern itself with the "various matrices" or points of origin and interconnection from which Shakespeare derived the material for the play. Coming from "outside the formal boundaries of the play," these matrices might include the kinds of legal arrangements about the dispensation of properties that aging parents made with their children, child-rearing practices in the Renaissance, or political debates about whether disobedience to a legitimate ruler was ever justified (Greenblatt 1990, 230).

Textualities

In cultural studies, then, a text is not a comfortable place where we find a balanced and orderly worldview; it is, instead, a "field of operations" that challenges "the category of literature." In such a field, Catherine Belsey explains, "meaning is never single, eternally inscribed in the words on the page" (as the formalists claim), and a "text is not an empty space, filled with meaning from outside itself" (as it is in some versions of reader response). Reading becomes a "quest" for meanings that, rather than being centrally located in texts, are often located on the margins. Meaning in cultural studies is disunified, discontinuous, and plural; and the text is a construction, a creation: "the text as it never was . . . dispersed, fragmented, produced, politicized." As the text is constructed, the traditional canon of literature disappears (Belsey 1988, 408–09). In this valuation of texts and canon, then, young adult literature does not have to compete with Shakespeare's plays, Dickens' novels, and the poetry of Robert Frost to be "worthy" of inclusion in the secondary curriculum. It is valued as another way of seeing and constructing the world, another social apparatus among many.

Cultural Studies and Ways of Reading

The field of cultural studies contains a variety of methods for making meaning and for exploring the ways in which meaning is constructed. These methods, though, are not "fixed and formalized". Instead, the cultural studies discipline uses an open-ended approach that is constantly subject to change, "positioning itself for revision and reshaping." Students do not "learn *about* cultural studies; they can only learn to *do* cultural studies" (Berlin and Vivion 1992, xii-xiv).

Two ways to "do" cultural studies involve historical perspectives. In either way, we do not have to begin, as we often do in the English classroom, with the literary text. In the first approach, we investigate political, historical, and literary events that were happening at the same time that the literary text was produced or during the period that the text represents. We may begin with the literary text, or we may first pursue interdisciplinary investigations that will provide a context for the later study of the literary text. In the second approach, we begin with the literary texts, perhaps texts that represent different genre, such as fiction, poetry, and autobiography, and that range over a broad period of time. As the analysis of these texts proceeds, we cross the borders into other disciplines that provide contexts and intertexts for the literary texts (Belsey 1988, 409). In our analysis of *Night Kites*, we will use the second approach, beginning with the contemporary novel and crossing disciplinary borders into philosophy, science, political activism, history, and film.

Reading *Night Kites*

An Introduction to the Novel

M. E. Kerr's *Night Kites* (1986) tells stories of a family in crisis, a young adult's struggle for identity, and young romance, all woven together in a confrontation with disease. Kerr explores how a difference in sexual orientation threatens to destroy the carefully constructed world of the Rudd family when Peter—twenty-seven-years old, gay, and suffering with AIDS—comes home to die. In this context, Erick, the novel's narrator and central character, undergoes an identity crisis in which he learns what it is to be a loner, different, in love, and outside his circle of friends.

The novel investigates differences created by disparities in economic and social class. The Rudds of Seaville, New York, are well-to-do as a consequence of Mrs. Rudd's inherited wealth and Mr. Rudd's rise from a poor beginning to an executive position on Wall Street. Family tension and conflict emerge from the parents' disparate economic backgrounds as well as from Peter's failure to complete an advanced education and secure a position of which his father can be proud. Peter writes science fiction stories; Mr. Rudd does not value this kind of work because, he believes, it offers neither status nor financial security.

Class differences emerge in the contrast between the worlds of the Rudds and the Marrs, families who represent different ways of living. Nicki Marr, the girl with whom Erick has his first sexual experience, lives on the margins, literally (the outskirts of town) and metaphorically (the fantasy world of her mother's creation). In contrast to Mr. Rudd's conservatism, Nicki's father, Cap, enjoys a flamboyant, nontraditional lifestyle in his bar and motel, The Kingdom by the Sea, a world constructed out of the images of Edgar Allan Poe's poem "Annabel Lee."

Another group of characters represent difference and play a smaller role in the novel; these are Peter's gay friends who enter and exit Seaville, usually in support of him in his illness, but also anxious to move on and construct other worlds for themselves. Nicki's world includes Charlie Gilhooley, a stereotypical "fairy" who often frequents Cap's bar and motel, gets drunk, and is subsequently beaten up by "straight" men.

The plot weaves together three narrative strands: (1) the Rudd's ways of coping with Pete's gay lifestyle and AIDS; (2) the knowledge that Erick gains about his brother and about himself as he deals with Pete's illness and imminent death; and (3) Erick and Nicki's romantic involvement, with the attendant damage to Erick's friendship with his former girlfriend Dill and his best friend Jack, who, at the beginning of the novel, is Nicki's boyfriend. Other stories are threaded through these major strands: Nicki's construction of herself in the mode of a popular culture icon and her involvement with macho types; Peter's fascination with *Star Trek* and his career as a science fiction writer; and a trip that Erick, Dill, Jack, and Nicki take to New York to see a Bruce Springsteen concert.

The Title and the Metaphor

Kerr frames the novel with references to night kites as signs of difference. In Chapter 2, Erick explains the meaning of the metaphor with
a story that happened when he was five. Peter, then fifteen, constructed a diamond-shaped kite equipped with small lights so he could
fly it at night. When Erick questioned, childlike, whether the night kite
might be scared of the dark, Peter explained that some kites "are different," that they "go up alone, on their own." He makes an analogy
between kites and people, a lesson lost on his five-year-old brother.
Night kites, he says, are "not afraid to be different. Some people are
different, too" (12). Erick recalls asking Peter if he were a night kite or
a day kite, to which his brother replied, "Oh, I'm a night kite." Erick
remembers: "I figured myself for the regular day kind" (16).

In the last chapter of the novel, Erick recalls the childhood episode, remembering how the night kite "took off in the darkness,
blinking out over the ocean, its phosphorescent tail glowing under the
stars" (209). This recollection of the image symbolizes not only Peter's
sexual difference, but it also foreshadows his death as the novel draws
to a close.

A Cultural Studies Reading

The Social Construction of Family

Erick's father tries to construct an ideal world for his family—a world,
Erick realizes, where his father has "always wanted to fit in" and
where Mr. Rudd "always says our family is first" (15). His father rules
in an absolutist patriarchal world in which he instructs his sons to
"sow a lot of wild oats *before* you marry," because, he says, "Rudds
marry forever!" (16). This implies, in the language of cultural studies,
that the Rudds are not social constructions, that they are not fluid;
instead, Mr. Rudd believes, they are completely formed, stable, pre-
dictable. In his instructions to the boys, Mr. Rudd perpetuates the stereotype of the male who is free to experiment sexually before he
marries the chaste virgin who will provide him with children in a
world where everybody will live happily ever after—because that's
the way he wants it. This is, of course, a fairy tale.

Mr. Rudd also attempts to construct meaning in his prescription
for success. When Erick challenges his father's disdain for Pete's writing and reminds him that he refused to support Pete through the
completion of a Ph.D. program, Mr. Rudd retorts that he paid for his

own M.B.A. with part-time work. Their father's construction of reality is so familiar that Erick and his brother have classified the elements of their father's work ethic, and this prescription for success is one of them: "Pete and I called this rap #2, the Pull Yourself Up by Your Own Bootstraps rap, twin to Rap #3, the Learn the Value of a Dollar rap. Rap #1 was The Family Is First" (40). In cultural studies terms, Mr. Rudd believes in the philosophy that success is preordained if you work for it—a reflection of his ideology, the American Dream.

When Mr. Rudd learns that Pete has AIDS, he devotes himself to protecting the world he has constructed. His principal tactics are silence and secrecy. He tells Erick, for example, never to discuss Pete's illness with anyone. Erick notices that his father has trouble actually saying the word *AIDS*. This is his father's form of denial; not naming something is a way of trying to negate its existence. Because AIDS has the power to destroy his conception of himself, his family, and his world, Mr. Rudd refuses to put the name to the disease, even in the privacy—and secrecy—of his home.

Mr. Rudd is not alone in his perspective; Erick's mother also constructs an ideal world in which she refers to the family as "the Waltons, or the Lawrences on *Family*" (93), families in popular 1970s television dramas. In these programs, the Waltons and the Lawrences exhibit qualities that Mrs. Rudd admires. The Waltons enact the solid virtues of a struggling farm family, while the Lawrences represent the best traits of an upper-middle-class urban family. Both families are always, in every episode, able to survive the most trying situations. Pete recalls that The Waltons, for example, are able to wrap up "every problem from adultery to abortion in sixty minutes flat, with time out for commercials" (93). Neither family, however, has to deal with AIDS. And the people who populate those television worlds are themselves social constructions, people scripted into being. From the perspective of cultural studies, these television programs serve as *intertexts*, "readings" from the popular culture through which we can investigate images of the American family in conjunction with our study of *Night Kites*.

Growing more nervous as Pete's disease worsens, Mr. Rudd attempts to protect the family's social status by isolating them. No one, he instructs, is to be taken into the family's confidence about the situation at home. Typical of the way in which he sees the world in financial terms, he constructs an analogy for his family's dilemma: "Another person's secret is like another person's money: You're not so careful with it as you are your own" (133). As tension escalates, Mr. Rudd offers a simplistic explanation of the problem, suggesting that if the family had "paid a little more attention to what Pete was doing when he was Erick's age," they would not be facing this disaster (134).

This offers us, as readers, an intriguing paradox. In a world where he thinks heterosexual behavior is normal, Mr. Rudd implies that sexual preference is a social construction, but only in the context of blaming Pete's disease on Mrs. Rudd: "The only way that Pete runs true to type is that he's always been a mama's boy" (134). The problematic terms in his language are the words *true* and *type*. The first assumes that *a* truth exists, and the second assumes that people are classifiable into simple categories. One of the lessons of poststructuralist thought is that absolute truth does not exist, and one of the lessons of cultural studies is that difference is enriching, not stigmatizing. A deconstructive reading of this novel might explore how Mr. Rudd's vision of an idealized reality (the American Dream) unravels in the context of AIDS. In a deconstructive image, Erick tells us that his father's world is disintegrating: "We were coming apart at the seams" (185).

Class Differences: Marginalization and Power. The field of cultural studies inquires into marginalization, how people are constructed outside the mainstream of society. In addition to Peter, another character who represents marginalization is Nicki's mother, Annabel Lee Marr. Nicki's world, The Kingdom by the Sea, stands in opposition to the upper-class world of Wall Street that Erick's father inhabits. It was constructed by her mother who believed that she was a reincarnation of Edgar Allan Poe. Poe's "Annabel Lee," from which Mrs. Marr is named, laments the speaker's loss of his youthful bride and her unconditional love after a mysterious wind blew out of a cloud, "chilling and killing" her. The poem suggests class differences, too. Annabel Lee's "highborn kinsmen" arrive to take her away from the distraught speaker who now nightly goes to lie by her tomb "by the sounding sea" (Poe 1956, 46–47). What has this poem to do with *Night Kites*? It is, first, an intertext about love that is unconditional, different, and misunderstood; it is about loss, about being on the outside, living on the shore, on the margin of the world. It is, apparently, about class difference—about the poor speaker and his beloved's "highborn kinsmen," and it is about death. All of these subjects echo throughout the pages of Kerr's novel.

Nicki lives in a suite named "the Dream Within a Dream." A plaque there reads, "All that we see or seem / Is but a dream within a dream," a quotation from Poe's "A Dream Within a Dream," which presents two contrasting worlds:

> I stand amid the roar
> Of a surf tormented shore,

And I hold within my hand
Grains of the golden sand. (Poe 1956, 8)

These lines are also intertextual commentaries on the worlds in the novel. The speaker might be Mr. Rudd, realizing that he is losing the "golden sand" of the world he has constructed. The speaker could be Peter, too, lamenting the loss of his life, the grains of sand, unable, as is the speaker in the poem, to "save / One from the pitiless wave" (8). Other rooms in The Kingdom by the Sea take their names from Poe poems, including "The Bells" and "The Raven." These poems, other works by Poe, and the poet's life provide sites for cultural studies work with *Night Kites*. So, also, do the signs of contemporary culture in Nicki's room—posters of modern music groups, including U2, Wham!, and Sting and stars such as Bruce Springsteen, David Lee Roth, and David Bryne. A cultural studies approach might investigate what these groups represent in American popular culture and how they connect to Nicki and the world of the novel.

The Kingdom by the Sea houses Annabel's Resale Shop, which is at the center of the tragedy of Annabel Marr's death, a story which illustrates the cultural studies' focus on power relations between the dominant and the marginalized elements of society. Her family in financial trouble, Mrs. Gaelen, the mother of Dill's friend Jeannie, sells some of her clothes to Annabel Marr. According to Dill, a number of Seaville women get money by selling to the Resale Shop, but they do it secretly to avoid blemishing their social standing. This is another version of Mr. Rudd's insistence on secrecy about Pete's disease, because he wants to preserve his social position and the power that attends it. To avoid the embarrassment of being seen in Annabel's shop, the Seaville women had Annabel pick up the clothes at their estates (kingdoms of a different sort). A "sickly type" (like Poe's heroine), Annabel had a heart attack while at Mrs. Gaelen's house. Fearful that her friends would discover her "secret," Mrs. Gaelen called Cap Marr instead of an ambulance. Cap arrived too late, and his wife died on the way to the hospital. Because she did not get the immediate medical attention she needed, Annabel Lee Marr became the victim of power, of a social image, an economic and social construction.

The connection between social power and religion emerges in an incident concerning the prestigious Seaville Hadefield Club to which the Rudds belong. The family minister, Reverend Shorr, resigns from the club because of its discriminatory practices against Jews, who may not visit the club, even in the company of members. When Pete and his father argue about Shorr's resignation, Mr. Rudd complains that Shorr has made an issue of some of the club's traditions, to which Pete responds, "Like the tradition of being rich, and privileged, and

prejudiced?" His father constructs the situation differently by changing one word in his son's description: "There's nothing wrong with
being rich and privileged and selective" (127). Powerful men may
consider themselves highly "selective" rather than "prejudiced" in the
insulated world that wealth and social status allows them to build
around themselves.

Pete offers a social criticism of the club's view of the world in a
shirt he gives to his father, a gift that angers Mr. Rudd. The back of
the shirt reads:

WHOEVER HAS THE MOST THINGS
WHEN HE DIES, WINS. (128)

This language is coded with respect to power relations, and we can
read it semiotically. First, "HAS THE MOST THINGS" indicts the mate-
rialism of the wealthy. Second, "HE" identifies the source of power in
patriarchy. Third, "WINS" inscribes the ideology of the survival and
dominance of the fittest. Life is constructed in the sentence and, in
Mr. Rudd's world, as a game in which material wealth and power
allow people to "win."

In contrast to the world of power that his father has constructed,
Pete constructs an alternate world in the science fiction he writes. His
short story "On the Skids" is the subject of a number of conversations
in the novel. "On the Skids," published in *Fantasy* magazine, takes place
in a world where sexual difference does not marginalize its citizens.
Peter, a loyal fan of *Star Trek*, enjoys writing science fiction, which we
might read as an indication of his desire to exist outside the restrictions
of his father's world where sexual difference marginalizes him.

"On the Skids" takes place in Farfire, the world of the Farflicks,
who are distinguished by their ability to self-fertilize. Almost all of the
inhabitants are androgynous, except characters who are called Skids;
either male or female, Skids need each other in order to reproduce.
The conflict revolves around two Skids who fall in love and are
hunted because they have made love, or "skidded," which is illegal. In
his story, Pete reverses the world in which he has been punished for
being sexually different. In "On the Skids," heterosexuality, not
homosexuality, is an aberration.

Peter is working on another science fiction story that appears only
as a fragment in the novel. "The Sweet Perfume of Good-bye"
describes a utopian world without murder or illness, and without fra-
grance, except an "exquisite perfume" associated with death. Death is
not a catastrophe; it is "the great change" that comes randomly to
inhabitants of the story's world (175–76). The perfume, appearing
one year before a death, might be read as a metaphor for appreciating
life and the change to death. A complete version of this story appears

in *Visions: Nineteen Short Stories by Outstanding Writers for Young Adults* (Gallo 1987). The setting is Farfire, and the story makes a good complement to *Night Kites*.

The Social Construction of Self: Nicki as Madonna. Nicki's flamboyant clothes may be read semiotically as signs of her difference. For example, when she accompanies Erick to the school's traditional ring dance, she dresses exotically, constructing herself in the image of the popular icon Madonna. She wears all black, from her high heels to her "dalmatian-dotted stockings" to her "off-the shoulder corset dress." She complements her clothes with "beads and crosses and chains," "crucifix earrings in her right ear," "black lace fingerless gloves," and a "rhinestone ankle bracelet." The whole outfit is topped with a jacket that shows a "traffic accident on the back" (185). Ironically, in the conservative world of Erick's friends, Nicki must seem like an accident herself.

From the cultural studies perspective, however, we can read Nicki's decision to look like Madonna as a sign of her power, as a sign of her ability to construct herself against the norms of the dominant ideology. While the dominant culture attempts to marginalize her, like many other young girls who were called Madonna wanna-bes in the late 1980s, Nicki's alignment with Madonna gives her what cultural studies critic John Fiske (1989) calls a "source of power." Her physical appearance is "a means of constructing and controlling social relations and thus social identity" (163–64). Nicki's excesses in makeup and jewelry, like Madonna's, may be read semiotically as her critique of the dominant ideology; wearing too much jewelry, for example, "questions the role of female decorations in patriarchy." Madonna's religious name and the religious icons she wears can be read, not as an attack on Christianity or in support of it, but as a sign that she "makes her own meaning out of the symbolic system available to her"; in other words, she demonstrates "*her* ability to make *her own* meanings" (167).

Discussing Madonna's lyrics, Fiske observes an important principle of cultural studies. Woven throughout the lyrics of "Like a Virgin," he suggests, are puns that play with "at least four discourses—religion, particularly religious love, sexuality or physical love, romantic love, and a discourse of street wisdom, of urban survival." A cultural studies reading resists closure, and what Fiske says about Madonna's language in this song is central to that idea: The relationship between the discourses is open and unresolved. Reading the lyrics requires, Fiske continues, "active productive readers," and the similarities and differences that exist among the discourses are "left reverberating and active, not closed off" (169). In other words, these contextualities and intertextualities are ways of opening up Madonna's construction of herself, her world, and, in context, our world. Fiske concludes that "Madonna offers her fans access to semiotic and social power" that works first through fantasy and then empowers "the fan's sense of self," an empowerment that "reverses social norms." Fiske notes that fantasy should not be written off as simply escapism because under certain conditions it can "constitute the imagined possibilities of small-scale change" (172). Perhaps Nicki (like Peter) cannot change the world that the Rudds and powerful people like them control, but she can construct herself differently so that she can negotiate life on her own terms. This is real power.

Constructing Erick. Erick changes more than any character in the novel as a consequence of his location in the worlds defined by the Rudds' traditional conservatism and by Nicki's fantasy and in the worlds of sexual difference defined by heterosexuality and homosexuality. After he breaks up with Dill and becomes entangled with Nicki, Erick feels the differences taking place in him as he fluctuates wildly from being "down so low sometimes I felt like a complete stranger to myself," to being "*up*, soaring, lost somewhere with her" (151). As he loses contact with the comfortable conservative world he has inhabited with his school friends, he feels a connection to Pete as he gets a taste of living in his own "private little world" (176). He has his first sexual experiences with Nicki, and these increase his sense of isolation, his feeling that he and Nicki exist "in our own cocoon" (183). The cocoon is a double symbol here of both Erick's isolation from the world he has known and the process of metamorphosis he is undergoing as he experiences what it is like to be different. When Nicki ends their relationship because she cannot construct herself in a world with AIDS, Erick realizes that "finally I was completely on my own" (215). Actually, he is not completely on his own; though he will be constructed by the opposing forces that swirl around him, he also possesses the power to make himself different.

The Social Construction of AIDS. *Night Kites* appeared in 1985 and was one of the first young adult novels to address the issue of AIDS. Kerr works details about the disease into her story, for example, its symptoms: amoebic dysentery (26), diarrhea (33), swollen lymph nodes and purple bruises (98), and Kaposi sarcoma lesions (129, 175). She explores legal issues related to the disease. For example, after being diagnosed with AIDS, Peter has experienced tensions at his job, and although he could not legally have been fired from the job, he has negotiated medical benefits and a leave of absence in return for leaving the job immediately (155). Kerr examines the social stigma of AIDS when Peter reveals that after he told a "friend" who lived near him about his illness, she circulated a petition to get him out of his apartment. Misinformation about the transmission of AIDS appears in a scene between Nicki and Erick after Nicki learns that Peter has AIDS. Nicki tells Erick that her father does not want him to come to the Kingdom anymore because he has used bad judgment by swimming in the pool "with something like that [AIDS] in your family" (205).

In addition to providing information on AIDS and the social stigmatization surrounding it, Kerr's novel describes the silences that attend the disease, especially in Mr. Rudd's pact of loyalty and silence within his family. The field of cultural studies extends the boundaries of the text, and now we will examine some ways in which American culture, contemporary with the publication of *Night Kites*, was constructing the disease in its language practices.

Crossing the Borders of *Night Kites*

Illness is the night-side of life, a more onerous citizenship. Everyone who is born holds dual citizenship, in the kingdom of the well and in the kingdom of the sick. Although we all prefer to use only the good passport, sooner or later each of us is obliged, at least for a spell, to identify ourselves as citizens of that other place.

Susan Sontag

Philosophy as Intertext

The epigraph above opens Susan Sontag's essay about her struggle with cancer, her passing from the kingdom of the well to the kingdom of the ill. Her metaphor of the "night-side" of life recalls Erick's memory of his brother's lesson on night kites and what it means to be different. Sontag's kingdoms remind me of the two "kingdoms" of *Night Kites*: the literal and metaphorical Kingdom by the Sea and the "kingdom" ruled by Mr. Rudd, its perfection preserved by social status, economic security, and the image of propriety. Sontag's language turns Kerr's novel into a passport with which we travel into the land of the sick. Her essays on illness and AIDS are the first interdisciplinary and intertextual borders we cross in our cultural studies approach to *Night Kites*.

Sontag (1990) traces the "dual metaphoric genealogy" of AIDS (105). First, a military metaphor of invasion describes the contraction of the disease; and second, a pollution metaphor of plague describes the transmission of the disease.

The Military Metaphor. In the military metaphor, which Sontag quotes from a June 7, 1988 article in the *New York Times*, the virus is a tiny "invader," a "foreigner," whose presence in the body is sensed by "scouts," cells of the body's immune system. These scouts "alert" the system, which "mobilizes" antidotes to "defend" against the threat of invasion. This metaphor, Sontag suggests, is made of "the language of political paranoia, with its characteristic distrust of a pluralistic world" (106). This metaphor of invasion also represents Mr. Rudd's perception of the effect of AIDS on his family and the body of his world. AIDS invades his carefully constructed social reality, and he sets out to mobilize his family against the invader. His weapon is silence.

Another version of the military metaphor connects directly to Peter and his interests in science fiction. Peter is a *Star Trek* fan, and Sontag develops the AIDS metaphor with respect to images from this popular television show and film series. Sontag observes that the AIDS infection is "high tech warfare": The virus drops into a "receptor," "docking" like an "alien" on the cell's surface where it produces more AIDS viruses ("alien products") in the "cellular machinery" (106–07). A world of high technology has been, ironically, unable to discover a cure for AIDS.

History as Context. At one point in the novel, Peter tells Erick, "I'm a little like a leper" (156), contextualizing himself in the history of disease. Sontag develops a plague metaphor, tracing diseases through history. She discusses leprosy as plague (1050–1350) as well as syphilis (late fifteenth century). She notes that writers such as Erasmus described the repulsiveness of syphilis in 1529, and that Daniel Defoe's *A Journal of the Plague Year* (originally published 1722) was written as if its narrator were an eyewitness to the bubonic plague in London in 1665. She includes Edgar Allan Poe's "The Masque of the Red Death" (originally published 1842), based on a ball held during the 1832 cholera epidemic in Paris (Sontag 1990, 132–42). Poe's story becomes a metaphor in which one of its most pervasive symbols, the clock, strikes the death knell for all who attend the ball. Any of these texts make good cultural studies intertexts for *Night Kites*. Defoe's *Journal* and Poe's eerie story are standards in many secondary school anthologies.

Other AIDS Intertexts

Anthropology/Stigma. Michael Quam's essay "Stigma" (1990) provides an anthropological intertext for *Night Kites*. Quam defines *stigma* in two ways: first, in its origin in Greek where it means "bodily signs designed to expose something unusual and bad about the moral status of the signifier"; and second, in its contemporary usage, where it refers "more to the disgrace itself than to the bodily evidence of it" (Goffman 1963, 11). Both meanings of *stigma* apply to Peter in *Night Kites*. His body literally bears his stigma in the purple bruise under his arm and the Kaposi sarcoma lesions on his legs and feet. His father feels the disgrace of these stigmata more than Peter does. Quam says that the "extreme stigmatization of AIDS derives in part from its associations with deviant behaviors" (680). Throughout the novel, Mr. Rudd casts himself as the figure of "normal" behavior; Peter tells us that his father "can't stand the word 'gay'" (90), and he encourages Erick to say the word *AIDS* because their parents are "calling it a thing, a bug, everything but AIDS" (98). The point is clear: They refuse to name it because of the blemish that it places on their carefully created world. Peter's deviation from the social norm threatens Mr. Rudd, threatens what Quam calls "social security and personal identity" (686).

History/The Pink Triangle. Nicki Marr refers to a logo that has become a symbol of gay activism when she is talking about one of her favorite rock groups, the gay Scottish trio Bronski Beat who wear "pink triangles like the ones homosexuals were forced to wear by the Nazis" (153). With this reference, she opens up a number of cultural studies approaches to the novel: contemporary music groups as texts in their construction of identities, for example, in their physical appearance, often outrageous to traditionalists; historical texts that deal with the Holocaust and other historical movements in which people have been persecuted for racial and ethnic difference. From this historical angle, Bette Greene's *The Summer of My German Soldier* (1973), set in the early 1940s in Jenkinsville, Arkansas, examines what happens when Patty Bergen, a young Jewish girl, helps a German soldier who is a prisoner of war. Patty aids the "enemy" to the consternation of her family and the townspeople who call her a Jew Nazi, and she learns how racism has the power to destroy. Greene's *The Drowning of Stephan Jones* (1991), a novel for more mature readers, examines the tragic consequences of a small town's hatred of homosexuals.

Political Activism/Logos. Another cultural studies border crossing involves both history and modern political activism, especially the work of the group ACT NOW, the AIDS Coalition to Network, Organize, and Win. The logo of AIDS activists is the equation SILENCE = DEATH printed in white underneath a pink triangle, all of this set against a black background. Nicki's reference to the Nazis is part of the historical knowledge that is necessary to understand the logo. The pink triangle turned upside down stigmatized gay men in Nazi concentration camps. The gay movement has appropriated the triangle as a symbol of oppression, reversing its direction to symbolize the silence surrounding AIDS that must be broken (Crimp and Ralston 1994, 709). Silence is Mr. Rudd's principal weapon, and he believes that it will protect his public image and his family's social status.

Film Intertexts. Randy Shilts' book *And the Band Played On* (1988) and the film version (1993) cross political borders as intertexts for *Night Kites*. Shilts indicts the Reagan administration and its budgetary practices for refusing to adequately fund AIDS research despite the fact that the number of deaths was mounting steadily across the nation. This book is not fiction; its carefully designed structure juxtaposes times, dates, and places all over the world as the virus was discovered and spread to epidemic proportions. Mr. Rudd's character in the novel symbolizes the politically and financially well-placed who made the decisions that affected the health of a nation as disease invaded its borders and killed its citizens. Another film, *Philadelphia* (1993), also makes a poignant intertext for the novel because it deals with the dramatic changes that occur in the life of a promising young lawyer who contracts AIDS. The story of how he loses his job connects to Peter's story of his own job loss and the loss of his apartment. In *Philadelphia*, the young lawyer fights the system, and in his last days, he beats it. The award-winning title song and the music video of it are also powerful intertexts for several reasons. First, the singer is Bruce Springsteen, the star that Erick, Jack, Nicki, and Dill go to hear in a New York concert. Second, the song lyric and the music video introduce new kinds of cultural texts to read, nonliterary texts that dissolve the boundaries of the novel as the two films do.

In cultural studies' contexts and intertexts, reality as social construction is a function of narrative: "Social reality is a vast network of narratives that we use to make sense of experience, to understand the present, the past, and the future" (Watkins 1992, 183). As cultural studies readers and interpreters, we entangle ourselves in the network of multidisciplinary narratives as ways of "reading" the world. We are far removed from the formalists, delighting in the work of art as container of meaning, in the language of the single text, in its patterns and systems, its ways of tying the world up in a tidy package. Instead, as readers we weave the texts of our interpretation. In the process, often messy and always unfinished, we realize that we, too, are texts that, like the whole world, are being constantly written and rewritten.

Joining the Conversation

This approach to reading and teaching young adult texts perhaps offers the easiest access to the theoretical conversation because it might remind us of the traditional historical research in the study of literature.

The biggest difference in that kind of research and cultural studies is that historical research sent us on an intellectual adventure to find facts related to the author, the period, or the ideas of the text or to uncover and explore discrepancies in the "facts." The cultural studies approach, however, begins with the assertion that knowledge is socially constructed; therefore, when we pursue this approach, we are also constructing knowledge, not just trying to learn all that we can from experts so that we can "know" an author or a period or a book. In cultural studies, we see the young adult novel as a cultural production, too, and we want to study it in the context of its own historical period of production or in the context of other texts that have preceded it. The possibilities here are enormous, and in the remainder of this chapter, I will suggest some ways in which you might join the conversation.

Sexual Orientation/AIDS

One way to pursue cultural studies with young adult fiction is to take the approach I have in this chapter, namely, to read a young adult novel in the context of other texts that relate to it. For example, if we continue with the issues of sexual orientation and AIDS that *Night Kites* opens up, Robert F. Williams offers contexts for our inquiry. He suggests that adults who deal with adolescents should find ways to bring books about sexual difference to students' attention in ways that do not threaten their privacy. In "Gay and Lesbian Teenagers: A Reading Ladder for Students, Media Specialists and Parents" (1993), Williams includes fiction and nonfiction that represent both the traditional literary canon and young adult literature. He cites *Changing Bodies, Changing Lives* (Bell et al. 1988) as "perhaps the finest and most comprehensive book for teenagers on sex and relationships" (Williams 1993, 14). On the issue of homosexuality, he includes Morton Hunt's *Gay: What Teenagers Should Know About Homosexuality and the AIDS Crisis* (1987); this comprehensive text is based largely on scientific research (14–15). For older readers, he suggests John Reid's 1977 autobiography about growing up gay, *The Best Little Boy in the World*. Williams categorizes sexual issues and provides a useful annotated list of young adult novels that explore them. Representative examples are as follows. For lesbian relationships, see Nancy Garden's *Annie on My Mind* (1982) and Sandra Scoppettone's *Happy Endings Are All Alike* (1978); for gay young men, see Aidan Chambers' *Dance on My Grave* (1982), (and for older readers, see David Leavitt's *The Lost Language of Cranes* [1986]); for straight teens with gay family members, see Norma Klein's *Breaking Up* (1980) and *Learning How to Fall* (1989) as well as *Night Kites*. Williams also provides suggestions with which we can cross disciplinary borders in our cultural studies. *Bridges of Respect: Creating Support for Gay and Lesbian Youth* (American Friends Service Committee 1988) is a basic resource that summarizes issues facing gay youth; it provides extensive lists of resources and related materials.

These issues and texts will surely present censorship problems in many places; but as Alan B. Teasley points out in "YA Literature About Aids: Encountering the Unimaginable" (1993), "our teenagers *are* at risk; HIV infection is preventable; and, in the absence of a cure, education is the best hope of fighting the disease" (19). Teasley annotates titles in young adult fiction, among them Alice Hoffman's *At Risk* (1988), and Gloria Miklowitz's *Good-Bye Tomorrow* (1987). To his list, I add Fran Arrick's *What You Don't Know Can Kill You* (1992), which differs dramatically from *Night Kites* in the reaction of the Geddes family to the knowledge that Ellen has tested positive for HIV.

Teasley also annotates drama, poetry, biography and nonfiction, health guides and instructional materials, as well as general resources for research projects for students and teachers. He includes film, videotape, and audiotape resources. His article provides rich materials for cultural studies inquiry. One powerful and unique site for this work is *Epitaphs for the Living: Words and Images in the Time of AIDS* (1989) compiled by photographer Billy Howard who invited each of his subjects to write a statement in their own handwriting to go under their photograph (Teasley 1993, 20). Howard's book crosses the borders of disciplines in the way celebrated by cultural studies.

Cultural Differences

Short stories for young adults provide an excellent way to begin cultural studies inquiry on a small scale. One of the best collections for this purpose is Joyce Carol Thomas' *A Gathering of Flowers: Stories About Growing Up in America* (1990). In her introduction, Thomas explains that she selected fiction about Anglos, Hispanics, Asians, Native Americans, and African Americans to provide "a rich sampling of the rich colors and voices that make up today's America" (xi). The characters in these stories are often literally crossing borders as far as their identities are concerned, and the texts open up many possibilities for inquiry. This collection contains Thomas' "Young Reverend Zelma Lee Moses," which was discussed in Chapter 8. Its usefulness in both African American and cultural studies contexts illustrates the overlap of theoretical stances. Both feminism (Chapter 7) and African American criticism are cultural studies enterprises, although each takes a specific category for the locus of its inquiry, whereas the field of cultural studies includes a broader spectrum.

Gerald Vizenor's "Almost a Trickster," in Thomas' collection, invites an examination of the Native American trickster, "a character in stories, an animal, or a person, even a tree at times, who pretends the world can be stopped with words" and who "frees the world in stories" (Thomas 1990, 5). In Vizenor's story, the concept of adolescent identity is intertwined with the culture of the Chippewa tribe. Students might examine tribal traditions and explore how they are manifest in the story, especially tribal teachings about the "almost world," which the main character Pincher says "is a better world, a sweeter dream than the world we are taught to understand in school" (6). From a cultural studies perspective, this "almost world" is always being constructed; it is never finished. Vizenor's tale offers a good opportunity to inquire into the nature of storytelling and the role it plays in a culture. Students might extend the story by exploring Native American storytelling traditions or, for example, the rich storytelling traditions of the Appalachian Mountains.

Lois Lowry's "The Harrington's Daughter," also in Thomas' collection, offers the opportunity to explore social-class perceptions. In the upper-class East Coast world of Nina's grandparents, the mental illness of a neighbor's daughter is a stigma that the grandparents will not discuss, telling Nina, "You'll understand that better when you're older" (30). The grandparents' language marginalizes Nina because of her age (seventeen). From a cultural studies perspective, students might investigate attitudes toward mental illness in their class, family, and community, as well as engage in research in other disciplines to support their discussion of the story. Again, this approach focuses on the concept of difference and how we construct it in our world.

Thomas' collection contains Kevin Kyung's "Autumn Rose." Culture clashes and generational conflicts are the subject of this story, in which a father stands in the way of Rose, a young Korean girl who dreams of the perfect future with Steve Campbell, a Stanford University student. Rose understands that "dating a *white* boy" is "the worst thing I can do, like spitting at the father's reverend face" (81). The story also explores class and socioeconomic differences when Rose visits the boy's home and discovers that the world of a hardworking dry cleaner (her father) cannot mesh with the world of a family who can provide their son a BMW.

Jeanne Wakatsuki Houston's "After the War," another story from Thomas' collection, is about the relationship between Reiko, a girl detained during World War II in a Japanese-American internment camp, and Sara, Boston born, the child of an alcoholic mother and a father in denial. The story abounds in cultural clashes, which Houston contextualizes in the opening scene with a playground struggle between black Willie Jackson, "king of the school, a sleek panther reigning over a jungle playground," and Peter Novak, whom Willie calls a "polack" (155). Racial issues emerge from this small war and continue as the story unfolds. Economic and class issues develop

because Reiko is embarrassed to take Sara to her house with its mea-
ger furnishings and the pungent odors of "tsukemo—fermented vegetables" and fish drying in a bedroom. Reiko envies Sara's life in what
she perceives as "a roller-coaster world of laughter, noise, and crazi-
ness" (161) symbolized by family drives in a sleek Packard sedan. Students might explore racial stereotyping (Willie and Peter), the
difficulties of cultural adaptation to new environments and the
attempt to preserve tradition (Reiko's grandmother), the history of
the Japanese-American internment camps, and the image of the perfect American family, which Reiko discovers is not so perfect. The
story opens up the issue of alcoholic addiction and its effects on the
family members who refuse to accept it as a disease.

　　Gary Soto's "First Love," which is retitled "Broken Chain" in *Baseball in April and Other Stories* (1990), invites an inquiry into the theme
of adolescent identity and its construction in the popular culture. Sev-
enth grader Alphonso suffers from teeth so crooked that he imagines
they look "like a pile of wrecked cars" as he tries "to push them" to
where he thinks "they ought to be" (137–38). He dreams of a body with
"cuts" like those on the Aztec warrior whom he has seen on a
calendar—a "man standing on a pyramid with a woman in his arms".
He likes Prince's looks and dreams of "his hair razored into a V in the
back and streaked purple" (137). These images occur on the first page
of this very short story, but they open up possibilities for discussing the
concept of physical beauty that the mass media presents to young
adults. A collection of calendars celebrating the perfect face and form,
posters of rock stars, record jackets, and advertisements from the print
and electronic media are just a few of the sites for cultural exploration
that this story suggests. A valuable resource for this kind of inquiry is
Joe Foreman and David R. Schumway's essay "Cultural Studies: Reading Visual Texts" (1992). Foreman and Schumway present specific
questions to guide students in the critique of visual texts: questions
about the production of the text, the key elements of the text and how
they are constructed, and ideological structures—the social, economic,
and political interests that the text serves (240–61).

　　I remember the bravado with which one of my ninth-grade students introduced himself to our English class one year with an "Ob-
session for Men" poster; he had swaggered to the front of the room and
turned sharply to face us with a sly grin. The poster seemed to give him
confidence; but perhaps the whole moment was a cultural production,
either the realization of a dream or a cover-up, or maybe a symbolic
exercise in the kind of tooth straightening that Alphonso attempts.
Soto's *Baseball in April and Other Stories* makes a good site for the beginning of a cultural studies inquiry into Latino culture. Many of the

stories contain Spanish words and phrases (a glossary is provided), and the collection is a good place to consider the role that language plays in the construction of identity. Students might inquire into issues of bilingualism in the Unites States, into the issue of whether or not Spanish should be declared an official language in this country.

Film: Racism and Ethnicity

Film is an excellent place to practice cultural studies border crossing with young adult literature. Gretchen Schwarz (1995) suggests a number of films and young adult texts that work well together for exploring racism and ethnic conflict. She suggests, to use our metaphor, putting the British film *A World Apart* (1989) into conversation with young adult texts. In the film, an adolescent white girl experiences racism and the suffering it causes in the apartheid of South Africa in 1963. Among the novels that Schwarz includes are Fran Arrick's *Chernowitz* (1983), which examines antisemitism in middle America, and Sonia Levitin's *The Return* (1987), which tells the story of a black Jewish girl's escape from Ethiopia during Operation Moses, a secret 1984–1985 airlift that transported 8,000 refugees to Israel from Sudan. In Lois Lowry's *Number the Stars* (1989), a young Danish girl and her family help Jews escape from the Nazis. In *Zlata's Diary* (1994), Zlata Filopovic tells her story about ethnic cleansing in Sarajevo. The clash of Chinese and American culture depicted in *A Great Wall* (1985) may open a dialogue with young adult novels that have the "caught-between-cultures" theme, such as Gary Soto's *Taking Sides* (1991), in which Lincoln Mendoza leaves the barrio for the white suburbs and is torn between his new basketball team and friends from his former school. Lorene Cary's autobiography *Black Ice* (1991), set in 1971, deals with a young black woman's adaptation to a New Hampshire prep school after she moves from the streets of Philadelphia. Linda Crew's *Children of the River* (1989) is a novel-length version of Kyung's "Autumn Rose"; the young female protagonist's wish to date a white boy comes in conflict with her family's expectations (Schwarz 1995, 40–42).

One use for film in the cultural studies approach is to study a young adult novel and then to study the film version of it, working with the film as text. Students might inquire into how the film realizes the novel in a different medium, what elements of the text are omitted, what new nontextual elements are added to the film, and the reasons for such omissions and additions. Other elements of filmmaking, such as casting, lighting, set design, cinematography, and scriptwriting, are fertile ground for exploration. The film version of

Isabelle Holland's *The Man Without a Face* (1972) is a good choice because it makes some powerful additions to the text, particularly in its reconstruction of the end of the novel; students could consider whether these changes enhance or detract from the fictional world that Holland has constructed.

Schwarz suggests the 1970 film of Richard Bradford's *Red Sky at Morning* (1969) and the 1982 adaptation of Chaim Potok's *The Chosen* (1982) as further examples of culture clashes. Both of these young adult texts about difference will set students and teachers onto multiple paths of inquiry. *Red Sky* deals with mixed ethnic groups in New Mexico during World War II, and *The Chosen* examines the roles that education, Orthodox and Hasidic Judaism, family, and friends played in the process of growing up in New York City during World War II.

Religion

A fascinating cultural studies project could be developed around the study of the religious upbringing and education of Jewish youth in *The Chosen* in relation to the Protestant upbringing of the sisters in Katherine Paterson's *Jacob Have I Loved*, the novel that is the subject of the next chapter.

Other young adult novels in which religion plays a prominent role could serve as the beginnings of cultural studies work for older students. Examples include Rudolfo A. Anaya's *Heart of Aztlan* (1976), in which a legend of spiritual renewal contrasts sharply with the realities of existence when the Clemente Chavez family loses its land, moves to a barrio, and its children become victims of the evils of the city. This novel shares elements with Alan Paton's *Cry, the Beloved Country* (1948), in which the life of the city (Johannesburg) destroys the spiritual values that a Zulu family has taught its children in the South African veld. Hermann Hesse's *Siddhartha* (1972) presents Buddhist thought in the context of the hero's quest for spiritual fulfillment. Chinua Achebe's *Things Fall Apart* (1988) examines the impact of Christian missionaries and British colonialism on the cultural values of the Ibo village of Umuofia in eastern Nigeria. And finally, to loop back to an earlier chapter, Gary Paulsen's *Dogsong* (1985) invites an inquiry into the effects of Christian missionaries on the cultural traditions of the Eskimos.

A final note about two new and helpful texts. Lois Stover's *Young Adult Literature: The Heart of the Middle School Curriculum* (1996) makes connections between young adult literature and other disciplines that should provide ideal sites for cultural studies inquiry, and Alan Teasley and Ann Wilder study young adult literature and film in *Reel Conversations: Reading Films with Young Adults* (1996).

Works Cited

Achebe, Chinua. 1988. *Things Fall Apart*. Portsmouth, NH: Heinemann.

"AIDS Virus Found to Hide in Cells Eluding Detection by Normal Tests." *New York Times*, 7 June 1988.

American Friends Service Committee. 1988. *Bridges of Respect: Creating Support for Gay and Lesbian Youth*. Philadelphia: American Friends Service Committee.

Anaya, Rudolfo A. 1976. *Heart of Aztlan*. Berkeley, CA: Tonaitiuh, Quinto Sol International.

Arrick, Fran. 1983. *Chernowitz*. New York: Signet.

———. 1992. *What You Don't Know Can Kill You*. New York: Dell.

Bathrick, David. 1992. "Cultural Studies." In *Introduction to Scholarship in Modern Languages and Literatures*, 2d. ed., ed. Joseph Gibaldi, 320–40. New York: Modern Language Association.

Bell, Ruth et al. 1988. *Changing Bodies, Changing Lives*. Rev. ed. New York: Vintage.

Belsey, Catherine. 1988. "Literature, History, Politics." In *Modern Criticism and Theory*, ed. David Lodge, 400–10. London: Longman.

Berlin, James A., and Michael J. Vivion. 1992. Introduction to *Cultural Studies in the English Classroom*, eds. James A. Berlin and Michael J. Vivion, vii–xvi. Portsmouth, NH: Boynton/Cook.

Bradford, Richard. 1969. *Red Sky at Morning*. New York: Harper Perennial.

Cary, Lorene. 1991. *Black Ice*. New York: Knopf.

Chambers, Aidan. 1982. *Dance on My Grave*. New York: Harper and Row.

Crew, Linda. *Children of the River*. New York: Dell.

Crimp, Douglas, and Adam Rolston. 1994. "AIDS Activist Graphics: A Demonstration." In *Signs of Life in the U.S.A.*, eds. Sonia Maasik and Jack Solomon, 718–10. Boston: St. Martin's, 1994.

Defoe, Daniel. 1992. *A Journal of the Plague Year: Authoritative Text, Backgrounds, Contexts, Criticism*. New York: W.W. Norton.

Filopovic, Zlata. 1994. *Zlata's Diary*. New York: Viking.

Fiske, John. 1989. "Madonna." In *Reading the Popular*. Boston: Unwin Hyman. Reprinted in David Bartholomae and Anthony Petrosky, eds., *Ways of Reading: An Anthology for Writers*, 3d. ed., Boston: St. Martin's, 1993, 156–75.

Foreman, Joel, and David R. Schumway. 1992. "Cultural Studies: Reading Visual Texts." In *Cultural Studies in the English Classroom*, eds. James A. Berlin and Michael J. Vivion, 244–61. Portsmouth, NH: Boynton/Cook.

Gallo, Donald R. 1988. *Visions: Nineteen Short Stories by Outstanding Writers for Young Adults*. Dell/Laurel-Leaf Books.

Garden, Nancy. 1982. *Annie on My Mind*. New York: Farrar, Straus, and Giroux.

Goffman, E. 1963. *Stigma: Notes on the Management of Spoiled Identity.* Harmondsworth, England: Penguin. Quoted in Michael D. Quam, "Stigma," in *Signs of Life in the U.S.A.,* eds. Sonia Maasik and Jack Solomon, Boston: St. Martin's, 1994, 661–78.

Greenblatt, Stephen. 1990. "Culture." In *Critical Terms for Literary Study,* eds. Frank Lentricchia and Thomas McLaughlin, 225–32. Chicago: University of Chicago Press.

Greene, Bette. 1973. *Summer of My German Soldier.* New York: Dial.

———. 1991. *The Drowning of Stephan Jones.* New York: Bantam.

Hall, Stuart. 1994. "Cultural Studies: Two Paradigms." In *Contemporary Literary Criticism: Literary and Cultural Studies,* 3d. ed., eds. Robert Con Davis and Ronald Schleifer, 610–25. New York: Longman.

Hesse, Hermann. 1972. *Siddhartha.* Trans. Hilda Rosner. New York: Bantam.

Hoffman, Alice. 1988. *At Risk.* New York: Berkley Books.

Holland, Isabelle. 1972. *The Man Without a Face.* New York: HarperKeypoint.

Houston, Jeanne Wakatsuki. 1990. "After the War." In *A Gathering of Flowers: Stories About Growing Up Young in America,* ed. Joyce Carol Thomas, 153–73. New York: HarperKeypoint.

Howard, Billy. 1989. *Epitaphs for the Living: Words and Images in the Time of AIDS.* Southern Methodist University Press.

Hunt, Morton. 1987. *Gay: What Teenagers Should Know About Homosexuality and the AIDS Crisis.* Rev. ed. New York: Farrar, Straus, and Giroux.

Kavanagh, James H. 1990. "Ideology." In *Critical Terms for Literary Study,* eds. Frank Lentricchia and Thomas McLaughlin, 306–20. Chicago: University of Chicago Press.

Kerr. M. E. 1986. *Night Kites.* New York: Harper.

———. 1987. "The Sweet Perfume of Good-Bye." In *Visions: Nineteen Short Stories by Outstanding Writers for Young Adults,* ed. Donald R. Gallo. New York: Dell.

Klein, Norma. 1980. *Breaking Up.* New York: Pantheon.

———. 1989. *Learning How to Fall.* New York: Bantam.

Kyung, Kevin. 1990. "Autumn Rose." In *A Gathering of Flowers: Stories About Growing Up Young in America,* ed. Joyce Carol Thomas, 79–98 New York: HarperKeypoint.

Leavitt, David. 1986. *The Lost Language of Cranes.* New York: Bantam.

Leitch, Vincent. 1992. "Reconnoitering Birmingham Cultural Studies." In *Cultural Criticism, Literary Theory, Poststructuralism,* 145–61. New York: Columbia University Press.

Levitin, Sonia. 1987. *The Return.* Fawcett.

Lowry, Lois. 1989. *Number the Stars.* New York: Dell.

———. 1990. "The Harrington's Daughter." In *A Gathering of Flowers: Stories About Growing Up Young in America,,* ed. Joyce Carol Thomas, 21–34. Chicago: University of Chicago Press.

Menges, Chris. 1989. *A World Apart.*

Miklowitz, Gloria D. 1987. *Good-Bye Tomorrow.* New York: Delacorte.

Paterson, Katherine. 1980. *Jacob Have I Loved.* New York: HarperTrophy.

Paton, Alan. 1948. *Cry, the Beloved Country.* New York: Scribners.

Paulsen, Gary. 1985. *Dogsong.* New York: Puffin.

Philadelphia. 1993. Directed by Jonathan Demme. 119 minutes. TriStar Pictures. Videocassette.

Poe, Edgar Allan. 1956. "A Dream Within a Dream." In *Selected Writings of Edgar Allan Poe,* ed. Edward H. Davidson, 8. Boston: Houghton Mifflin.

———. 1956. "Annabel Lee." In *Selected Writings of Edgar Allan Poe,* ed. Edward H. Davidson, 46–47. Boston: Houghton Mifflin.

———. 1956. "The Bells." In *Selected Writings of Edgar Allan Poe,* ed. Edward H. Davidson, 47–50. Boston: Houghton Mifflin.

———. 1956. "The Masque of the Red Death." In *Selected Writings of Edgar Allan Poe,* ed. Edward H. Davidson, 174–80. Boston: Houghton Mifflin.

Potok, Chaim. 1982. *The Chosen.* New York: Ballantine.

Quam, Michael D. 1994 "Stigma." In *Signs of Life in the U.S.A.,* eds. Sonia Maasik and Jack Solomon, 679–87. Boston: St. Martin's.

Reid, John. 1977. *The Best Little Boy in the World.* New York: Ballantine.

Schwarz, Gretchen. 1995. "Growing Up, Reaching Out: Multiculturalism Through Young Adult Literature and Film." *ALAN Review* 22 (Spring): 40–42.

Scoppettone, Sandra. 1978. *Happy Endings Are All Alike.* New York: Harper and Row.

Shilts, Randy. 1988. *And the Band Played On: Politics, People, and the AIDS Epidemic.* New York: Penguin.

Shulman, Arnold, and Edward Teets. 1993. *And the Band Played On.* New York: HBO Home Video.

Sontag, Susan. 1990. "AIDS and Its Metaphors." In *Illness as Metaphor and AIDS and Its Metaphors,* 88–183. New York: Anchor.

———. 1990. "Illness as Metaphor." In *Illness as Metaphor and AIDS and Its Metaphors,* 3–87. New York: Anchor.

Soto, Gary. 1990. *Baseball in April and Other Stories.* San Diego: Harcourt Brace Jovanovich.

———. 1991. *Taking Sides.* New York: Harcourt Brace Jovanovich.

Stover, Lois. 1996. *Young Adult Literature: The Heart of the Middle School Curriculum.* Portsmouth, NH: Boynton/Cook.

Teasley, Alan B. 1993. "YA Literature About AIDS: Encountering the Unimaginable." *ALAN Review.* 20 (Spring): 18–23.

Teasley, Alan B., and Ann Wilder. 1996. *Reel Conversations: Reading Films with Young Adults.* Portsmouth, NH: Boynton/Cook.

Thomas, Joyce Carol, ed. 1990. *A Gathering of Flowers: Stories About Growing Up Young in America*. New York: HarperKeypoint.

———. "Young Reverend Zelma Lee Moses." In *A Gathering of Flowers: Stories About Growing Up Young in America*, ed. Joyce Carol Thomas, 99–134. New York: HarperKeypoint.

Watkins, Tony. 1992. "Cultural Studies, New Historicism and Children's Literature." In *Literature for Children: Contemporary Criticism*, ed. Peter Hunt, 173–95. London: Routledge.

Williams, Raymond. 1976. *Keywords*. Glasgow: Fontana.

Williams, Robert F. 1993. "Gay and Lesbian Teenagers: A Reading Ladder For Students, Media Specialists and Parents." *ALAN Review* 20 (Spring): 12–17.

Vizenor, Gary. "Almost a Trickster." In *A Gathering of Flowers: Stories About Growing Up Young in America*, ed. Joyce Carol Thomas, 3–20. New York: HarperKeypoint.

Ten

Theory as Prism
Multiple Readings of *Jacob Have I Loved*

Literary theory functioned in my education as a prism, which I could turn to refract different spectral patterns of language use in a text, as one does daylight. Turn the prism this way, and one pattern emerges; turn it that way, and another pattern configures.

Henry Louis Gates Jr.

The Prism of Literary Theory

This chapter demonstrates how combining several theoretical approaches leads to multiple readings of a young adult novel. The preceding chapters have shown how the reading strategies of literary theories weave us in and out of texts, some of them implicating us in the intertextualities of both the novel and the world. Now, we explore how turning the light of Gates' theory prism on a single text allows us to read it differently and enjoy the possibilities that its language opens up to us and our students.

To elaborate on the prism metaphor in the epigraph (Gates 1987, xvii), various beams of light will not illuminate each text in the same way. That is, readers read differently and, consequently, construct different readings, even though they practice the same theory. Light refracts through the prism as a consequence of many factors, including the quality of the light and the setting in which it shines. In other words, the light that illuminates a text is the individual consciousness with all its attendant powers and limitations. We "eye" the text as a function of the "I" that we are and are becoming. Jonathan Culler's view of how theory works in practice offers another refractory angle.

Actually, he says, we may consider each theory ("methods of interpretation or ways of approaching literary works") as "a partial vision,
more appropriate to some books than to others" (Culler 1992, 225).

The prism of theory becomes a brilliant jewel in the English classroom because of the colors it casts on the study of young adult literature. Our reading of Katherine Paterson's *Jacob Have I Loved* (1980)
will illustrate how theory illuminates this text and allows us to construct multiple interpretations and multiple meanings. As we work
with the novel, we turn the prism one way to examine the biblical
archetype that governs the whole novel. Then we turn it another
way, shining a feminist light on the developing character of Sara Louise Bradshaw. In yet another way, focusing our cultural studies beam,
we contextualize the novel in World War II history. As we read, theories overlap to reveal the rich tapestry of the novel.

Reading *Jacob Have I Loved* from Multiple Perspectives

The novel is set in a fishing village on the island of Rass in the Chesapeake Bay, where, in 1941, Sara Louise Bradshaw and her twin sister,
Caroline, live with their parents, Truitt and Susan Bradshaw, and with
their aging and senile grandmother. Except for McCall (Call) Purnell,
Sara Louise's childhood playmate who eventually marries Caroline, the
other significant characters in the novel are older inhabitants of the
island. Hiram Wallace is a former resident who comes back to live on
the island and restore his family's home; he marries Trudy Braxton, an
aging and ill resident whose money helps Caroline realize her musical
ambition to attend the Juilliard School in New York.

Sara Louise, the narrator, tells the story in retrospect, focusing on
her rivalry with Caroline, who is beautiful, musically talented, and the
epitome of femininity. In contrast, Sara Louise feels unattractive and
unfeminine, preferring men's work to women's work. Against the
backdrop of a real war, Paterson plays out the psychological warfare of
the sisters' difference as Sara perceives and reports it. The novel begins
when the girls are thirteen and follows them into adulthood, although
most of the action occurs in the painful years of adolescent uncertainty
when Sara Louise struggles to construct her identity.

Archetypes: Sibling Rivalry

Isaac's Sons. From the perspective of archetypal theory, Paterson's
story transforms the Old Testament tale of sibling rivalry between Jacob
and Esau, twin sons of Isaac and Rebekah (Genesis 25:19–35:29), a
rivalry that begins before the sons are born, when Rebekah feels them

struggling in her womb. Their birth symbolizes future conflict; Esau is born first, but Jacob is holding onto his foot. By right of primogeniture, Esau is entitled to claim headship of Isaac's clan. When the twins reach manhood, however, Jacob twice tricks his brother and succeeds in stealing away his birthright. Aided by his mother, who favors him, Jacob secures his father's blessing and becomes lord over all his brothers. According to tradition, the passing of the birthright is an act that cannot be reversed. Esau is so filled with rage that Jacob, fearing for his life, flees. Years later, the brothers reconcile, each having become the head of a large and prosperous family.

Paterson transforms the ancient text, replacing the twin sons with twin daughters: Sara Louise/Esau, Caroline/Jacob. The central conflict of the novel is symbolized in a story, often told in the family, of the twins' births. In the story, Sara, first born and strong, receives little attention, while Caroline, who almost dies at birth, is lovingly cared for by her mother. From this story, Sara carries around an image of herself as the rejected twin, "washed and dressed and lying in a basket. Clean and cold and motherless" (19). As a child, she lives in the shadow of Caroline; and throughout the novel, she copes with her isolation, eventually believing that she hates her mother for favoring her twin.

Dreams and Jacob's Sons. Paterson weaves another biblical archetype of sibling rivalry into her narrative as Sara's dreams reflect her struggle to create an identity. In her "wildest daydreams," Sara takes a scene from the Genesis story of Joseph in which his brothers and parents bow down before him. Sara imagines trying to force Caroline to bow down to her. At first, Caroline laughs and refuses; but then "a giant hand" descends from the heavens and shoves Caroline to her knees (40). The giant hand symbolizes simultaneously Sara's wish to exercise power over Caroline and Sara's realization that she alone is powerless.

This daydream has its complement in Sara Louise's dreams at night, in the psychical manifestations of thoughts that she cannot allow to exist in the daylight. Her dreams are unacceptable in her Christian worldview, where "to hate was the equivalent of murder" (74). She dreams often of the different ways in which Caroline might die. In one dream, the ferry to the mainland sinks with both Caroline and her mother aboard; in another, a taxi crashes and flames consume Caroline's "lovely body" (75), erasing the beautiful sister from existence. In Sara's dreams, her mother, who has protected and favored Caroline, is also destroyed.

In the most horrifying dream, Sara becomes a murderer, using the tools of her work to free herself from her sister's domination. When Caroline comes to the shore and begs for a ride in her sister's skiff,

Sara takes the heavy pole with which she guides the boat and beats Caroline to death. Caroline's mouth makes the shape of a scream, but Sara Louise hears nothing but her own laughter. When she awakens, the dream laughter turns to sobbing that shakes her whole body. This dream imagery links her psychological state to that expressed in the Joseph daydream. She wants to be the smiting hand, and, above all, she wants to enjoy it. The dream connects her story to the first arche- type of the sibling rivalry in the Old Testament: "I'm a murderer. Like Cain" (75). Sara cannot imagine her life outside the patriarchal poli- tics of power in the Christian myth that governs the worldview of her family. Even when she rages against God for having "pets" like David, Moses, and Paul, she succumbs to remorse for her unforgivable wick- edness, asking God "to have mercy on me, a sinner" (76).

Feminism

Reading Gender. As we turn the prism of theory to read Sara Lou- ise's efforts to construct her identity on the island, poststructural the- ory and feminist theory overlap, an example of one of the realities of theorizing texts. A poststructural reading investigates "how social and public systems of meaning constitute individual identity." Feminism takes gender as the central category of investigation, and gender is the key issue in Sara's struggle for identity. Poststructural feminists theo- rize "gender roles as performances, improvisations within a culturally defined system of gender-specific signs" (McLaughlin 1991, 264).

Thirteen years old and suffering from comparisons to Caroline, Sara Louise identifies with her father: "He needed a son and I would have given anything to be that son" (21). On the island, however, men's work and women's work are distinctly separate, and her father's boat is considered an inappropriate place for Sara. The roles appropriate to island women are clearly defined; women are not sup- posed to be attached to the water, to love it, because water is "the wild untamed kingdom" of men. This kingdom marginalizes women; according to Sara Louise, even though "water was the element in which our tiny island lived and moved and had its being, the women resisted its power over their lives" (43). The language of the passage locates women not only in opposition to men but in opposition to a natural power of the world. The effect is to render women powerless, to subdue them by a male power that is actually a social construction of their culture.

Sara Louise is juxtaposed with two images of women in the novel: the dutiful spouse and the glamorous Caroline. Sara articulates her identity in the social context of island women. She cannot bear, for example, to think of herself as the dutiful spouse with a "lifetime of passive waiting"—waiting for the men to come home from work in the evening, for the birth of children, for the years of raising them, and "waiting at last, for the Lord to take me home" (44). If read from a feminist perspective, this passage reveals how patriarchal cultures marginalize women. On the island, women wait for men, produce heirs for them, and finally, even in death, are at the mercy of an omnipotent male. The final image is devastating. Some men may die heroically in the struggle against the natural forces of the universe, but women waste away in the enclosures men make for them, entombed in their own housekeeping. This is, at least, how Sara Louise reads it.

Paterson also juxtaposes Sara Louise and Call Purnell, whose maturation defines another possibility of identity for Sara. Eventually Call drops out of school to work with Sara's father; but when Caroline befriends Call, he and Sara grow apart. Sara is jealous as Call matures physically, losing his childhood pudginess and growing taller and thinner. These changes are symbolized by the "rough brown bark" look of his hands as he becomes a waterman. Sara Louise registers his pride as he comes "at last into a man's estate" and as he becomes the sole supporter of the women who have raised him. Her attraction to him grows stronger as he goes "deep into the world of men"—a place that Sara felt she "could never hope to enter" (172–173). Her language tells the story. "Man's estate" connotes rank, social position, political power, property, and ownership. The image of Call's entrance into the depths of a man's world implies that women are somehow shallow, surface creatures.

When Call joins the navy, Sara finally gains entrance into her father's world. At fifteen, she replaces Call as her father's helper, dresses in men's clothes, and does a man's job. Her hands become rough and weathered, and she effects a symbolic gender shift. One morning as her mother serves them breakfast, Sara thinks, "No one said anything about my not being a man—maybe they'd forgotten" (187). The mother as servant emphasizes the difference in power that gender constitutes.

Reading the Body. Sara first acknowledges her sexual self in an encounter with Hiram Wallace, a man in his sixties who has retired to the island. A storm devastates the island and completely destroys the house that Hiram Wallace has been restoring with the help of Sara and Call. After the storm, Sara rescues him in her boat, and they set out to survey the damage. When she sympathetically embraces him, "an alarm" clangs inside her body as she goes "hot all over" and hears her heart "banging to be let out of my chest." She interprets this sensation as a "deadly sin" (132). Attempting to control her feelings, she

concentrates on Hiram's hands, but they do "the same wild things to
the secret places" of her body that the embrace has done (133). She
fears losing control because, according to Sara, she has always prided
herself—like a closed oyster—"on keeping the deepest parts of me
hidden from view" (136).

After this encounter, Sara confronts a dilemma. She cannot tell
Hiram how she feels, and she cannot talk to her mother—cannot, she
says, possibly reveal "the wildness of my body or the desperation of
my mind" (142). Thinking herself crazy, Sara imagines the worst—
that Hiram will marry Trudy Braxton and that she will lose him forever. Later, Hiram does marry Trudy in a mutually satisfactory
arrangement: He is homeless, and she is ill with no one to take care
of her. Trudy later suffers a stroke and dies, but by that time (Chapter 14) Sara understands how unrealistic her secret love has been.

Unwittingly, Hiram betrays Sara's devotion to him by using some
of the money in Trudy's legacy to finance Caroline's musical education. The archetypal source of the novel's title is clarified by this episode: When Sara learns of Caroline's good fortune, her grandmother
whispers the text of Romans 9:13 to her: "As it is written, Jacob have
I loved, but Esau have I hated" (178). When Sara interprets her
grandmother's comment in light of Sara's relation to Caroline, Hiram
becomes the father figure in the Old Testament story—the father who
chooses one child over the other. Sara has always believed that Hiram
Wallace was different from the other men on the island, but now, like
everybody else, he has preferred Caroline over her: "Since the day we
were born, twins like Jacob and Esau, the younger had ruled the
other" (180). When she looks up the biblical passage that her grandmother has quoted, she learns that the speaker is God, and her guilt
deepens. Even God seems to be against her.

Cultural Studies

Work and Identity. Sara's identity emerges as a function of her
cultural milieu, defined on the island primarily by work. She finds
herself by working with her father. Years later, telling and interpreting this story, she recalls those adolescent years as the happiest of her
life, and she remembers that she was content for the very first time
because men's work "sucked from me every breath, every thought,
every trace of energy" (188). She is so comfortable with her new
identity that she locates herself in the patriarchal genealogy of the
island, among the tongers who stand on their tiny boats "just as our
fathers and grandfathers had before us" and who are careful not to
disturb the bottom of the bay so that they can "provide a bed for the

oysters that would be harvested by our children's children" (189). Work is the defining element of this existence, and she feels that the valuable work of sustaining life is men's work.

The way in which Sara reads her work opens up feminist inquiry into gender roles on the island. She describes how a good oyster, hitting the culling boards, stays tightly closed while a dead one, already open, is thrown away. We can interpret these images from work as a metaphor for the sisters' sibling rivalry. When Caroline comes home for Christmas, grown up and radiant, she is powerless, Sara Louise says, "to get under my shell" (189–90). Alive and strong, Sara sees herself as the good oyster, her closed shell protecting her from her sister. She is not "open" for communication or for hurt in comparison to her sister's successes.

This image of the closed oyster shell recalls an earlier moment in the novel when Sara recollects a childhood photograph of the twins. The laughing face of the tiny and exquisite Caroline is framed in golden curls as she reaches out to the person taking the photograph. In contrast, Sara sits hunched over "like a fat shadow," with her thumb in her mouth, cutting her eyes toward Caroline as her hand covers most of her face. In addition to their sharply different physical features, the details of the photograph indicate the contrasting psychological worlds that the sisters inhabit. Caroline is open, reaching out, communicating. Sara's hand over her face erases her identity, and her hunched position in the early photograph prefigures her body inside its metaphoric oyster shell. Sara's memory of herself as a "fat shadow" denies her body, both its substance and its shape. Her eyes, averted from the camera, tell the most: She wishes to be unseen, and even she is looking at the beautiful Caroline. Sara's thumb in her mouth makes the perfect foil for her sister's smile.

Reading Popular Culture

Paterson's text is a manifestation of historical consciousness. Sara Louise constructs herself in the framework of the popular culture of her day, including the text of an advertisement for Pond's hand cream: "She's lovely, she's engaged, she uses Pond's" (142). The advertisement depicts two beautifully manicured hands, a diamond ring sparkling on the left one. During her infatuation with Hiram Wallace, Sara imagines his hand putting the diamond ring on the soft "Pond's-caressed female hand" (133). Consequently, she reads the popular advertisement as a devaluation of herself as far as her idea of what men want in a woman is concerned: "A man with strong clean hands would never look at me in love. No man would" (142–143).

One of her youthful characteristics is that she constructs life as this kind of either/or situation. She thinks she must either be all girl, like Caroline, or all boy, like Call. She does not see what lies between extremes or understand the value of difference.

The radio is an important cultural symbol in the novel. When Franklin Roosevelt's announcement of the attack on Pearl Harbor brings World War II to the island, Sara immediately weaves herself into the historical moment. She assumes a male role, putting herself to sleep at night with fantasies of "performing incredible feats of daring" for her country, with visions of herself heavily decorated for her valor (60–61). She and Call play games of counterspying, for which she receives the Congressional Medal of Honor from Franklin D. Roosevelt, who, in her dreams and in her imagination, is her immediate superior and personal friend.

Reading World War II. In telling her story, Sara's images attest to the power of the war in her island world. Remembering her response to Caroline's singing at a Christmas concert one year, for example, Sara recalls that "a sharp report of applause suddenly rattled the room like gunfire" (35). She remembers that her grandmother asked her once why she was looking at her "with bullets in your eyes. Like you want to shoot me dead" (45). Sara recollects that during the storm that destroyed Hiram's home, the rain came down "like machine-gun fire" (120), and when Caroline tells Sara that Hiram has married Trudy Braxton, the news explodes "like shrapnel" inside Sara's stomach (160). Hearing about D day from her mother, Sara contextualizes her struggle for identity in the war years, as she thinks, "It was not the European war that concerned me" (193). Her entire life has been a psychological war for selfhood.

Paterson uses the distinction between the European war and the personal war to draw *Jacob Have I Loved* to a close. The first sixteen chapters deal with the years between 1941 and 1944, but the author takes only four short chapters to narrate the remainder of the story. Sara and Caroline finish college and settle into very different lifestyles. Caroline marries Call, becomes an opera star, and lives a glamorous life. Sara completes her medical studies and becomes a midwife in the Appalachian community of Truitt, where she marries Joseph Wojtkiewcz, the father of three children. Away from a world that has narrowly constructed her, she finds herself reconstructed by Joseph who asks her, "Why would a woman like you, who could have anything she wanted, come to a place like this?" He places her in a context that she has never imagined: "God in heaven's been raising you for this valley from the day you were born" (236). In Joseph's words, her youthful Joseph dream materializes, but not as she had imagined. No one bows servilely before her; instead, her skill allows her to serve others in a community that appreciates her gifts.

Formalism: The Narrative Circle

The last event of the novel brings the story full circle and completes it, unifies it in a way that formalists would applaud, but that some readers would think is too tidy in its coincidences. In Truitt, Sara serves as midwife to a young mother who delivers twins. The first twin, a boy who weighs nearly six pounds, comes easily; but the second, a girl, nearly dies. Without an incubator, Sara improvises a way to keep the second baby alive by stuffing an iron pot with rags and laying the baby in it, just inside the oven door. Fearing that the child will die, the young father pleads for baptism; and since the parents have not chosen names, Sara baptizes the weaker child Essie Susan, uniting the names of the baby's mother and her own mother. In this act, Sara brings together her past, present, and future since it is clear that she will live in Truitt and watch the twins grow up. When Sara learns that the stronger child is "in the basket," exactly where Sara had lain in the story of her own birth, she urges the male child's grandmother to give him to his mother to nurse. She refers to Essie Susan as "my baby" and nurses her from her breast, since she is also nursing her own son, Truitt, named for her father.

As Sara leaves the young couple's house late in the evening, the final moment affirms her identity, her sisterhood, and her connection to all the worlds of the novel. Once at a Christmas concert, Caroline sang a simple, plaintive song that began, "I wonder as I wander." At the concert, Sara described her sister's voice as being "like a single beam of light across the darkness" (34); the song was so beautiful then that Sara tightened her arms against her sides "to keep from shaking, perhaps shattering" (35). As the novel ends, she hears that same song, this time in the setting where it originated. "I Wonder as I Wander" is an Appalachian Christmas carol, an elegant and simple expression of the worldview of mountain people who wonder why Christ was born into the world to die for them in their unworthiness. Its words bridge the island and the valley, the lives of the two sisters, the two families, the Truitts and the Wojtkiewczs. The words also bring Sara's Christian childhood into focus in her adult life. As she walks out into the cold night air, she hears a melody "sweet and pure": Paterson writes over her own words, echoes the beginning of her novel in its ending, as Sara tells us, "I had to hold myself to keep from shattering" (244). No longer in the shadow of the singer, Sara hears the song in the world to which it belongs and in which, finally, she belongs.

Joining the Conversation

In earlier "Joining the Conversation" sections, I have suggested other novels that might be read from each chapter's theoretical perspective. Here, rather than discuss new texts, I turn several of the texts examined in previous chapters under the prism of theory to illustrate the rich possibilities of multiple readings. I suggest ways of reading without developing those ways in any great detail, and I do not apply each theory to every text.

M.C. Higgins, the Great

From an archetypal perspective, M.C. goes on a psychological quest during the course of the novel. This is a quest to understand how the world works and his role in the world; it is a quest that results in the loss of innocence through the harshness of experience. The physical journey is small, but symbolic: We first meet M.C. flying high on his gleaming steel pole, with Harenton and all the natural world beneath him, his is the power to construct the world he sees. As a consequence of his complex psychological quest, he descends the pole to the earth below; and as a result of the knowledge that he gains, he sets out to change the shape of the earth and to protect his home, his family, and his history.

The chapter on formalism is organized around how M.C. achieves a vision of reality from the worldviews represented by significant characters in the novel. A semiotic reading could address the specific language of these characters and the cultural mythologies that their language represents. I go into this in some detail in the case of Mr. Killburn's philosophical worldview, but there are many other possibilities. For example, the way in which James K. Lewis describes the ravages of strip-mining, or the way in which he describes the urban nomads who have tried unsuccessfully to leave the mountains and come to the city, makes a good site for semiotic inquiry, as does Lurhetta's language about economic realities and the independent life she lives in the wider world beyond M.C.'s narrow perspective.

Reading the novel from the angle of black theory invites opportunities to explore the folklore of the African American tradition and the way in which Hamilton signifies on the well-known African American folktale "The People Could Fly." In the folktale, the people escape slavery by flying over their master's head to freedom. Hamilton's use of the image of flight may suggest that since M.C.'s ancestor Sarah fled across the Ohio to freedom, M.C.'s obligation is to preserve that freedom. Hamilton invites us to explore her signification on music as well, especially in the fragment of the African song that Jones sings to M.C. and in Banina's songs, among them the blues and the Juba Song, the latter perhaps reflecting the complex rhythms of the juba dance that Southern plantation slaves performed. The novel may also be contextualized in African American history, a contextualization that Gates suggests is necessary if readers are to understand the text from the black perspective. Sarah's escape across the Ohio in the history lesson that Jones gives M.C. reminds me of the journey that Sethe makes in Toni Morrison's *Beloved* (1987). Sarah carries a bundle, her baby, the future of the family, and Sethe, pregnant, crosses the river and journeys away from her past and into the future.

A Lesson Before Dying

Although our analysis of Gaines' novel focuses on its signifyin(g) practices in rhetoric, spirituals, and slave narratives, the novel is rich ground for further semiotics work. The analysis of language and especially imagery in the diary that Jefferson keeps is one way to explore the social construction of his reality as a black person in a world dominated by the cultural mythologies of white people. Another productive angle would be the comparison of the language of the untutored Jefferson and the language with which college-educated Grant Wiggins tells the story of how his life becomes intertwined with Jefferson's. The fabric of American history from the time of slavery to the 1940s setting of the novel offers many opportunities for cultural studies inquiry. The conflicting worldviews of Grant and Reverend Ambrose might spark an inquiry into the role of religion in the novel and in the black community of the rural South. A cultural studies perspective contextualizes Claude McKay's sonnet "If We Must Die" on which Gaines signifies (Chapter 8). Poet Nikki Giovanni does that in *Shimmy Shimmy Shimmy Like My Sister Kate: Looking at the Harlem Renaissance Through Poems* (1996). She discusses McKay's Jamaican background and the maroon's practice of cooking wild boars on open fires in the mountains after the maroons had escaped from the plantations below. The maroons, she says, were a fighting people who would not give in (33–34), who would not "die like pigs." Her historical approach to the poem provides us another intertext with which to contextualize a powerful image in *A Lesson Before Dying*. The roles played by Aunt Emma and Tante Lou in the novel will richly reward feminist inquiry into the ways in which these women use the power of their history, their presence, and their language to construct and transform the world in which they live.

Dogsong

Further inquiry into *Dogsong* might explore (1) the complex structural design of the novel as a device for achieving unity (formalism), (2) the role of women in Eskimo culture (feminism), (3) the oral tradition in Eskimo culture and the creation of written literatures, (4) the impact of outsiders on Eskimo traditions, and (5) the geography of the tundra and its portrayal in the novel (cultural studies).

Fallen Angels

Myers' novel is an excellent example of the archetypal journey of the hero, with its emphasis on home as the destination after the trials and tests of the journey. Richie Perry refers many times to his brother and his mother and to his desire that home remain the same so that he can return to it after the traumatic experiences of the war. He undergoes the rite of passage that transforms him as a consequence of his experience; and in the final scene of the novel, he reflects on the mental photographs he has taken during his tour, affirming his place in a community of heroes, dead and alive. When he returns to "the World," as he refers to home during the novel, we know that he is a changed man and that what he has learned will change the way he constructs his life.

  Fallen Angels especially invites cultural studies inquiry, and one outstanding source of materials with which to work is Larry R. Johannessen's *Illumination Rounds: Teaching the Literature of the Vietnam War* (1992), which offers an extensive bibliography of literature and film related to the Vietnam War. Naturally, a cultural studies approach could also contextualize Myers' novel with other war novels in an investigation of the causes and costs of war. Such an approach would be a good opportunity to incorporate young adult literature into the traditional curriculum alongside such familiar texts as *All Quiet on the Western Front*, and *The Red Badge of Courage*. Film versions of these novels offer new cultural texts for students to explore; Nilsen and Donelson (1993) recommend Lewis Milestone's 1930 film on Remarque's novel and John Huston's 1951 adaptation of the Crane book (266).

  Other novels that could lead to a cultural studies inquiry into war from the perspective of young adult characters include Howard Fast's *April Morning* (1961) (Revolutionary War), Irene Hunt's *Across Five Aprils* (1964) (Civil War), Bette Greene's *Summer of My German Soldier* (1973) and Katherine Paterson's *Jacob Have I Loved* (1980) (World War II), Sue Ellen Bridgers' *All Together Now* (1979) (Korean War), and Katherine Paterson's *Park's Quest* (1988) (Vietnam War).

  Nonfiction texts that could be included in a cultural studies inquiry into the Vietnam War include Terry Wallace's *Bloods: An Oral History of the Vietnam War by Black Veterans* (1984), Morley Safer's *Flashbacks: On Returning to Vietnam* (1990), and Elmo Zumwalt Jr.'s *My*

Father, My Son (1986). Mark Jury's *The Vietnam Photo Book* (1986) includes stories and photographs about the men and women who "were overlooked by the television cameras" during his tour of duty in Vietnam (Nilson and Donelson 1993, 264–65). It offers students the chance to learn to read visual texts and to better understand the intertextuality of cultural studies.

Works Cited

Bridgers, Sue Ellen. 1979. *All Together Now*. New York: Bantam.

Crane, Stephen. 1982. *The Red Badge of Courage*. New York: Norton.

Culler, Jonathan. 1992. "Literary Theory." In *Introduction to Scholarship in Modern Language and Literature*, ed. Joseph Gibaldi, 201–35. New York: Modern Language Association.

Fast, Howard. 1961. *April Morning*. New York: Crown.

Gaines, Ernest. 1993. *A Lesson Before Dying*. New York: Vintage.

Gates, Henry Louis, Jr. 1987. Introduction to *Figures in Black: Words, Signs, and the Racial Self*, xv–xxxii. New York: Oxford University Press.

Giovanni, Nikki. 1996. *Shimmy Shimmy Shimmy Like My Sister Kate: Looking at the Harlem Renaissance Through Poems*. New York: Holt.

Greene, Bette. 1973. *Summer of My German Soldier*. New York: Dial.

Hamilton, Virginia. 1974. *M.C. Higgins, the Great*. New York: Macmillan.

———. 1985. "The People Could Fly." In *The People Could Fly: African American Folktales*, 166–73. New York: Knopf.

Hunt, Irene. 1964. *Across Five Aprils*. New York: Grosset and Dunlap.

Johannessen, Larry R. 1992. *Illumination Rounds: Teaching the Literature of the Vietnam War*. Urbana, IL: National Council of Teachers of English.

Jury, Mark. 1986. *The Vietnam Photo Book*. New York: Vintage.

McKay, Claude. 1971. "If We Must Die." In *Black Literature in America*, by Houston A. Baker Jr., 166. New York: McGraw-Hill.

McLaughlin, Thomas. 1991. "Theory as Equipment for (Postmodern) Living." In *Practicing Theory in Introductory College Courses*, eds. James M. Cahalan and David B. Downing, 261–70. Urbana, IL: National Council of Teachers of English.

Milestone, Lewis. 1930. *All Quiet on the Western Front*.

Morrison, Toni. 1987. *Beloved*. New York: Plume.

Myers, Walter Dean. 1988. *Fallen Angels*. New York: Scholastic.

Nilsen, Alleen Pace, and Kenneth Donelson. 1993. "History and History Makers." In *Literature for Today's Young Adults*, 4th ed., 251–99. New York: HarperCollins.

Paterson, Katherine. 1980. *Jacob Have I Loved*. New York: Harper Trophy.

————. 1988. *Park's Quest.* New York: Penguin.

Paulsen, Gary. 1985. *Dogsong.* New York: Puffin.

Platoon. 1986. Directed by Oliver Stone. 120 minutes. Herndale Film Corp. Videocassette.

Potok, Chaim. 1982. *The Chosen.* New York: Ballantine.

The Red Badge of Courage. 1951. Directed by John Huston. 69 minutes. MGM. Videocassette.

Remarque, Erich Maria. 1929. *All Quiet on the Western Front.* Trans. A. W. Wheen. Reprint, New York: Little, Brown. 1975.

Safer, Morley. 1990. *Flashbacks: On Returning to Vietnam.* New York: Random House.

Wallace, Terry. 1984. *Bloods: An Oral History of the Vietnam War by Black Veterans.* New York: Random House.

Zumwalt Jr., Elmo, and Elmo Zumwalt III (with John Pekkanen). 1986. *My Father, My Son.* New York: Macmillan.

Inviting Theory: End Thoughts

Inviting literary theory into the English classroom can transform our approach to young adult literature and all the literatures we teach.

Theory can help us teach our students to become better readers, to read differently, and to dwell in the possibilities and uncertainties of texts.

Theory can help us foster the development of interpretive communities in which we belong as the most mature reader but not the reader with all the answers.

Theory can lead students to deeper understandings of how young adult texts connect to their lives and to the wider world beyond the classroom.

Theory can show students how young adult texts can be catalysts for the study of other disciplines and other ways of knowing. In examining closely how texts are made and how we trace their weave as we read them, students can explore new ways of constructing their own texts, both analytical and imaginative.

Inviting theory can help teachers put into practice Gilbert Highet's notion of what they do:

> Teaching is not like inducing a chemical reaction: it is much more like painting a picture or making a piece of music, or on a lower level like planting a garden. (1950, vii)

Let us, then, paint pictures with young adult literature, a literature that helps students color their worlds.

Let us make music with a literature that sings the joys and sorrows of youth.

Let us plant gardens, and let us watch students grow as they flower in their language, in their learning, and in their becoming.

Works Cited

Highet, Gilbert. 1950. Preface to *The Art of Teaching*. New York: Vintage Books.

1588